THE WALTZ KINGS

Johann Strauss, Father & Son,
and Their Romantic Age

THE
WALTZ KINGS

Johann Strauss

Father & Son, and
Their Romantic Age

by Hans Fantel

WILLIAM MORROW & COMPANY, INC.

New York 1972

fantel waltz at16139

FOR SHEA

Regards

This book came into being mainly for and because of two people. One is my Viennese father, who bequeathed to me his love for Vienna and who paid for his loyalty to that city with his life. The other is my American wife, whose love and generosity of spirit reconciled me to my native city after seventeen years of embittered separation.

Others helped.

Fred Hennings, that excellent Viennese historian, not only guided my search for source materials in Austrian archives and libraries but enlivened my vision by being himself a paradigm of the bygone world reflected in this book.

Carol-Coe Conway Mueller, who read part of the manuscript, helped in several ways: as a historian she averted imminent collisions between my prejudices and historic fact; as an editor she occasionally untwisted my language; and as a friend she sustained the creation of this book by her critical reassurance and her uncritical encouragement.

Mill River, Massachusetts
September 1970   H. F.

Vienna in Waltz Time

Illustrations follow page 96

The meaning of a certain music lies not only in *what* it is but, often more importantly, in *why* it is.

EDUARD HANSLICK

For many of us, some of our most important "new" experiences are discoveries about the hitherto unknown past.

W. H. AUDEN

When the ten thousand things have been seen in their unity, we return to the beginning and remain where we have always been.

TS'EN SHEN

Prelude:

The Land of the Waltz

The Viennese traditionally live in two countries. One is on the map. The other is the imaginary region where wine flows, love triumphs, and everything is silk-lined. This is the land of the waltz.

A century ago, during the sunset years of Austria's thousand-year-old empire, there was no clear demarcation between the real world and that mythical land of the waltz. The two realms merged along the hazy boundary that never quite separates fact from fancy in Vienna.

This region of the Viennese mind is not just a shallow, sybaritic fantasy. Like Viennese music itself, it embodies a substantial premise. If melody could be translated, a Viennese waltz would add up to a hundred ways of saying that, all considered, and with due allowance for everything, simply being alive is a cause for celebration.

At its surprising best—in such creations as *The Blue Danube*, the *Emperor Waltz*, or *Tales from the Vienna Woods*— the waltz is perhaps the closest description of happiness ever attained in any art.

Paradoxically, the music is not merry. A haze of wistfulness lies over the sunniest tunes, and their sweetness sometimes touches on melancholy. Though the dance is a swirling embrace, the music countermands sensual abandonment. It insists on grace; it remains pensive in the midst of pleasure. And in this blending of the sensual with the reflective, the Viennese waltz expresses and creates a condition of durable bliss—a measured joy.

For almost a hundred years, while the last Habsburg emperors ruled the real Austria, the land of the waltz had its own dynasty—the Waltz Kings. Both were named Johann Strauss.

Johann Strauss I ruled over this mythical realm of music during the first part of the nineteenth century. A generation later, his son, Johann Strauss II, extended the scope of the waltz to symphonic proportions, writing dance music in the form of orchestral tone poems that transformed the ball-room into a concert stage.

These two men welded their city and their music into a single identity, making Vienna and the waltz almost a single thought. Viennese historians are fond of florid meta-phors suggesting that Johann Strauss—father and son—did not so much compose their waltzes as ineffably transmute their city into music. Such notions seem altogether plausible to the romantic Viennese, including the younger Strauss himself. "If it is true that I have talent," he wrote during the latter part of his life, "I owe it, above everything else, to my beloved city of Vienna . . . in whose soil is rooted my whole strength, in whose air float the melodies which my ear has caught, my heart has drunk in, and my hand has written down."

Sentimental, yes. Unrealistic, no. Strauss's own assessment of his creative act is probably accurate. *Zeitgeist* and *genius loci*—the spirits of time and place—have always whispered to the creative imagination, and Strauss, being a musician, surely had a fine ear for such promptings.

It is impossible to weigh such ephemeral influences, but one can hardly dispute the perceptive comment made by

Marcel Brion on Vienna's matchless array of musicians: "They would not have been what they were, what they had to be, if chance had forced them to live anywhere but in Vienna."

Music, like wine, takes its flavor from the soil and the season in which it grows, and the roots of the waltz were nourished by a moment of history in which an aging civilization had reached the peak of mellowness. No other city has ever been so suffused by an art as Vienna was by music. Painting, perhaps, was of similarly intense concern to the Florentines of the Renaissance. But this enthusiasm was confined to a relatively small circle of aristocratic sponsors centering around the Medicis, and it seems unlikely that painting played a major part in the life of the ordinary Florentine.

By contrast, Vienna's involvement with music was shared by its shopkeepers and janitors. The barriers between serious and popular music had not yet become impassable. There was no "music business" in the modern sense, for commercial pressures had not yet debased and polarized public taste. In the crowds who thronged to hear performances of Beethoven symphonies, Haydn oratorios, or Mozart operas, burghers and artisans easily joined princes of the realm. Conversely, in the little rustic inns tucked among the hillsides of the Vienna Woods, members of the nobility mixed quite casually with lesser folk to dance to the sweet and giddy folk tunes of the region. Here lay the tree-shaded courtyards of the *Heurigen,* the vintners' houses where the Viennese sampled the new wine. And if the white wines that grow along the Danube lack the finesse of more famous vintages from the Rhine or the Moselle, they have a tart freshness and a light headiness that make them all the more inviting for casual tippling.

During the long spring and fall seasons, and during the mild summers, these spacious gardens and courtyards were filled daily from about four in the afternoon until the early hours, and their mood of easy conviviality shaped the pattern of Viennese leisure. Drunkenness was not tolerated; the typical Viennese was a thoughtful drinker who made a glass last a long time by puffing between sips on a pencil-thin, foot-long cigar that he smoked through a straw. Groups of strolling musicians would pass from one to another of these inns, entertaining the patrons with tunes of the Austrian countryside—the lilting *Ländler*, which was the rural precursor of the not yet invented waltz, and the *Schnadahüpfl*, a jaunty country hop. Here, too, the sound of music created an instant democracy of manners, and class barriers melted in the balmy atmosphere of relaxed hedonism.

This aspect of Vienna's life invariably amazed foreign visitors, particularly those from France, where such casual friendliness between people of widely different social standing was unthinkable either before or after the revolution. "Ancestors and rank seem to be forgotten," reports one traveler, "and aristocratic pride laid aside. Here we see artisans, artists, merchants, councillors, barons, counts and excellencies dancing together with waitresses, women of the middle class, and ladies."

At private concerts, too, there was congenial mingling of persons from different social strata. Tradespeople with sincere musical interests often found access to the musical soirées which were the chief entertainment in the baroque town houses of the high bourgeoisie.

In an ancient monarchy whose minutely graded class structure might otherwise have calcified into social arthritis, music thus served a vital limbering function. In an order where status—being mostly fixed by birth—could rarely be achieved, music provided the safety valve that kept the pressure of social unrest from building up and enabled absolutism to maintain its sway over Austria long after the American and French revolutions had shaken other thrones.

For centuries, the Habsburg rulers maintained a tradition of fostering the arts. The theater, as long as it confined itself to entertainment and did not become a platform for ideas, received royal encouragement, as did the pictorial arts, sculpture, and above all, music, architecture, and landscaping.

The implicit tenet was that beauty begets pleasure, and pleasure begets contentment. The great cities of imperial Austria—Vienna, Prague, Salzburg, and Budapest—owe their splendor to the endearing assumption that civic beauty is the key to civic tranquillity.

To accuse the Habsburgs of prostituting art for political aims would be unjust. Its furtherance was no cynically contrived policy. In fact, it was no policy at all, never having been consciously formulated. The state of the arts in Austria sprang quite naturally from a naïvely mystic faith—not uncommon in Catholic countries—that aesthetic grace was akin to divine grace, and that to invest a country with outward beauty would somehow bestow civic virtues that would hold it together inwardly. This sort of intuition is legitimate to statecraft. What, after all, is a nation but an agreement on style and a cohesive sharing of myths?

Under these conditions, the whole country seemed pervaded by a certain musicality—an innate, casual feeling for form and harmony. It was evident in the visual charm of the Austrian baroque that left its mark not alone on the great cities but also on many of the smaller towns and villages.

A feeling for the baroque and its later, lighter variants, with their graceful, almost melodic lines, was by no means confined to the leading architects employed in the design of palaces and manors. It filtered down to the humblest mason molding garlanded cherubs above the gate of an ordinary house. It shaped the vision of the local builder who quite matter-of-factly bestowed an exquisite harmony of proportions. It guided the hand of the cabinetmaker who filled the house with the playful curves of rococo and Biedermeier furniture. It influenced the gardener and blacksmith alike, one arranging flowerbeds like calligraphy, the other echoing the scrolls in wrought iron. The tailor and the pastry cook shared a concern for graceful shape, and even the gestures of ordinary citizens reflected a certain elegance as they went about their business.

Industrial manufacture had not yet cast its equalizing pall on the design of objects that fill the household and pass through hands in daily use. Far longer than the more industrialized countries to the west, Austria retained the practice and attitudes of individual craftsmanship. The decorative merit of a product ranked at least as high as its utility. Beauty had market value, and the combination of commercial worth and aesthetic joy bestowed on tradesmen and their customers alike a measure of dignity and satisfaction.

In such an ambiance, the ear, too, became attuned to the refinements and delights of form. Music derived from the surroundings. It was inescapable. It lay before the eyes.

Vienna, and much of Austria, thus became a natural breeding ground for musicians. A contemporary chronicler, Eduard Bauernfeld, observes that "every hole is full of musicians who play for the people. Nobody wants to eat his *Bratl* at the inn if he can't have table music to go with it." No feast or celebration was complete without a special overture composed for the occasion. Virtually every bourgeois family could muster a passable string quartet among its members, creating a constant demand for new scores. More than sixty piano factories flourished in the city, which numbered a mere quarter-million inhabitants, and next to good looks and a dowry, musical talent was considered a girl's chief asset.

Every Sunday, the churches resounded with musical settings of the Mass—"operas for the angels," as Mozart called them. Performed by choirs and orchestras of remarkable proficiency, these compositions by Mozart, Haydn, and Schubert were splendidly melodic, and the occasion, despite its ecclesiastical setting, was often more of a public concert than a divine service. The clergy never objected to mixing devotion and enjoyment. In fact, the monasteries

owned some of the best vineyards and maintained some of
the coziest inns to dispense their wine. Austrian Catholicism
had been spared the more Puritan notions of sin that had
shaped the restrictive attitudes of northern Europe. It had
also escaped much of the cruel virulence of the Counter-
Reformation. Austria's faith, touchingly expressed in countless sculptures of smiling, childlike Madonnas, never really
clashed against that other trinity in Vienna's heaven—wine,
women, and song.

Perhaps the most significant aspect of Vienna's musical
life was the attitude of the typical listener. In Paris or London, for example, music was regarded as an entertainment.
Not so in Vienna. Here it was a personal necessity, an in-
dispensable part of everyday life. In its lighter forms, music
was a needed refreshment; in its more demanding forms, an
exercise of the spirit in search of illumination.

All this presupposed the placid political climate which,
at the outset of the nineteenth century, still prevailed in
Austria. Marcel Brion, in his excellent book on Vienna,
suggests the political feeling of that time in a perceptive
précis:

"God in His gracious Providence has given us rulers on
whom He bestowed all the qualities necessary to govern well.
He ought therefore to respect them as children do their
parents, obey them and accept their decisions as being the
most conducive to the good of the country. . . ." The almost
universally practiced Catholicism led to a quietism that canceled spiritual anxiety, and the monarchy was based on a
political sort of quietism. The citizen, little inclined to insist
on his theoretical and abstract rights and primarily anxious
to enjoy life in peace and comfort . . . was unconcerned about
physical systems, and his special philosophy was to live and
let live.

Unlike the populace of Paris, the Viennese had no griev-
ance against their aristocracy. On the contrary, the Viennese
tended to admire their aristocracy in much the same way as

later generations would idolize public entertainers—as symbols of freedom and glamour beyond the sphere of everyday life. And a notable number of aristocrats lived up to their expected role. Through the splendor of their palaces and gardens laid out like fanciful stage sets, their carriages, their attire, their sponsorship of the arts, as well as in a certain unaffected grace of deportment they set an example of civilized life.

It is hardly surprising that such a society left considerable room for individuality. The forces of regimentation and efficiency were traditionally resisted, thus preparing the ground for Vienna's famed *Gemütlichkeit*, the characteristic attitude of unhurried bonhommie.

Without this accepting and forgiving attitude of *Gemütlichkeit*, the Viennese might have considered themselves oppressed by their rulers and even resented the goodwill and familiarity of their aristocrats as an insidious form of paternalism. Yet whatever loss of liberty the benevolent despotism of the Habsburgs entailed, it was borne lightly at the time. Few among the bourgeoisie felt their personal freedom seriously restricted. Because industrialism, just then beginning in western Europe, had not yet reached Austria, a large proportion of Viennese burghers and craftsmen were still self-employed, and, as such, enjoyed considerable independence. Many lived by selling their own products made in a workshop at the back of the store. Often they had no help other than their apprentices and journeymen, with whom they stood in a close personal relationship. The degrading impersonality of industrial employment was still unknown, as were the alienation and social resentments of an industrial proletariat.

An employee in a Viennese workshop still had well-justified expectations of being taken into partnership or someday opening his own shop. His attitude, therefore, was bourgeois rather than proletarian, and his politics conservative rather than radical. To a considerable degree, the employee shared the same pleasures and maintained the same cultural aspirations as his master. Thus the whole of society was unified, posing no barriers to communication between classes.

As for the shop proprietor, merchant, or small entrepreneur, he experienced little interference from the authorities in the conduct of his business or private life and probably enjoyed a greater sense of personal freedom under the Habsburgs than today's corporate minions in nominally democratized countries. Since his condition of life was generally satisfying, he would happily forgo forbidden ideas of political freedom (such as representative government, which he didn't quite understand, anyway) for the life of a self-employed burgher well rewarded by his social environment. Rather than outright oppression, the sheer pleasantness of life was the root of old Austria's political tranquillity.

No doubt the most benign economic influence on the social climate was the virtual absence of extreme poverty. To be sure, Vienna had its share of improvidents and people suffering ill fortune. But the causes of their plight were personal rather than built into an exploitive system. Hence their number was small and they did not constitute an embittered group endangering the balance of the community. Where in Paris a Jacobin majority marshaled the envy and fear of the deprived into an orgy of class hatred, the Viennese joined all classes in self-indulgent epicureanism.

Even lowly citizens ate well in Vienna. A surviving restaurant menu lists a complete meal for thirteen *Kreuzer*— the equivalent of about twenty-five cents. For this modest sum one could regale oneself on soup, smothered liver, roast beef, vegetables, bread and a quarter-liter of wine. A remarkable document survives in the City Archives showing that during one typical year (1786) some 200,000 Viennese managed to do away with 42,197 oxen, 1,511 cows, 66,353 calves, 43,925 sheep, 164,700 lambs, 96,949 pigs, 12,967 suckling pigs, 454,063 buckets of local wine, 19,276 buckets of

Hungarian and Tyrolean wine, and 382,478 buckets of beer. No one seems to have made per-capita comparisons, but this document is generally taken as historic proof of an ample appetite.

Such statistics are not irrelevant to music, for they bespeak a love of life and a general greediness for good things, be they products of art or of the kitchen.

With comforts of mind and body abundant and readily available, economic incentive never was honed to an irritant edge. Material possessions alone could not change one's social standing in a fixed-status society, and since the public environment was generally delightful, there was less need for private luxury. Consequently, acquisitive drive, the dominant motivating force in open and industrial societies, rarely inspired the Viennese. Their motivation was not so much material success but satisfaction with the task at hand, or, quite often, simply the leisurely enjoyment of the day. To the Viennese, this was the utmost practicality and realism.

As long as external conditions supported this mode of existence, remarkably little cruelty or vulgarity crept to the surface of Austrian life. The feral substrate at the bottom of any society remained nicely covered. And those who, by dark intuition, knew it was there said nothing of it.

Of course, not even an unfailing surfeit of music and *Wiener Schnitzel* could remove all challenges from life, but in an age of indulgent epicureanism, these challenges could usually be surmounted by not trying too hard. That, too, lies in the music. The cardinal rule for playing a waltz is the same as for mastering other phases of life in Vienna: Don't push it—and keep the tempo loose.

Its cushioned resilience made Vienna relatively crisis-proof —at least until the final, cataclysmic collapse of the empire. Nonchalant self-irony lent Vienna, and all of Austria, the buoyancy to clear minor hurdles. For example, during a government scandal involving payoffs at the ministerial level, the noted Viennese journalist Karl Kraus soothed tempers by explaining that the accused civil servant "took such small bribes as to border on incorruptibility."

Scanning a thousand years of Austrian history, John Gunther observed that the country "in its own inimitable, slippery way wriggled out of any difficulty. Something of the very softness of the Austrian character had been a factor of strength, because the horns of a crisis were apt to disappear through absorption—the crisis lost its point, melted in the prevailing solvent of easygoing compromise."

This is hardly a country to be admired by moralists. Philosophers may not find it much to their liking, either. But poets and musicians have always felt at home there, for the land pulses with the heartbeat of humanity.

Here Johann Strauss was born. He felt that pulse and shaped it into a special music that lifted Vienna from its moorings on the map, wafting the city across that misty line between reality and dream into the land of the waltz.

1

The Dawn of Waltz Time

Before it reaches the city, the western wind sweeps over vast Alpine forests, taking from them the fragrant essence that makes Vienna's summer air as heady as its wine. But in winter, the wind carries the chill from snowy peaks just beyond the horizon. On such a day, March 14, 1804, the first Johann Strauss was born. The midwife, delayed by glare ice and an untimely display of *Gemütlichkeit*, nearly missed the occasion. She arrived just in time to keep frail little Johann from by-passing this world altogether.

The scene of his arrival was The Good Shepherd (Zum guten Hirten), a shabby, one-story tavern in the Leopold-stadt, one of Vienna's poor districts on an island bounded by two branches of the Danube. The dank, low-ceilinged inn offered shelter and beer to riverboat sailors coming down from Linz, having traversed the yet untamed rapids of the mountainous Wachau, where castles at every turn still bore witness to the robber barons who once laid chains across the river to exact toll from travelers. Other patrons of the inn slowly worked their way upstream from the Hungarian plains, bringing to Vienna grain-laden barges drawn by trains of powerful Pinzgau horses, each as massive as a buffalo.

The little boy's father, Franz Strauss, owned the tavern jointly with his wife Barbara, and as innkeepers they were counted among the lower, but still respectable, ranks of the bourgeoisie. Little is known of Franz Strauss except that he was uncommonly moody, giving rise to rumors of suicide when a few years later his body was found in the Danube.

Johann's mother died when he was only seven, and his father's drowning shortly after a second marriage left the boy orphaned. He stayed on at The Good Shepherd with his widowed stepmother, who eventually remarried. Johann's new stepfather, a man named Golder, seemed genuinely fond of the boy, and his genial temperament soon changed the formerly dour atmosphere of the tavern. Strolling musicians now were invited to play a few tunes for the customers before moving on to the next alehouse, groping by the dim light of their pig-fat lanterns through the dark lanes among the steep-roofed stone houses of the Danube district.

A pair of violins, a cello, and a zither—or perhaps a lap harp similar to the Irish harp in shape and size—would make up the more imposing of these groups. At other times, a solitary "beerfiddler" would scratch out a dance in exchange for some goulash.

Whatever the level of such performances may have been, the very sound of music created a private paradise for Johann. Night after night, Golder recalled, the child sat huddled in the background amidst barrels and ham hocks, listening as if in a trance.

Noticing the boy's musical bent, Golder gave his stepson a violin for St. Johannis Day, in accordance with the Austrian custom of giving children presents not merely on their birthdays but also on the calendar day named for their saint. The fiddle was little more than a toy, made in the woodcarving village of Berchtesgaden near Salzburg, then famous for its manufacture of cheap musical instruments. It had a dry, buzzy sound, but Johann soon discovered a way to improve the tone. He would grab a mug from one of the tavern tables and pour beer into the *f*-holes of the violin.

The beer-soaked fiddle became the focus of his life. Nothing else aroused his interest. He taught himself to play the tunes he had heard from the strolling players in the tavern. More and more he withdrew into music as if into a shielding armor.

He did badly at school. The fiddle distracted him. Always he kept it under his desk, and during recess he played it in the yard. Golder cursed that violin. What he had given as a toy had become an obsession. A perceptive schoolteacher, convinced of Johann's overwhelming musicality, suggested music lessons for the boy. But Golder bridled at the idea. He had seen too many besotted fiddlers at his inn. His boy wouldn't wind up that way. Johann was to learn a solid trade.

So, at the age of thirteen, Johann was apprenticed to a bookbinder. He detested the smelly glue, boiled down from the bones of freshly killed animals. He wept and shouted, refused even to touch the work, and once dashed the hated glue pot to the ground. His master, a decent though thick-skulled man with the typically Viennese name of Lichtscheidl, did not know how to handle the alternately wild and melancholy boy. The usual discipline of whipping seemed to have no effect. He resorted to incarceration. But Lichtscheidl's wife took pity on the boy, and one day in her husband's absence she opened the door to the dark storeroom where Johann was kept. Like an animal sprung from a cage, he dashed out, grabbed his fiddle, and ran off.

He headed west, toward the Vienna Woods. There, he knew, were the *Heurigen*—the vintners' inns with their shady courtyards. Surely, a young man of fourteen who played as well as he could earn his keep with his violin. But when he reached the village of Grinzing, whose onion-domed steeple marked the center of the *Heurigen* district, he felt too shy to enter the guest-filled gardens. He walked on toward the slopes of the Kahlenberg, that last gentle echo of the Alps rising above Vienna like the heel of a huge hand whose palm cradles the city.

Along the way Johann may have met a frequent wanderer in these parts—a leonine man striding with his hands behind his back, whose tortured face suggested that he was not native to this genial land but an immigrant from a harsher, northern region. Those who encountered Ludwig van Beethoven on his walks shied away from the gruff man who refused all companionship rather than admit that he was deaf.

But the landscape sang in Beethoven's ears: vineyards and gardens patterning the hills, and the meadows where the sun lifted reflections from the green water of small brooks. And in the distance where the ribbon of the Danube unites mountain and plain, Vienna lay like a jewel in a vast setting. Amidst the Baroque abundance of copper-green domes, the solitary gothic spire of St. Stephen's rose like a marker, signifying that under all the world's skies there is no other such place.

Almost daily, Beethoven walked here from his room in the suburb of Heiligenstadt, often heading toward a wooded grove inexplicably named the Krapfenwaldl (Little Forest of the Buns). It was here that the un-Viennese stranger distilled the sublime allegory of Vienna's landscape: the Pastoral Symphony.

Other musicians, too, had been profoundly affected by the spell of this singular region. Schubert, too chubby to do much hiking through the countryside, liked to spend his afternoons at the *Heurigen* here, sharing a jug of *Nussberger* with friends, flirting with the waitress, and—in the absence of napkins—jotting down deathless music on his cuffs. Some years later, Robert Schumann, on visiting Vienna, wrote at length in his diary how the vista from the Kahlenberg had stirred his mind.

This particular view is a recurrent theme in the imagination and awareness of the Viennese. It was not only artists and musicians who possessed this special responsiveness to form. During that period, quite ordinary people took part in a tradition of feeling that lets the line of a hill speak a language both intimate and explicit. From this derives the mystic notion that landscape is destiny:

Hast du vom Kahlenberg das Land dir rings besehn
So wirst du was ich bin und was ich schrieb verstehn.

(If from the Kahlenberg you looked into the land
My being and my writing you will understand.)

So wrote Beethoven's friend, the poet Franz Grillparzer.

Indeed, the view from the Kahlenberg encompasses the diverse regions from which Vienna, the heart of Europe, draws the vital juices of its life: the Alpine West with its Germanic influence; the eastern plains stretching endlessly toward Asia, adding Slavic and Magyar elements to the Viennese mix; and to the south, beyond the mountain pass of Semmering, perhaps the first hint of the Mediterranean.

Slowly Johann climbed toward the small castle at the crest of the mountain. He made his way among the weather cannon, a typically Austrian type of artillery emplaced in the vineyards. With their huge, funnel-shaped mouths gaping straight up at the sky, these enormous, squat howitzers never fired a shell. Their sole purpose was to make the loudest possible noise by firing blank charges. As everyone knew, this scared off hailstorms that might otherwise damage the grapes. Rationalists supported this article of faith with a theory that sound belching from these grotesque guns shook up the clouds.

But on that balmy afternoon in 1818, the weather cannon lay silent. By the time Johann gained the heights above the vineyards, it must have been late in the day. The sun would already have stood low, illuminating the red tile roofs and green copper domes of the city below. The runaway boy was tired from walking and from the excitement of his venture. He fell asleep by the wayside as the warm summer night settled over him.

By fateful coincidence, it was a professional musician, a certain Herr Polischansky taking his evening walk, who found the sleeping boy. The fiddle clasped in Johann's arms aroused his curiosity. He wakened the boy, and soon the two were chatting happily about music. For the first time in his life, Johann was speaking with a man initiate to the mysteries of tone that had so entranced him. How different he was from those inarticulate beer fiddlers at the tavern! Polischansky must have seemed to him like some higher being from another world.

Having won Johann's confidence, Polischansky was able to persuade him to return home. Convinced of Johann's talent, he also promised to give him free lessons and to talk with Johann's stepfather about a musical career for the boy.

Meanwhile, Johann's stepparents were desolate. Remembering the presumed suicide of Franz Strauss, they imagined that the boy had inherited his father's bent toward self-destruction. After Lichtscheidl had told them of Johann's extreme behavior at the bindery and of his own drastic measures to discipline him, they felt sure that Johann had done himself some harm.

In his joy and relief at Johann's safe return, Golder readily accepted Polischansky's offer to develop the boy's musical gifts. True, he insisted that Johann should at the same time continue his apprenticeship as a bookbinder. But now that Johann was at last able to devote his main attention to music, he no longer detested that glue pot and eventually won his journeyman's papers.

As a violinist, Johann soon outgrew Polischansky's ability to teach him. He surmounted even the knottier problems of technique with a sort of natural knack that made conventional teaching superfluous. After only one year of formal study he landed his first professional job. At the age of fifteen he became a violist in Michael Pamer's string orchestra —Vienna's most famous dance-music ensemble.

Pamer was a capable musician, but a drunkard who suffered from a curious delusion. He believed that during a drinking bout he had somehow swallowed a Capuchin monk alive. Not intentionally, he assured everyone; and often at inconvenient moments he was overcome by tears of remorse for this cannibalistic gulp. Also linked to his toping were fits of foulmouthed rage vented at his musicians. One reason Pamer resorted to hiring fifteen-year-old fiddlers was that, at that point in his life, older and more established players just wouldn't put up with him. Yet for all his personal failings, Pamer's place in the history of the waltz is pivotal. It was largely through him that the waltz gained a foothold in Vienna's glittering ballrooms.

Three-quarter time, the triangular essence of the waltz, was not native to Vienna. As far as can be determined, it originated in the Black Forest and the Danube uplands, where it formed the basis of such folk dances as the *Ländler* and *Schnadahüpfl*—simple-minded and short-breathed rustic tunes with no hint of the languorous grace that was to mark their Viennese descendants. But they rollicked with the persuasive *oom*-pa-pa that impelled dancers to turn, turn and keep turning.

The swirling music reached Vienna by boat. Long before the railroads usurped their role, Danube ships plied between Vienna and the upstream city of Linz. Of course, to the Austrians a boat ride without music would be inadequate transportation, and the standard equipment of ships included a deck orchestra, usually consisting of a pair of fiddles, a zither, a double bass, and sometimes the newly invented clarinet.

Docking in Vienna, the musicians would pick up a little extra money by playing their upland tunes in various riverfront taverns. Some of the dances harked back to the Middle

Ages, as attested by a verse dating roughly from the year 1000, apparently the earliest recorded comment on the compelling power of the three-four beat:

Rudolieb hub an zu spielen und sang ein Lied dazu,
Es hätte hüpfen mögen das Kalb im Leib der Kuh.

Roughly translated:

Rudolieb began to play a little ditty now
So merry that it caused the calf to jump inside the cow.

Indeed, jumping was the salient feature of these outdoor dances, for the heavy boots worn by country folk and the rough ground made it necessary for the dancers to be up in the air while executing their turns. Each leap was functional: it served as an antifriction device. But such sportive maneuvers seemed too strenuous for the fashionable Viennese, and the precursors of the waltz were banished to the simpler suburban inns while the minuet and other more restrained dances still dominated the genteel establishments of the inner city. But then Napoleon unwittingly prepared the triumph of the waltz.

In 1809 the "Corsican Ogre" overran Austria. After their victory at Wagram, French troops stood at Vienna's gates. The Viennese dealt with this crisis in their own fashion. Far too fond of their city to expose even a single plaster cherub to Napoleon's cannoneers, who were already lobbing cannonballs into the suburbs, Vienna surrendered.

But it was Napoleon who was conquered. The Viennese treated him with the same cheerful courtesy as they would any visiting monarch. Of course, their own emperor, whose dynasty had ruled for centuries, had more than two thousand royal ancestors while Napoleon had none. But under the circumstances, the Viennese were willing to overlook such social nuances.

Napoleon, in turn, showed the Viennese every possible consideration. He further endeared himself to the population by his fondness for music, his frequent visits to concerts and the opera, and by posting an honor guard at the house of Vienna's most revered musician, the octogenarian Haydn. Rumors that the French emperor breakfasted on newborn children soon lost their credibility, and in a strange emotional turnabout, the Viennese began to take pride in the fact that the terrible Napoleon evidently liked their city and admired its artistic life. French officers were welcomed into the drawing rooms of "good families" where they danced with the Viennese girls, and on his trips from Schönbrunn palace, Napoleon found that he could move about Vienna without special security provisions. In fact, when a young German radical tried to kill Napoleon—having come to Vienna especially for this purpose—the Viennese were outraged at such an unmannerly breach of decency and hospitality. While Napoleon urged clemency for his would-be assassin, it was the Viennese who insisted on executing the rather appealing and fervently idealistic young man. The strange relation between conqueror and conquered culminated in 1810, when Napoleon married the Austrian archduchess Marie Louise, thereby becoming an in-law of the House of Habsburg.

But Napoleon was too restless to become Viennese either by marriage or by adoption. The devouring ambition that had raised the Corsican peasant to the throne of France now drove him eastward against Russia and to his doom in the terrible winter retreat of 1812. By 1814 he was exiled on Elba while his enemies gathered at the Congress of Vienna under the aegis of his royal father-in-law to forge a Holy Alliance against him.

The Congress had a hard time getting down to business. In fact, it never really did. There were simply too many distractions in Vienna, and the festive assembly of crowned heads soon degenerated into a sort of long-run Mardi Gras.

When one of the delegates, the Prince de Ligne, was asked, "How goes the Congress?" he replied tartly, "It doesn't go; it dances."

It was a festive time for Vienna. The citizens thoroughly enjoyed the panache and pageantry, grumbling only faintly about the extra taxes imposed on them to pay for it all. They were rewarded by the colorful sight of six royal delegations and their uniformed retinues riding daily through the streets, and the seven hundred foreign diplomats who took up local residence contributed to the life of the city mainly by being idle and rich.

Parties, plays, parades, concerts, horse shows, and fireworks crowded the calendar. The Viennese gawked at the bibulous King of Würtemberg, who was so huge that he was quite a spectacle in himself; they watched the miserly King of Denmark haggle with shopkeepers, laughed at Lord and Lady Castlereagh's outlandish clothes, and wondered at the quirks of Talleyrand, who always traveled with his own pianist to play for him wherever he went. Best of all, there was an endless stream of delicious gossip, preserved for later generations in the files of Vienna's meticulous secret police, who even intercepted imperial love letters and organized everybody to spy on everybody else.

Thanks to these over-enthusiastic security provisions, no secret—diplomatic or otherwise—was safe. For example, everyone knew about the odd parlor games played by Alexander, Czar of All the Russias, with his lady friends, whom he had brought with him, along with their respective husbands. They knew that furtive man with the big round hat drawn over his face who nightly walked certain streets in obvious search of company was really the Grand Duke of Baden. And they heard about the dinner party at Count Zichy's, where the Czar engaged the sprightly young Countess of Wrbna-Kageneck in an argument as to whether men or women spent longer over their toilettes. To settle the question, they withdrew together to undress and dress again, an incident often discussed by the papal nuncio, Monsignor Severoli, who disapproved. History does not record the results of the experiment.

In the wake of the official dignitaries trundled an army of courtiers, servitors, adventurers, con men, pickpockets, and otherwise respectable mothers anxious to peddle their daughters to the highest title or the highest bidder. In its expectant holiday mood, this motley horde displayed an almost pathological craving for nonstop entertainment.

Night after night, dance-mad crowds filled Vienna's ornate ballrooms. It was in one of the largest and most resplendent of these, the famous Sperl, that Michael Pamer's orchestra held forth. To satisfy the public's demand for new and more exciting music, Pamer, Johann's hard-drinking mentor, borrowed some of those rustic three-quarter-time dances that the riverboat musicians had brought to the outlying country inns. In deference to downtown decorum, Pamer slowed the tempo. Thus, on polished parquet floors and in light urban footwear, the Viennese could replace rural hops and leaps with a supple gliding step. As in the older country dances, the couples kept turning. And because swirling is easier when you have something to hold on to, the town dancers soon copied the old country trick of embracing one another.

This radical method of mutual stabilization made the new dance instantly notorious. It certainly was a startling change from the minuet, in which couples touched only at their fingertips. But moral outcries, at least in Vienna, were stifled in the licentious atmosphere of the Congress, which had already softened many of the more rigid restraints on social behavior. Of course, a name had to be given to the new dance, and an obvious designation soon gained currency: *Walzer*—"revolving dance."

Whether bandleader Pamer deserves principal credit for urbanizing the waltz from country dance to city vogue is open to question. Contemporary sources are understandably confused, for the waltz swept the city like an epidemic whose point of origin could only be surmised. But it is certain that Johann's conductor was one of the main carriers of this musical contagion.

Vienna's waltz fever continued even after the Congress disbanded in alarm and dismay at the chilling news that Napoleon had escaped from his island exile and was reconquering France to the rousing tune of the *Marseillaise*. But imminent disaster never kept the Viennese from their pleasures, and even more spacious ballrooms had to be built until their total capacity amounted to more than 50,000. Since they were invariably sold out, this meant that in a city of about 200,000 adult inhabitants every fourth person was out dancing.

The public dance halls offered ordinary citizens the opportunity to spend evenings amid splendors comparable to those of the great aristocratic palaces they knew only from the outside. The popular Apollo-Säle, for example, held 4000 dancers in five huge halls lined with graceful marble pillars arrayed against mirrored walls that multiplied the brilliance of the crystal chandeliers. For the foot-weary, or those in search of privacy, there were forty-four intimate drawing rooms furnished in rococo style, three flower-filled garden pavilions domed with glass, artificial grottos with waterfalls and live swans, and thirteen kitchens. Half a dozen other such establishments vied with each other in lavishness.

The waltz mania was not confined to these pleasure palaces. Even the humblest inn had to have an orchestra of sorts to attract trade. In this ready and constantly shifting market for musicians, it is hardly surprising that young Johann Strauss did not stay long with the monk-swallowing Pamer, whose fits and fantasies were fast getting the better of him. In Pamer's orchestra, Johann shared a desk with Josef Lanner, another talented musician only three years older than himself. A glover's son, Lanner had been playing with Pamer since the age of twelve. But his sensitive, poetic nature was revolted by Pamer's alcoholic coarseness. Soon after Strauss joined the orchestra, Lanner quit to form an ensemble of his own. The group was modest enough, a trio of two fiddles and a guitar, consisting of Lanner and two brothers named Drahanek. Their meager bookings in small coffeehouses hardly kept them alive; but Lanner, feeling the need for fuller sound, resolved to expand his trio into a quartet and asked Johann Strauss to join as violist.

As the junior member of the group, it was Strauss's job to pass the tin plate among the patrons at the end of each concert, a painful chore for the proud youngster. But the sheer exhilaration of making music with a congenial group made up for the hardships of his life, and both he and Lanner found in lightheartedness a natural antidote to penury.

It wasn't that they didn't make any money. After all, even the stingiest Viennese would gladly toss a couple of *Kreuzer* to a bunch of likable chaps who fiddled as sweetly as Lanner's quartet. It was just that they somehow never managed to bring any of their money back home.

To cut overhead, Lanner and Strauss moved into the same room at No. 18 in the Windmühlgasse. Such joint residence also enabled each to deny the other's presence to pursuing creditors. They even shared each other's clothes, which led to difficulties in August 1821, when their affairs were such that they had only one shirt between them. They took turns wearing it, and when they went out together, one of them, despite the summer heat, had to wear his coat buttoned to the neck and his collar turned up.

From that particular nadir, their fortunes rose swiftly. Matching Lanner's sweetness of tone with Strauss's rhythmic verve, they fashioned a distinctive style of captivating musicality. In Vienna, such qualities were quickly recognized and rewarded. In their swift ascent from the small coffeehouses to the great ballrooms they expanded their group to a well-drilled orchestra of some twenty players that was Vienna's most celebrated musical attraction.

The orchestra owed much of its popularity to the waltzes Lanner composed. Vienna had never heard such music before. These waltzes were altogether different from the hastily varnished country hops with which Pamer had mesmerized the Congress. Lanner interlaced several distinct and contrasting waltz melodies, arranging them into a garland of tunes framed by a formal introduction and ending. With this musical structure, Lanner created the essential bridge between the crude, fragmented waltz tunes of the Congress period and the extended musical form characterizing the Viennese waltz in its maturity.

The friendship between Lanner and Strauss survived their sudden affluence. They took turns in conducting the orchestra, and the Viennese public delighted in the contrast of their personalities. The slender, flaxen-haired and fine-featured Lanner projected an air of romantic delicacy. The dark Strauss, now nearing twenty, with his full lips, burning eyes and jet-black curls, embodied the image of romantic passion. The audience dubbed them with special nicknames: Lanner was "Flaxhead" (*Flachskopf*), Strauss "Blackamoor" (*Mohrenschädel*). As if to compensate for the time of shared shirts, both now lived in comfortable apartments, and their colorful tailcoats and cravats were always in the latest fashion. So many girls were smitten with the young men that the quick turnover simply left no time for jealousy.

Lanner was in the habit of composing a new number for every special occasion, usually jotting down a few ideas the evening before the concert and rehearsing the new piece on the morning of its premiere. So intimate was the rapport between him and his players that they read his mind more than the sketchy scores he provided. One evening Lanner felt ill and asked Strauss to take over the morning rehearsal.

"But what about a new number for tomorrow?" Strauss exclaimed.

"Why don't you think of something?" Lanner suggested nonchalantly.

That, according to his own account (later recorded by his son), is how Johann Strauss became a composer.

Strauss's first waltz and several succeeding ones appeared on the programs under Lanner's name. But the enthusiasm of the audience encouraged him to shed the role of ghost composer and to acknowledge his own work. Soon he and Lanner ruled Vienna's musical life on equal terms.

Jointly they expanded not merely the form of the waltz. They also revised the attitude of the music. By the eighteen-twenties, romanticism unfolded in early bloom. If you went out dancing, you looked at a girl in a different way. Gone was the frank, ribald lustfulness of the eighteenth century. Don Juan had given way to Werther, and the standard specifications for love were drastically revised toward the ethereal.

The unvarnished sensualist of the Congress period welcomed Pamer's quick-stepping waltzes as a handy pretext for getting a tight grip on a girl. But the flowery swain of the next decade wanted something else besides. For him, plain sex had no savor. He wanted it garnished with illusion and ceremony, and relied on the music to add an element of reverie, sketching with insinuating tenderness the contour of romantic longing.

Lanner and Strauss belonged to a generation already attuned to this shift. The aim of their melodies—if melodies can be said to have a purpose—was not to seduce but to enchant. After all, for the true romantic, seduction was merely banal. What he desired lay not within but beyond the girl: it was not the promise but the *context* of her smile—the essence that surrounded the gesture of the smile. To extend that moment, that was the real music.

It takes a bit of magic to stretch a flash of happiness over the whole span of a tune. Even Lanner and Strauss couldn't always bring it off. But their average ran high enough to intoxicate a city. Each of their new works was anticipated like a holiday. The distinctive and contrasting qualities of the two composers were constantly mulled over in the press, in coffee houses, and on the street. Complete strangers would strike up conversations about some new offering by Lanner or Strauss.

Of the two, Lanner was more lyrical. A man of quiet, matter-of-fact piety, he claimed God as his co-author. Each new score was inscribed: "With God—Josef Lanner." Though his melodies were lacy, they were never effete; though their emotion was reticent, it was nonetheless glowing.

Lanner's waltzes were love songs in three-quarter time. Those of Strauss, by contrast, were racy and flirtatious. They excelled in rhythmic snap and spicy syncopation. And the tunes, though less tender than Lanner's, were more catchy and had a spellbinding ebullience. One contemporary critic pinpointed the difference: "With Lanner, it's 'Please dance, I entreat you!' With Strauss, it's 'You must dance, I command you!'"

With their contrasting personalities, Lanner and Strauss extended the emotional range of the waltz over a broad spectrum of temperamental shades. But the public, instead of rejoicing in the complementary diversity of their talents, turned the artistic relationship of the two composers into a contest.

Like the aficionados of Spanish bullfighters, the Viennese admirers of Lanner and Strauss split into fiercely partisan camps, playing one off against the other by demonstrative acclaim and by treating the two as rivals. Unable in their spiritual vulgarity to comprehend subtler and more creative relationships, the public subverted the friendship of the two men.

The inevitable clash came in the fall of 1825. Strauss and Lanner were playing at The Ram (Zum Bock), an inn they favored for the excellent acoustics of its arcaded courtyard. It was long past midnight. Everyone was tired and nervous. Suddenly the hot-tempered Strauss took exception to what he considered a slighting remark by Lanner. Right in front of the audience, he leaped at his friend. The musicians, trying to separate their leaders, somehow became themselves embroiled in the skirmish, and the stage turned into a battlefield. Flutes and clarinets served as dueling rapiers while splintering cellos and basses provided heavier weaponry. Even the great gilt-framed mirror, the pride of the establishment, was shattered in the melee. Fortunately, human casualties were confined to a few bruises.

A few days later, the remorseful Strauss composed a *Reconciliation Waltz* dedicated to Lanner. Lanner countered with a *Separation Waltz* that opened with a lament. The twin constellation was sundered.

Both men retained their personal fondness for each other, but never again did they appear together. At the age of twenty-one, Strauss was on his own.

2

The Politics of Dancing

Strauss was on his own, but hardly alone. Anna was pregnant.

The dark-haired girl who seated herself next to the orchestra nearly every night was pretty enough to have caught Strauss's eye even if she hadn't so obviously sought his attention. Of course, there were always girls flirting with Strauss, trusting their coquetry to usher them into those floating regions of romance delineated by Strauss's music, and it appears that Strauss, as a bachelor, made the most of such opportunities. But with Anna, things were different.

When he finally spoke to her, he discovered to his surprise that she was not just another *Backfisch*—some pert little virgin to whom men and music were indistinguishable parts of a single mental miasma. Anna had critical intelligence and was unafraid to show it. At twenty-four, she had no more education than other lower-class women, but her way of speaking frankly and perceptively about everyday concerns must have been striking at a time when the prescribed female fashion called for swooning rather than thinking.

Strauss was also impressed by Anna's musicality. She was an excellent guitarist and, more significantly, she had keen musical judgment. When she praised one of Strauss's waltzes she could give precise reasons for liking it, pointing out this or that harmonic modulation, certain shifts in rhythm, or some particular melodic turn. For Strauss, who had known only blind adulation and empty badinage from women so far, the combined attraction of sex and shoptalk proved irresistible, and it would probably be mistaken to assume that Anna's pregnancy was the only compelling reason for their marriage.

But the schedule was inconvenient. The wedding was in July. The baby was due in October. And the fight with Lanner left Strauss jobless in September.

He needed money, but none could be expected by way of dowry. His bride was the daughter of Josef Streim, an ex-coachman turned innkeeper. As owners of the Red Cockerel (Roter Hahn), Anna's parents had a fairly comfortable existence but no extra cash.

Anna liked to embellish her prosaic descent with a romantic, if questionable, history. Her mother, she claimed, was the child of a Spanish grandee who fled his country after killing a member of the royal family in a duel, found refuge at the Bohemian estate of Duke Albert of Saxe-Teschen, where he changed his name, became a cook, and soon died from the burden of his sorrows. This story is lovingly detailed in the Strauss family papers, with names, dates, and places, which can be neither verified nor disproved.

Anna's appearance, judging by a youthful painting and a much later photograph, lent some credence to her claim. Like her husband, she had an uncommonly dark complexion that stood in exotic contrast to the predominantly fair-skinned Viennese. Her jet-black hair, full lips, and slightly almond-shaped eyes might well have been Iberian. She owned a beautiful guitar unquestionably of Spanish origin, which she said was a family heirloom—the only one of her grandfather's possessions passed on to her. But, on balance, the story of her noble descent attests to the quality of Anna's imagination rather than the quality of her ancestors. Certainly, the invention of such a pedigree is in keeping with the character of a girl whose high spirits and resolute ambition were as much a factor in establishing a veritable dynasty of the waltz as the genius of her husband and sons.

The child was born on October 25, 1825. If the young father could have known that his son's fame would soon surpass his own, he might not have christened him Johann also. By his desire to perpetuate the name he saddled posterity with the perennial chore of sorting out the Johann Strausses.

Strauss had little time to devote to his new family, by then living in a flat at Lerchenfelderstrasse 15. He was busy building an orchestra of his own. Strauss figured with characteristic directness, that raiding Lanner's group might be a good start. What promises and persuasions he used is anyone's guess, but fourteen of his former colleagues left Lanner and joined Strauss. Some, no doubt, were influenced as much by Strauss's personal magnetism as by hope of material gain. He booked the group under his own name at the Two Pigeons, an inn at the corner of the Heumarkt in the inner city that was just at the verge of becoming fashionable.

Despite the following he had gained, success was by no means assured. He was known, after all, as Lanner's partner; alone he might produce a different response. Michael Deiss, the owner of the Two Pigeons, was taking a chance on Strauss and said so. To mollify him, Strauss wrote the *Pigeon Waltz* for his debut, replete with phrases depicting the cooing, nodding, and tripping of Vienna's abundant turtledoves.

Whatever apprehensions the innkeeper may have felt (it is doubtful that Strauss ever felt anything but reckless self-confidence), they vanished in the shouts and applause as Strauss leaped to the podium, signaled the downbeat and, with demonic intensity, fiddled along with his players while indicating rhythm and phrasing by the motion of his hips and shoulders. His magic still worked. A mere handful of his hypnotic measures welded the audience into a single body swaying under his rhythmic spell.

From that day on, Strauss always had more offers than he could handle. If only he could be in two places at once! Then he could collect two fees. So great an idea had to be implemented—somehow.

He divided his nominal presence. Hiring extra musicians, he split the orchestra, booked two halls, and appeared in each for half the evening. The rest of the time each orchestra was entrusted to an assistant.

Of course, this system could be further refined. With mounting demand for his appearance at private balls as well as public functions, the mytotic process continued until, by 1830, he had two hundred musicians under contract, deploying them like an army in divers engagements, each contingent numbering some twenty-five players. A corps of lieutenants drilled these musical squadrons, leaving it for Strauss merely to apply the final touches that marked his unmistakable style.

Strauss parlayed this pre-electronic system of musical omnipresence into a virtual monopoly on Viennese dance music. On a typical evening he would race by fiacre from place to place, conduct the same meticulously rehearsed sequence of waltzes in each location, fight his way out through adoring crowds, and hurry on to the next assignment,

By about three in the morning he would arrive home, not exhausted, but tingling with the excitement of the hours just passed. In this state of feverish stimulation he would cover his notebooks with ideas for the new waltzes his public constantly demanded. A brief sleep around daybreak sufficed to refresh him for the next rehearsal.

Lanner, lacking the taste and stamina for this type of bigbusiness operation, might well have felt envy for his former protégé, whose success now overshadowed his own career. But Lanner's more patient merit was rewarded in 1829 by his appointment as Director of the Imperial Court Balls, the highest distinction the emperor could bestow on a musician in the lighter vein.

Not to be upstaged, Strauss scored a triumph in a different arena—not at court, but at the amusement palace. At an unprecedented fee, he entered into an exclusive contract with Sperl, Vienna's biggest dance hall where as a boy of fourteen he had played viola under Michael Pamer. Now, in 1833, at the age of twenty-six, he returned on his own terms.

At Sperl, Strauss crossed the limits of local celebrity. Here he was on view to the world; for Sperl was Vienna's pre-eminent tourist showplace. The constant flow of foreign visitors included Richard Wagner, a nineteen-year-old youngster from Saxony who had already composed two operas. This music, Wagner felt, was something to write home about:

"I shall never forget the almost hysterical response evoked by every piece of Strauss's in these curious people. A demon within the Viennese populace seems to be summoned anew at the beginning of every waltz. The shudders of sheer pleasure in the audience are unquestionably due to the music rather than the wine, and the frenzied enthusiasm for the magic music master struck me as frightening,"

Wagner was astonished that all this merriment continued right through a cholera epidemic. Hundreds died daily, but, as Wagner reports, "nobody dreams of altering his life and the places of amusement are crowded." As always, Vienna's response to imminent catastrophe was to make music while there still was time.

At the onset of the epidemic, Wagner wrote a frightened letter, describing a horrifying vision of a hollow-cheeked Fury grasping him with bony hands and turning his limbs to ice. But the waltzing soon sweated his fears out of him. Night after night, Richard Wagner, creator of gods and heroes, defied death at Sperl to the music of Johann Strauss, and ran up bills so high that he eventually had to skip town —a pattern of financing repeated by the great composer throughout his life.

One visitor in particular spread the fame of Strauss beyond Austrian borders. He was Heinrich Laube, a roving journalist from Leipzig, who filed with his paper, the *Elegante Zeitung*, a piece of reportage all the more remarkable for having been written at the dawn of modern journalism:

Under illuminated trees and in open arcades people are seated at innumerable tables, eating, drinking, laughing, and listening. In their midst is the orchestra from which come the new waltzes . . . that stir the blood like the bite of a tarantula. In the midst of the garden on the orchestra platform stands the modern hero of Austria, *le Napoléon autrichien*, the musical director Johann Strauss. The Strauss waltzes are to the Viennese what the Napoleonic victories were to the French, and if only the Viennese possessed cannons, they would erect a Vendôme pillar to him at Sperl. The father shows him to his child, the Viennese lady shows him to her foreign lover, the host points him out to his guest.

I was very curious to see the Austrian Napoleon and it pleased me to find him in the center of the battlefield. He was just fighting his Austerlitz as we arrived. With his bow he was pointing to the heavens and the violins were acclaiming the rising of the sun.

All eyes were turned to him; it was a moment of worship. You will be asked, I said to myself, the generations of the future will ask: what does he look like, this Johann Strauss? If Napoleon's appearance was classically Roman and calmly antique, if Paganini's was as romantic and arresting as moonlight, so that of Maestro Strauss is African and hot-blooded, crazy from the sun, modern, bold, fidgety, restless, unbeautiful, passionate. These are adjectives from which the reader may make his selection.

The man is black as a Moor; his hair is curly; his mouth is melodious, energetic; his lip curls; his nose is snub; if his face were not white, he would be the complete king of the Moors from Ethiopia, the complete Balthazar. . . . Under Herod, Balthazar came bearing incense with which to capture the senses—and it is the same with Strauss; he, too, commands the wicked devils within our bodies, and he does it with waltzes. That is the modern way of swaying the senses.

The power wielded by the black-haired musician is potentially very dangerous; it is his especial good fortune that no censorship can be exercised over waltz music and the thoughts and emotions it arouses. The strange saying that it is possible to combine in one person a musical genius and a fool is applicable to him. This is not meant as an insult but as a form of congratulation. I do not know what other things besides music Strauss may understand, but I do know that he is a man who could do a great deal of harm if he were to play Rousseau's ideas on his violin. In one single evening the Viennese would subscribe to the entire *contrat social*. . . .

And now begin the preparations for the real dancing. Very characteristic is the beginning of each dance. Strauss intones his trembling preludes; panting for full expression they sound tragic like the happiness felt in childbirth while pain still reigns. The Viennese male partner tucks his girl deep in his arm and in the strangest way they sway themselves into the measure. For a time we hear the prolonged chest tones with which the nightingale begins her songs and enchants our nerves; then suddenly her resounding trill rings out, the actual dance begins with whirling rapidity and the couple hurls itself into the maelstrom. . . . The couples waltz straight through any accidental hindrances in their joyful frenzy; no god holds them back, not even the intense heat which is carried backward and forward in penetrating waves, as if driven by African desert winds.

It is a notable fact that Austrian sensuality is neither vulgar nor sinful; it is that of mankind before the fall, before the tree of knowledge. . . . These orgies last till the early morning . . . when the heated couples stream out into the warm night airs of Vienna and disappear with fond giggles in all directions.

Flamboyance was the literary fashion of the day and does not detract from Laube's credibility. Comparison of his report with other contemporary accounts shows that his exaggerations were of language, not of fact. In calling Strauss *le Napoléon autrichien*, Laube correctly implies that Austrians generally rely on music rather than the military to furnish their national heroes. Particularly significant is Laube's reference to Rousseau; for in Vienna the waltz was clearly a political phenomenon.

It is not mere coincidence that the minuet gave way to the waltz about the same time that the waterwheel was replaced by the steam engine. For while the minuet flourished in the private exclusivity of the palace, the waltz belonged to the public ballroom. As a dance form, it marked the rise of the urban bourgeoisie at the beginning of the industrial era.

In the eighteenth century, the social ideal was *la vie en château*—life as a nonstop house party at some exquisite mansion in the country. By invitation only, of course. By 1830 the archetype of glamour had shifted to places like Sperl, a setting more suited to the rising merchant class which sounded the cultural keynote in an age of incipient industrialism. Here you could get in by buying a ticket.

Compared to the minuet, the waltz embodied a wholly different set of premises. The minuet was a stylized *approach* between dancers, not in pairs but in groups: It was a hide-and-seek game. The waltz, by contrast, contained no trace of seeking. Having found what you wanted, you grabbed it, hung on, and whirled away—that's what the waltz was about in its earlier forms. The minuet was a game for aristocrats; the waltz was an analogue of capitalist go-getting.

The minuet was predictable. Once the rows of partners were facing each other, one knew exactly where each person would be at any moment of the dance. The proceedings were static and self-contained like the closed society they symbolized. The waltz, on the other hand, was open-ended. It was movement for its own sake, without a prescribed path or fixed ground rules.

One of the characteristics of three-quarter time is that the uneven number of beats per bar creates a forward thrust like that of a rushing stream. With each measure, momentum is renewed, reinforced to greater dynamism, whirling on and on with no end in sight. Fine music indeed for daring men building new worlds with their new engines and their new money.

Besides, a waltz is a strictly private enterprise—nobody's business but your own. What other couples do doesn't concern you, and while the music plays you are free to explore a considerable range of opportunities. One can imagine every gesture of a minuet taking place in polite society even without music. But could the breathless embrace of the waltz be tolerated in public without the extenuating circumstance of music? In sum, the minuet was convention. The waltz was the overthrow of convention—the music of the new economic *laissez-faire*.

If the Viennese at the time lacked the perspective to recognize this historically, they certainly felt it at a less intellectual level. To them, the music of Lanner and Strauss was the affirmation of their city and of themselves as citizens, as distinct from older forms of social structure based on rural aristocracy and their tenants. Not the least reason for the overwhelming importance of this music to the Viennese was its use as a symbolic assertion against—as well as escape from —a political climate that squelched most other forms of liberal expression.

During the Biedermeier period—the span from the Congress of Vienna to the revolution of 1848—Austria's throne was occupied by two emperors of notable incompetence. Unwilling and partly unable to function as rulers, Franz I and Ferdinand II placed the affairs of state entirely in the hands of their capable Chancellor, the lean-faced, elegant Prince Clemens von Metternich.

As steward of the crown, Metternich conceived his task in classic terms. He pictured himself as guardian of the Divine Right of Kings and devoted his ample executive talent to this foredoomed cause. For nearly four decades Metternich managed to keep Austria politically in the Middle Ages.

Metternich embraced political reaction not because he was unable to understand the new liberalism that was creating constitutional and parliamentary governments in western Europe either by reform or revolution. He comprehended these ideas only too well. Liberalism, he perceived, was the road to democracy, which, to him, was the ultimate horror and blasphemy.

Modern historians often cast Metternich in the role of a villain whose policy was inspired by contempt for the newly enunciated rights of man. But from the viewpoint of an Austrian traditionalist exactly the opposite was true. As he saw it, the power to rule over men was a trust so exalted that it could be bestowed on a mortal creature only by the grace of God as manifest in a monarch. "The basis of power in absolute monarchy is, paradoxically, not pride but humility," explains historian Reinhold Schneider.

Only if earthly power was anointed by the Church, and thereby deputized by the heavenly majesty, could there be any hope of surmounting human frailty in the conduct of the state. The system also carried a built-in check on corruption and the abuse of power, for deliberate misrule would imperil the ruler's soul.

To enfranchise the unanointed—the self-seeking commoners—through a parliament or some other form of representative government would be a dereliction of the divine trust of rulership and a disservice to the people. It would abandon the common man to himself and to the imperfections of human wisdom and virtue.

Clemens von Metternich was resolved to keep such misfortune from his country. He even refused to set forth a constitution, as kings elsewhere had done, to create a legal framework within which to manage the industrial properties of the rising middle class. For to put the emperor under rather than above the law would be to place limits on that divine grace which gives sanction to the Crown.

Beyond Austria's borders, a new age emerged. The philosophies of Diderot, Rousseau, Voltaire, and Locke were taking political shape. Consent of the governed and their participation in the governing process were already accepted principles in England and France. To guard Austria from the contagion of such ideas, Metternich imposed a censorship so strict as to choke off nearly all forms of public intellectual life. To deal with private dissent, he had another resource. At any sign of liberal thought within the land, Prince Metternich would reach for the brocade bellpull in his gilded office at the chancellery and ring for Sedlnitzky, the chief of the secret police.

But Metternich's subtlest and most insidious ally was not Sedlnitzky but Johann Strauss. He provided the chief instrument of pacification: Music To Not Think By.

"If I were a despot," wrote the contemporary Viennese poet Glasbrenner, "I would award a ton of gold to Strauss and Lanner to lull the heads of my subjects and halt all public discussion." Of course, he wrote in a cautious subjunctive, but the meaning was clear enough.

Again a paradox: the music of liberalism became the tool of reaction. Or, to paraphrase a later social critic, the waltz was the opium of the people, the dynamic antidote to the stifling air of a country where not too many questions could be asked. It was better to dance.

The Viennese, for the most part, accepted these conditions placidly. After all, Metternich's concept of divine rule by earthly proxy suited the Austrian temperament and world view: a humble, God-trusting pessimism—an existential resignation seeking solace in gaiety and pleasure.

None of this was lost on a sharp-eyed Englishwoman visiting at the time. Frances Trollope, having just finished her famous stay in the United States, felt sufficiently hardened to take on Vienna. In her book *Vienna and the Austrians* she observes: "The singularly strong *besoin* of amusement and music, and the manner in which it is not only unchecked, but cherished by the authorities, furnishes in my belief, one of the principal keys to the mystery of the superior tranquillity and contentment of the populace. . . ."

Mrs. Trollope reports on Vienna's waltz mania from the female viewpoint. It was not uncommon, she writes, for single women who were no longer young and attractive to hire partners for the evening. The price varied according to the skill and general appearance of the swain. Supper was to be included in the charge, so that for a really eligible partner one had sometimes to pay as high as two dollars, or even more. Mrs. Trollope tells of a middle-aged cook who gave this necessary expense as one reason why she was obliged to ask for an increase in her wages.

These were the good old times, the heyday of *Gemütlichkeit*, the fabled era of *Alt-Wien*. Shrugging off Metternich's police spies, the people on the whole were happy and untroubled. One must consider, of course, that accounts to the contrary would not likely have appeared in print. Still, the placid and joyful mood pervading the popular literature at the time seems genuine, and there can be no doubt that life in the Biedermeier era had a predominantly pleasing aura.

Something of this mood comes through in a travel report published in 1830 under the title *A Week in Vienna*. It contains a description of the festivities in the Prater on St. Bridget's day, complete with "short-skirted Tyrolean girls whirling like tops as they waltzed all by themselves in a kind of ecstasy, sharing the dance floor with trained monkeys and dogs dancing on their hind legs." The author, a certain Herr Kurländer, tells of restaurants throughout the great park featuring orchestras, acrobats, puppet shows, and clowns.

Of course, Strauss was there, playing at the largest of these establishments, and his manager, Carl Friedrich Hirsch, had once again displayed his special talent for achieving marvelous illuminations with the rather primitive lanterns then available.

"It was as if Birnam Woods from Macbeth had come alive again," writes Kurländer, rather foppishly parading his knowledge of foreign literature. "A rotating movement had seized on the meadow and all its surroundings as far as the eye could reach. The masses of people waltzed over the mountains and down into the valleys, stumbled on the grass and then went on waltzing. . . ."

More than forty thousand dancers thronged the park. What amazes Kurländer is that despite this enormous concentration of people of all sorts "there never was any disturbance or brawl. The art of pleasure was so highly developed in the Viennese that a vast number of people gathered to enjoy themselves would naturally keep their gaiety free of vulgarity and retain their decency and good nature." A later English historian, Alan Pryce-Jones, also sees the Viennese Biedermeier as an age characterized by "an extraordinary diffusion of kindly temper."

A significant element in creating this atmosphere seemed to be a sense of personal aesthetics. More, perhaps, than anything else, this was the factor permitting humane qualities to assert themselves in daily life to such an exceptional degree.

A common artisan taking his family on a Sunday outing would do so in style. Not lavishly, but with attention to manner and detail. Everywhere one found intimations of *grandezza*—a display of style and manner—scaled to fit the dimensions of ordinary lives. It might be seen in a waiter's bow conveying not servility but self-esteem, in a coachman's flourish as he opened a carriage door, or in a little girl's curtsy to her parents before she retired to the nursery. This transposition of aristocratic aesthetics into a broad, comfortable bourgeois sphere was the essence of Biedermeier. Throughout the social scale, there was a sense of the appropriate, of self-contained ease.

Thus the Viennese Biedermeier presents yet another paradox. In a world of stiffly reactionary politics, a kind of social democracy took root based on a shared feeling for style. Nobility became a matter of manner. Everyone could play.

Of course, the hereditary nobleman was still expected to excel. But the criteria of excellence were the same for him as for the bourgeois. As Brion lists them, they were "sensuous refinement, delicacy of feeling, rarefied taste, politeness, and discreet charm." With such social values, only one question suggests itself: Shall we dance?

In this context the waltz matured, taking shape as a social force. In turn, the prevailing social forces shaped the waltz, giving it the light Biedermeier grace that it retained even in its later forms. The politics of Metternich, producing a mental climate in which emphasis was laid on style rather than substance, were as necessary to the development of the waltz as were the social thrust of the bourgeoisie and the genius of Strauss that summarized these influences in musical terms.

If the Viennese have a special gift for happiness, they owe it partly to a political tradition that does not challenge them to anything else. Under benevolent despots they were relieved of all social responsibility beyond the care of their families. Unable to maneuver power to their advantage or exercise political foresight to avert misfortune, they were free to devote themselves entirely to their pleasures. Time and again, before Metternich and since, the Viennese have displayed that distinct quality of temperament that permits them to withstand oppressive authority but not to defy it. And all the while there is music, like an armistice between unseen forces.

3

The Making of a King

After Johann junior, Anna bore her husband five more children: Josef (1827), Anna (1829), Therese (1831), Eduard (1835), and the unfortunate Ferdinand, who died shortly after his birth. It is remarkable that she managed to see her husband long enough for all this fecundity. It wasn't just work that kept him away nights. There was also Emilie.

What he saw in her is a puzzle. Strauss, who could have had his pick among women, enmeshed himself with a plain-faced, ill-spoken, graceless and stupid hatmaker. Even her name, Trampusch, sounds cloddish. Her shabby flat in the Kumpfgasse, a dank medieval alley, must have seemed insufferably drab after the opulence surrounding Strauss at work and the solid comfort of his own home. Yet it was with Emilie in the Kumpfgasse that Strauss found repose.

All Emilie asked of him was money, which she frittered away on silly luxuries. Anna asked for things that were harder to give. After all, what first attracted Strauss to his wife, aside from her exotic good looks, was her clear-eyed intelligence, her depth of character, and her keen musical judgment. Anna was a person of considerable inner complexity and resources, and in time her maturing sense of values demanded something from life beyond mere glitter and pretty tunes. Strauss was apparently unprepared to meet these demands.

He was not a man to put his perplexities in words and left no documentary clue to his feelings. It is quite likely that the frenzied pace of his daily activity and the intensity of his creative life both as a composer and conductor left him spiritually drained and emotionally bankrupt. Whatever Anna's merits, Emilie was easier.

Anna had long accustomed herself to other women's pursuit of her husband. It appears that she kept prudent silence about many a passing fling. She would have understood Johann's attraction to any of the elegant and witty women of rank who fawned upon Strauss as a celebrity. But to see the man she loved, and of whom she was deeply proud, dragged nightly into a slum by a dull and ugly creature was to her more distressing than his infidelity as such.

Anna kept her composure in the face of gossip. She devoted herself to her children and the management of her spacious home in the new *Hirschenhaus*, Vienna's first large apartment building and a rather fashionable address for those of the upper bourgeoisie who preferred not to keep their own houses. Of course, malicious friends saw to it that she was duly informed every time Emilie flaunted herself at Strauss's concerts in her extravagant if tasteless clothes.

Anna's response was quiet and appropriate. She no longer appeared in public with her celebrated husband. Even the eagerly reported news of a spectacular diamond clasp Strauss had presented to his paramour failed to shake Anna's self-possession.

But her quiet endurance reached its limit when Emilie, who bore Johann's children as often as Anna, had the gall to name one of her bastards Johann. To Anna, this was blasphemy. At last, she confronted her husband with an ultimatum. Strauss simply packed up and moved into the Kumpfgasse. From then on, his relations with his family consisted mostly of sending a slender allowance of 500 *Gulden* (roughly equivalent to $500 in current value) on the first of each month. Emilie added her own grace note to the situation by announcing that Anna evidently lacked "the liberty needed by Strauss of the Waltz."

Supporting five legitimate children along with five bastards, plus keeping Emilie in her kind of pin money, strained the finances of even the fabulous Strauss. Throughout the late 1830s he took one group of musicians on extended concert tours while another part remained in Vienna to play under assistant conductor Franz Ammon. Ostensibly, these tours were to bolster his income. And if some of them didn't turn out to be as profitable as anticipated, they still afforded him the priceless fringe benefit of getting away from both his women.

In his journeys Strauss found surcease from his almost pathological restlessness. He needed the challenge of conquering strange audiences. His invariable triumphs reassured him, and perhaps masked the pain of his marital failure. In his music was happiness. And there was happiness mirrored in all the thousands of faces about him as he played in city after city. He created these people. They were inhabitants of worlds made anew each night. These happy crowds were his real children—everywhere.

Traveling itself was still a challenge. The newly invented railroads with their tiny wood-burning locomotives and their open-sided cars were a splendid adventure. The Viennese always had their own way of looking at progress. They regarded railroads as a new form of entertainment, in a class with such other excellent innovations as the steam-driven merry-go-round. The government declined to support such frivolities, and only the Baron Rothschild seemed to see any future in rail travel. He financed the first Austrian rail lines and, according to a perhaps apocryphal report, employed a unique signaling system along the tracks. Near refueling stops, where heaps of fast-burning pine cones awaited the hungry engines, watchful dachshunds were tied to stakes.

They could hear approaching trains long before human ears registered their puffing, and announced imminent arrivals with their frenetic barking. According to this account, the dachshunds were official railroad employees in Austria, with pension rights and the resounding title of *Zugsvormeldehund*. But like so many other railroaders since, they were soon replaced by mechanical devices.

At the time, most railroads chugged but a few miles beyond the major cities on short suburban runs. For long-distance hauls Strauss and his thirty-man orchestra still depended on hard-sprung stagecoaches bouncing over cobbled streets or lurching through mud. With luck, these "accommodations" covered fifty miles each arduous day. But the very discomfort of getting to his destinations was solace to Strauss—another morsel to feed his insatiable appetite for challenge.

The first of his longer journeys—in November 1834—took Strauss to Berlin, where his reputation assured him the privilege of playing before the King of Prussia at his court. The larger Berlin public was by no means predisposed toward any artistic import from Vienna, a city at the opposite temperamental pole from the stodgy metropolis of Germany's sober north. But they were culturally open-minded, willing to hear anyone out and judge him on his merits. Before long a Berlin newspaper critic exclaimed: "Look at little Strauss. He has turned all our good citizens into Viennese."

Night after night, lambent Viennese melodies, so unlike anything heard in the chilly North, melted the Berliners thronging the Königstädter Theater. After a concert on November 12, 1834, the well-known Berlin critic Oettinger seemed to lose control over his pen: "I am so happy, so joyful, so glad that I want to kiss the heavens with their stars; so recklessly, deliriously happy that I want to embrace the whole world and press it to my heart! And why? Because I have heard him! Because I have heard Johann Strauss!" It goes on from there.

On November 25, Strauss and his whole orchestra were

virtually kidnapped backstage after a public concert, bundled into carriages, and whisked off to the royal palace at Potsdam. The visiting Czar Nicholas of Russia and his Czarina had expressed the wish of hearing Strauss play. Their wish, it seemed, was Strauss's command. After the music, the Czar made amends for the importunity of abducting Strauss by presenting him with a magnificently engraved golden cigarette box. The next day, the King of Prussia also apologized in the only way a royal person may do so. He sent Strauss a satchel of money.

A day later, the Russian ambassador conveyed the Czar's invitation to St. Petersburg. His Imperial Highness wanted Strauss and all his musicians to join the imperial entourage on the way back to Russia. But Strauss declined this singular honor, pleading a prior engagement to play at Sperl in Vienna during the coming Carnival season. Very likely, he could have reneged on that obligation, but after the command performance at the palace, Strauss was perhaps a little apprehensive of the Czar's invitations.

His return trip to Vienna offered opportunity for concerts in Leipzig, Dresden, and Prague. At the last stopover, Strauss encountered a new dance that had just sprung up in Bohemia —the polka. According to local legend, the polka had been invented a short time before by a pretty peasant girl in the village of Elbeteinitz, a short way down the Moldau from Prague. Whatever the source, the invention proved immediately successful. Everywhere in rural Bohemia one could hear sweet-tooting brass bands pumping out polkas in the arcaded village squares and in the backyards of the country inns, next to the shingle-roofed, open-air duckpin alleys. Farm boys with shiny leather boots and blazingly colorful shirts would hop about with girls in countless lace-trimmed petticoats and flying braids. It was during his journey through Bohemia that Strauss gained the impetus for writing his own polkas, which later introduced this buoyant Czech dance to Viennese ballrooms.

By mid-December, Strauss celebrated his return to Vienna amidst the accustomed adulation at Sperl. But the success and stimulation of his tour, as well as his domestic problems, whetted his appetite for further travel. Within a year, he again set off on an extended tour that included many quaint capitals of the small ducal states that later were to form a unified Germany. Halle, Magdeburg, Brunswick, Hannover, Hamburg, Bremen, Cologne, Aachen, Mainz, Würzburg, Mannheim, Stuttgart, Nuremburg, and Augsburg were among his main stops. A lovely journey it must have been with all these towns still in the unspoiled bloom of their ancient charm, gabled and beamed, full of sculptured nooks, and innocent of a fate that a century later would obliterate all but their names.

Not everyone in these picturesque but often provincial cities welcomed Strauss. Especially in the Protestant North there was virtuous agitation against the waltz as a moral infestation from the Catholic South. The dance was decried as "an incitement to sinful passion," and denounced as "demoralizing and lewd." Some of the opposition adopted a medical guise and circulated a treatise splendidly titled in the current style of German scholarship: *Beweis, dass der Walzer eine Hauptquelle der Schwäche des Körpers und des Geistes unserer Generation sey. Deutschlands Söhnen und Töchtern angelegentlichst empfohlen* (Proof That the Waltz is a Main Cause of the Weakness of Body and Mind of Our Generation. Most Urgently Recommended to German Sons and Daughters).

From a medical point of view, the treatise was spurious. Yet it was demonstrably true that the new dance, in its more bacchanalian forms, induced occasional fainting, and was dangerous to the elderly or hypertensive with spirit more willing than flesh. A few fatalities occurred. Men seemed more prone to such risks than women—possibly the double task of grasping a girl while whirling in circles put them under combined emotional and cardiovascular stress. Judging by contemporary reports, strait-laced northerners seemed more seriously affected by this syndrome than the nimbler Viennese.

Local puritans, making the most of such clinical incidents, had prevailed upon several German towns to pass laws against waltzing as health ordinances. Others, notably Magdeburg, Prenzlau, and Frankfurt, simply issued police edicts against the "improper and horrible turning of women by men," particularly if done in a manner to "make skirts fly up and reveal too much."

But such statutes failed to stem the Straussian avalanche. The acceptance of the waltz was further hastened by the timely appearance of Halley's comet in April 1836, which, as is customary in the case of comets, was widely presumed to be on a collision course with Earth. Waltzing seemed the best possible preparation for the impending end of the world.

After his conquest of the German philistines, Strauss ventured further abroad, playing in Amsterdam, The Hague, Liège, and Brussels. Moving beyond the German-language region into areas culturally even more remote from his home grounds, Strauss began to realize that he was not merely a traveling entertainer. He came to understand that his music represented the Viennese spirit, and that his travels were in the nature of a missionary journey. As a Hamburg newspaper observed: "Vienna is not only in Vienna. It is wherever Strauss is." Strauss relished the role of cultural ambassador and readied himself for his toughest assignment—the journey to Paris and London.

At five o'clock in the afternoon of October 4, 1837, Strauss and twenty-eight of his musicians climbed into the overland coaches that were to take them to Paris. Their point of departure was the Wollzeile, a narrow, curved street lined with bookshops that winds through the center of Vienna between St. Stephen's cathedral and a tributary of the Danube. An almost hysterical crowd that had come to bid them farewell refused to make way for the horses. It was as if the

Viennese were afraid to let Strauss go, as if some premonition warned them that his absence might somehow leave the city unprotected, deprived of its very soul. Women wept and pushed their tear-stained handkerchiefs through the open carriage windows, along with small bouquets of flowers. It was nearly an hour before the coachmen were finally able to make headway, and the caravan rolled through the city gate into the autumn dusk.

Paris would be no pushover. Strauss was tackling the intellectual and artistic capital of the world, a city surfeited with excellence in every field. Parisian audiences had a reputation for being cool, critical, and cruel. Unlike cities where Strauss had played before, Paris wasn't likely to be grateful to itinerant purveyors of Viennese glamour. Paris had quite enough glamour of its own. Espeially in the field of popular music, it boasted the fabled M. Musard, who had ninety-six men in his orchestra, including a floor-shaking row of double basses and an astonishing oboe player with seemingly endless breath.

How would the Parisians react to Strauss waltzes? Their own popular music, dominated by the quadrille, tended to be crisp and pointed, emotionally the very opposite of the sentimental sweep of Viennese melodies. Besides, in Vienna it was generally understood that, in a mystic sort of way, love and the waltz were the same thing in different guises. No such amiable association existed among the French.

Understandably, Strauss's confidence wavered for the first time when he arrived in Paris on October 27. No sooner had he, along with his orchestra, taken up residence at the Hôtel Violette than a famous visitor announced himself. With the instinctive politeness of the French, his chief rival, M. Musard, promptly called on Strauss to welcome him to Paris. Soon the two musicians were engrossed in cordial shoptalk and their rivalry receded before their personal liking for each other. Still, the interview left Strauss wondering uneasily how his own puny group of twenty-eight would sound to a public conditioned by Musard's massed forces. His gloom deepened.

He was noticeably nervous when, on November 1, 1837, he mounted the podium for his opening concert. The Salle des Gymnases had been sold out despite raised prices. Luminaries of French music showed up *en masse:* Meyerbeer, Cherubini, Auber, Adam, and Halévy. And looking down from the stage Strauss recognized a wild mop of carrot-colored hair as the head of Hector Berlioz. Such an audience could make or break international reputations.

As tribute to his French hosts, Strauss began the concert with Auber's prelude to *Les Faux-Monnayeurs.* The composer listened with obvious pleasure and tossed Strauss a bunch of violets at the end. Next, Strauss launched into his own waltzes. His style of leading the orchestra, alternately conducting and playing along, intrigued the French, who had never seen anything of the kind. His physical abandon, as he swayed with his violin, bending forward and backward, tossing his head, and swinging his fiddle up and down in an effort to play and conduct simultaneously, seemed wild and exotic to the decorous Parisians. But the audience was carried along by the obvious musicality of the man and the charm of his waltzes. Long before the concert was over, Strauss knew that Paris was his.

Berlioz recorded his impressions of the concert in an essay analyzing the contrast in Viennese and Parisian styles of orchestral playing. Characteristically, he was intrigued by Strauss's use of the woodwinds, remarking on the sweetness of the Viennese clarinets. As might be expected of a man who revolutionized orchestration, Berlioz admired the wide range of tonal nuance Strauss was able to draw from his relatively small orchestra, and he clearly perceived the most essential element in Strauss's music—its rhythmic fluidity: "Strauss's musicians had more practice in overcoming the difficulties of rhythmic change than our own artists. Their waltzes in which the melody, self-intoxicated, chases and whips up the tempo, are difficult to play; but how easily the

Viennese accomplish it, how they charm us with their piquant rhythmic coquetry!"

Four days later, Strauss played at the Tuileries for King Louis-Philippe. As the orchestra entered the palace, they had to pass through a long hallway filled with soldiers, their rifles stacked in pyramids as if encamped before battle. The Viennese, whose own history up to that time had been more tranquil than that of the French, were alarmed at the sight of armed troops inside a royal residence and before a concert.

Other aspects of the French court seemed equally perplexing. When Strauss and his group were finally admitted to the royal presence, he made a deep bow and remained in that position, just as he might have done before a Habsburg emperor, awaiting the touch of a chamberlain as a sign to resume upright posture. But Louis-Philippe, the Bourgeois King, who prided himself on his democratic ways, expected no obeisance and had no one ready to straighten up Strauss. He remained bent until finally a genial bystander ambled over to him and broke up this grotesque impasse by suggesting that he might as well start the music. Later on, the progressive monarch mortified Strauss by saying to him graciously, in German: "Herr Strauss, you have done me an honor by appearing here personally." It was a strange country where a musician could do honor to the king. The world was changing here, but Strauss, like most Viennese, did not understand it.

After the concert Louis Philippe made an impromptu speech to his Viennese guests—a king addressing players!—and the orchestra was invited to mix socially with members of the court. The Duke of Orleans took the violin from Strauss's hands and scratched a few tunes on it, and the visiting King and Queen of the Belgians, a pleasant young couple, casually engaged Strauss in conversation. All this fashionable display of egalitarianism did not diminish the royal largesse. The next day the king sent Strauss two thousand francs and a diamond pin.

Meanwhile, Strauss and Musard, growing increasingly

fond of each other, buried their rivalry and decided to give joint concerts in which the gossamer texture of the Strauss sound made a pleasing contrast to Musard's large orchestra. The format was an immediate success, and the joint concerts were the highlights of Parisian musical life that season. From Musard Strauss learned to play quadrilles with an authentic Parisian accent and later introduced this elegant dance to Vienna.

A minor disciplinary problem arose from the nature of French wines. The vintages of Bordeaux and Burgundy proved more potent than Vienna's light domestic growth, and apparently Strauss's musicians failed to take account of this difference. After a few musical after-effects were traced to this circumstance, Strauss ordained strict wine rations. His men accepted these restrictions without grumbling. To them, Strauss was an absolute ruler, the complete autocrat. He enforced personal discipline and proper public deportment as rigidly as good musicianship, and if his men did not necessarily love him, they were deeply loyal and proud of their share in his glory.

The only thing ever to undermine the orchestra's morale was homesickness, a malaise endemic in all Viennese away from Vienna. Predictably, it broke out at Christmas. Those French didn't even have Christmas trees! And instead of going to midnight Mass, they were dancing in the streets. One orchestra member indignantly wrote home that he had seen a nun whirling about in the arms of a Capuchin monk. Besides, what good is *haute cuisine* when what you really want is *Tafelspitz, Zwetschkenknödl,* and *Kaiserschmarrn.*

It took all the persuasion Strauss could muster, along with a massive pay boost, to keep his band from deserting and somehow straggling back to Austria in the midst of winter. But Strauss was under contract to remain in Paris throughout the Carnival, alternating public concerts with playing in the fashionable private mansions of the Faubourg St. Honoré.

The Comte de la Garde captures the mood of these gatherings: "It has a mysterious power, this waltz. As soon as the first measures ring out, a smile steals upon the faces, the eyes light up, and all feel some inward expectation. The graceful pairs form and begin to move, interweaving their paths. One must observe the beauty of the women as they are carried along by this irresistible music, leaning on the arms of their partners, with the glossy silk and delicate gauze of their dresses sharing their every move in caressing waves. . . ."

Strauss played repeatedly at the home of the Baron Delmare, reportedly the possessor of a fortune of twenty million francs, who gave parties that lasted for thirty continuous nights and days. It was at Delmare's mansion that Strauss was approached by an ancient man whom he did not recognize but who was treated by everyone with great deference. The old man silently took Strauss's hand, smiled, and left again. Later, the host explained to Strauss that he had been greeted by Talleyrand, whose gift for political compromise had helped his nation survive the generation of turmoil from the Revolution, beyond Napoleon, to the Bourbon restoration. Years before, when Talleyrand dominated the Congress of Vienna, he had heard the fifteen-year-old Strauss playing his first waltzes in Pamer's orchestra. Now he wanted to pay his respects to the mature master.

Strauss's most memorable encounter during his Paris sojourn involved another old man, then near the end of his life, who rarely went out to concerts anymore. He sat inconspicuously in one of the back rows. But the audience immediately spotted Nicolò Paganini, and escorted him to a place of honor quickly vacated in the front of the hall. Strauss stood on the podium, about to begin the concert, but as soon as he recognized the unexpected guest, he left the stage and hurried down the center aisle to greet him. Paganini rose and embraced Strauss. Then Paganini spoke into the silence which had fallen upon the audience: "I am glad to meet a man who has brought so much joy into the world."

Before leaving Paris, Strauss ruffled the French by his ob-

stinate refusal to let his musicians appear in costume at the
traditional Masked Ball of the City of Paris. He rejected the
black dominoes prepared for them as beneath their dignity.
To the Austrian ambassador, who tried to explain the local
custom, he replied curtly that his men were musicians, not
buffoons. The French Minister of the Interior was called to
the scene and asked Strauss not to disturb the festivities. But
Strauss was obdurate, and finally, to the astonishment of the
Parisians, his orchestra took their seats in ordinary evening
dress. Strauss was a proper Austrian. He had been outraged
at the idea of his men mixing socially with the French court.
But he was equally outraged at the suggestion that his musicians were anything less than gentlemen.

At the end of the Carnival, the coming of spring once
again caused an acute flare-up of homesickness, driving the
orchestra to near-mutiny. But Strauss would not hear of returning to Vienna. The young Princess Victoria was to be
crowned Queen of England that spring, and Strauss—devout
monarchist that he was—would not forgo the chance to be
playing in London at that festive time. Again he raised his
players' pay, and to mollify their grumblings, he made every
possible provision for their comfort. "We have every kind
of convenience," one of the players wrote home, "equal to
anything enjoyed by rich travelers."

Yet the British venture started badly. The Viennese, like
most inlanders, have a strange feeling about the sea, compounded equally of legend and longing. They also fear it as
one fears the unknown and unfathomable, with a mystic, un-
quenchable horror. A first voyage would be a dubious
adventure for any Viennese, even under the best of circumstances. But on the night of April 11, 1838, a sea squall
churned the Channel, and one can surmise their state of mind
and stomach as Strauss and his orchestra held to the railings
of a tiny steamer whose paddlewheels spun impotently in the
air as the ship rolled from side to side.

On land, conditions proved equally unstable. The hotel in
which the orchestra was booked fell short of Strauss's accus-

tomed luxury. With typical impatience, Strauss gathered his men and they all marched out. They did not get far. The irate hotelkeeper had Strauss arrested for breach of contract. Strauss, on being shown some supposedly binding clause in the rental agreement, pleaded his inability to read English. That was no legal excuse, and it took the intervention of the Austrian ambassador to get Strauss free.

Sensing that the indignant Strauss was heading for further debacles, the ambassador cautioned him: "I warn you of two things—lawsuits and scandal. You are not in France, where publicity is a spicy adjunct to the person of an artist. In England it is always dangerous for a person to make himself conspicuous."

The ambassador, Prince Esterházy, was an unlikely person to give such advice, A latter-day scion of the family immortalized by Haydn, he had fathered a hundred bastards and was equally extravagant with money. Shortly afterward, his estates were sequestered. But he was quite right in anticipating more trouble for Strauss.

After trudging about the strange city, Strauss and his band at last found suitable lodgings at the Hotel Commerce in Leicester Street. The proprietor, sharing the customary British opinion of artists and musicians, demanded advance payment. When Strauss went to his room to fetch the money, he found that a thief had broken in and taken all his cash. He could not even pay expenses already incurred.

It was the time of early Dickens, and under Britain's notorious bankruptcy laws, Strauss's entire entourage might have been marched off to debtor's prison, had not a certain Mr. Cock turned up to take matters in hand.

Mr. Cock introduced himself as a music publisher. If Mr. Strauss would be so kind as to promptly write a waltz for him, he would see to it that everything was taken care of. Strauss explained that he had an exclusive publishing contract with the firm of Tobias Haslinger in Vienna. Never mind, said Mr. Cock.

Strauss, realizing that it would be easier to explain all this to Haslinger than to an English judge, sat down and wrote a short waltz. Cock paid the bill and ran off with his prize. Later, after Strauss's eventual success in Britain, Cock recouped his investment many times over.

As earlier in Germany, Strauss enjoyed a great deal of free publicity from self-appointed moral guardians. As in other Protestant lands, in England the Devil was known to be an active proponent of music and dancing. One London observer "could not help reflecting how uneasy an English mother would be to see her daughter so familiarly treated, and still more to witness the obliging manner in which the freedom is returned by the female."

Even Lord Byron, though rarely siding with pious causes, had some years earlier penned a poem that pictured the waltz as prelude to inevitable rape:

> Round all the confines of the yielded waist
> The strangest hand may wander undisplaced;
> The lady's, in return, may grasp as much
> As princely paunches offer to her touch. . . .
>
> Thus all and each, in movement swift or slow
> The genial contact gently undergo;
> Till some might marvel with the modest Turk,
> If nothing follows all this palming work?
> Something does follow at a fitter time;
> The breast thus publicly resigned to man,
> In private may resist him—if it can.

The notoriety his opponents gave him soon helped Strauss fill the halls that had been more than half empty at his first concerts, especially after London's competent reviewers, seemingly unafraid of the Devil, conceded the excellence of his music. But his most telling support came from the graceful nineteen-year-old girl who soon would be Victoria, Queen of England. The woman whose name was to become the signature of prudery was in her youth a charming and sprightly creature and very fond of dancing. At the great court ball at Buckingham Palace preceding her coronation, she waltzed with charming restraint to the music played for her by Johann Strauss.

Couriers and semaphores carried the news across half a continent back to Austria, where Strauss now appeared to his countrymen in a new aura. He didn't realize it, but when he played at Victoria's ball, the coronation had also been his own. It was during his triumphs in the West that the rather trite designation of Waltz King took on a new meaning.

The Viennese, painfully self-conscious about their eastern latitude and reluctant in their kinship to the Slavic sphere, rejoiced in the fact that their own star now shone over Paris and London.

The average Viennese knew little about either of these cities, but he was dimly aware that these capitals of the West were focal points of altogether new conceptions of life. To him, Britain and France were magic regions whence came steam engines, forbidden ideas of political liberty, religious skepticism, romantic novels, and heaven only knew what other tantalizing notions. Johann Strauss with his *echt-Wien* music had enchanted those fabled lands far beyond the snowy mountains. This bolstered Vienna's civic pride, and the stout burghers at the *Heurigen* patted their stomachs with reassured self-importance.

Had Austria marched on France, sailed against Britain, and hoisted the Habsburg emblem atop the Arc de Triomphe and the tower of Parliament, the Viennese would have shrugged it off as just another military byplay. But now Paris and London were dancing the waltz. That was a real conquest. Johann Strauss was a true king. He had earned his title.

Having played before the Queen, the Defender of the Faith, Strauss was presumably cleansed of devilish corruption. It was now safe for the good people of the English provinces to hear him, and he left London for a highly successful tour of Birmingham, Bath, Southampton, Brighton, and Portsmouth. Everywhere he was acclaimed with quite un-British fervor, and his honorarium reached the unheard-of sum of £200 per night.

Only in Scotland did he encounter difficulties. Strauss naturally considered Sunday as the best possible day for making music and having a ball. The Scottish Presbyterians thought otherwise. On this and several other points, Strauss and his Scot hosts regarded each other with profound mutual incomprehension, and he soon moved on to Ireland, where music and dancing were less suspect.

At the farthest point of his great journey, Strauss stood on the Irish shore and looked westward over the sea. Beyond lay new land—America—a curious country without kings and castles, the land where everything was yet to be. Across the water lay the last challenge. That was where he now wanted to go.

The clarinetist Reichman, his trusted confidant among the musicians, tried to dissuade him. The men were homesick again. Besides, the small wooden ships then in transatlantic service made the ocean seem doubly dreadful.

Yet Strauss was obsessed with that curious romantic yearning for the West that struck Europeans like a madness in the last century. Unwittingly, he must have betrayed his thoughts. Rumors sprang up among his players: Strauss, having broken with his family, never really intended to return to Vienna, and planned to drag his troupe into the murderous wilds of the United States.

One night the orchestra confronted Strauss with its suspicions and refused to go onstage. They had been absent from home for almost a year. They had played a killing schedule: eighty-six concerts within four months in France, seventy-two concerts in as long a span in England. They had followed Strauss implicitly. Now they had had enough.

It was an open revolt, and only Reichmann's mediation prevented a walkout. Grudgingly the players agreed to complete a scheduled tour of England, on condition that they would then go directly to Vienna.

They were home sooner than promised. A chill October fog defied the efforts of hotelkeepers to make their Viennese visitors comfortable. Open fireplaces, then the only heat source in British houses, warmed the men on one side only. Accustomed to the enveloping warmth given off by the massive tile stoves of Vienna, they developed persistent colds. A seven-day spell of rain overtook them in Scotland as they traveled in unheated coaches up to the axles in mud. Repeatedly, the entire orchestra had to get out into the downpour to lift their carriages from the mire. By the time they reached Edinburgh, a fever had spread among them. A local doctor prescribed plenty of claret, nutmeg, and ginger, "hot enough to wake the dead." The men shivered with fever and sweated from the medicine, but they played as scheduled.

Despite fever and a racking cough, Strauss conducted at Newcastle, Leeds, Hull, and Wakefield. At Derby he found himself unable to go on stage. A doctor tried to still his coughing spasms with the latest all-purpose medicine: he prescribed a massive dose of opium. Strauss almost died. Frightened, he fled the English and their climate, crossing to France. In Calais, he collapsed in a hotel corridor, uttering a scream of horror as he fell.

For days he lay in intermittent coma. Occasionally he became conscious long enough to announce to his doctors that he planned to conduct a concert in the evening.

Some Britishers looked upon Strauss's condition as a providential hint. London's leading music journal, *The Musical World*, managed to work some uplift into the story:

> As the hour of sickness is held to be a good time for the inculcation of a little morality, we shall, after the manner of the most orthodox divines, endeavor to improve the occasion, by a word of advice (which at present is much needed), to those who are disposed to make money too fast, and damage their constitutions, their fame, and—worse of all—their music, by a horrid greediness after the receipts of concerts. Be ye warned in time, ye itinerant speculators, observe what we shall say of the fate of Strauss and tremble:

Strauss, who is on his bed at Calais, finds himself very successful, much applauded, rich—and dying.

The article ran under the headline "Strauss's Last Waltz," and the editors seemed quite miffed when Strauss didn't properly cooperate. A few days later they noted peevishly that they had "not yet heard any fatal news of Strauss" and almost implied that it would be tactless of him to stay alive, because it would spoil the good moral of their essay.

The orchestra, taking desolate farewell of the man who had led them to worldwide fame, set off for Vienna. Only Reichmann remained with the sick leader. Again and again, Strauss begged his doctors to let him go home, too.

Giving in to the pleas of the presumably moribund man, the doctors permitted Strauss to attempt the long trip in a coach fitted with a cot. Only rugs shielded the sick man from the cold of winter. Sometimes the coachman tried to keep his passenger warm by piling trampled straw from the stables on top of him.

The carriage limped from hospital to hospital. Strauss was delirious most of the time. At Strasbourg physicians despaired of his survival. But when he crossed onto Austrian soil at Linz and once again heard familiar accents about him, he became alert and his condition improved.

Within sight of Vienna, at the town of Purkersdorf in the Vienna Woods, the trip ended abruptly. Something frightened the horses. They bolted and dashed the coach against one of the great acacia trees shading the highways of Austria. Miraculously, the sick man remained uninjured as the carriage splintered. Anna came from Vienna to fetch her husband, and thus Johann Strauss returned to his wife and family.

Under Anna's patient care, Strauss gradually regained his health. The whole city, anxious since the first news of his illness, now rejoiced at his recovery. As soon as he was able to stand on his feet, Strauss was back at Sperl.

One reason for his eagerness to resume concerts may have been his finances. The huge profits from his tour had been mysteriously dissipated. Not even his astute manager, Carl Friedrich Hirsch, a former student of Beethoven's, turned keen-eyed accountant, could ever figure out where it all went. Quite possibly, Strauss's ostensible loss may have been only a ruse to deceive Anna. He himself may have spirited the money to a secret depository, out of Anna's reach, in anticipation of his next move. When he no longer depended on Anna's care, he left her once more to resume his off-key idyll with Emilie. He never again set foot in his own home.

As before, Strauss enraptured his city and everything seemed as it once was. But it was not. The Vienna of the early 1840s was no longer quite the same city Strauss had left at the beginning of his travels. Beneath the bland harmonies and the happy tinkling, a new note was heard. Students, poets, and playwrights were passing forbidden books among themselves, whispering of "freedom of thought."

The whispers grew louder, and not even Metternich's police could muffle them altogether. Somehow, the seeds of liberalism had blown into the sealed land and taken root in the Biedermeier flowerbeds. The city no longer floated free of its time.

A new burden seemed to weigh on Vienna's spirit—not the official yoke, but the first inkling of something hitherto unknown to Vienna: the intellectual and social responsibility that inevitably accompanies liberal thought.

Vienna was still a joyous panoply for the celebration of life, but the silvery innocence had passed.

4

The Rival

It was an insurrection against royalty and the Crown Prince was the rebel. The scent of scandal, Vienna's favorite perfume, hung in the air and aroused the city.

The Waltz King had been challenged by his own son. Johann junior, barely nineteen, had hired a hall, assembled an orchestra, and plastered the town with placards:

ANNOUNCEMENT
INVITATION TO A SOIRÉE-DANSANT

which will take place on Tuesday, the fifteenth of October 1844, at Dommayer's Casino in Hietzing. Johann Strauss (the son) will have the honor of directing, for the first time, his own orchestra in a program of overtures and opera pieces as well as in a number of original compositions of his own.

Commending himself to the favor of his public,

Johann Strauss, Junior

Tickets available in advance for 30 Kreuzer; at the box office for 50 Kreuzer. It begins at six o'clock.

Agitated groups quickly formed around the street posters, discussing the announcement as if it were a political proclamation.

Normally, of course, it would be hardly remarkable if a talented son followed in his father's footsteps. But all Vienna knew that they were witnessing not a case of succession but an act of rebellion.

Emilie's blatancy had long made it an open secret that Strauss lived sumptuously with his mistress while keeping his family on a miserly allowance. But only lately had there been rumors that Strauss was pathologically jealous of his own son's musical talent.

At the age of six, little Johann picked out a waltz tune all his own on the piano at the family's summer house in Salmansdorf, a quaint almost toylike suburb at the foot of the Kahlenberg. This first hint of his son's musicality so disturbed the older Strauss that he forbade the child all further musical activity. But Anna, proud of her boy's precocity, fetched some music paper and secretly noted down the child's composition, thus preserving the first musical effort of the man who was to give the world *The Blue Danube*, *Tales from the Vienna Woods*, and *Die Fledermaus*.

That may have been the day when Anna Strauss, consciously or otherwise, conceived a plan to revenge herself on her husband. She would train little Johann to rival his father in his own field, so that someday he might dispute the Waltz King's crown.

As for young Johann, who like most Viennese boys of that name was called Schani, his innate eagerness for music made him a willing accomplice to his mother's scheme. Together they formed a conspiracy against the father. Anna would pinch *Kreuzer* from her household allowance to pay for Schani's secret music lessons. Franz Ammon, who conducted the Strauss orchestra in Vienna while Strauss toured with another group, was their collaborator. Recognizing the boy's unusual gifts, he agreed to become his surreptitious teacher.

It was from Ammon that Schani absorbed every nuance of the musical style his father had created. Secretly practicing the violin, Schani not only copied his father's gestures and mannerisms, he also developed his father's knack for tossing off those feather-light yet deeply yearning phrases, for striking that seductive balance between gaiety and languidness.

Schani knew but one kind of music—the waltz. Within the lilt of three-quarter time, he found the sensuous element that stirred his imagination. He was hardly more than a child when his playing already had what the Viennese call *Schmiss* —a curious witchery that makes music propelling, compulsive, ravishing, yet at the same time smiling and innocent.

When Ammon felt that Schani needed more solid grounding in music theory than he, a mere fiddler, could give him, Schani was taken to study counterpoint and harmony with Joseph Drexler, a renowned organist and composer of church music. Struck by the boy's talent, this rather monastic old musician was horrified to see it wasted on what he considered coarse and vulgar dances. He was also taken aback by Schani's playing waltzes on the church organ, occasionally confounding worshipers quietly praying in the dimly lit nave. "I meant to play a fugue," the boy would explain, "but somehow it slipped."

To break Schani of such habits, Drexler made him write a church cantata on the text *Tu qui regis totum orbem* (Thou Who Rulest the Whole World), hardly foreseeing how these words might someday apply, in a different sense, to the student himself. But this assignment went clearly against the boy's grain, and Anna, too, would have none of it. Schani was to challenge his father on his own grounds—not in the church but in the dance hall.

Paradoxically, it was this cantata, completed at Drexler's insistence, that cleared the way for Schani's bold defiance of the Waltz King. Before making a public appearance he had to obtain a license, and no city magistrate was likely to grant permission to a minor to play in a dance hall, especially if his name was Johann Strauss, Jr., and it was well known that the young man's famous father objected to such ventures on the part of his son. Surprisingly, Drexler helped Schani clear this hurdle. This gentle sixty-year-old music master would not stand in the way of young talent, even if he deplored the form of its expression. He endorsed Schani's license application, assuring the authorities that young Strauss was a "most modest and highly cultured youth," and he clinched the case by calling the magistrate's uncomprehending attention to the manuscript of *Tu qui regis totum orbem*. This, he argued, was proof of the boy's serious musical intentions. Impressed by Drexler's reputation as a noted composer of sacred music, the magistrate at last set his seal on the document that authorized the first public appearance of "Johann Strauss the Son."

Schani's entry into the musical profession did not take his famous father entirely by surprise. Years before, on one of his rare visits to his family's home, the elder Strauss caught Schani practicing the violin. He gave the boy a brutal whipping, shouting that he was going to beat the music out of him for good. Anna tore the whip from her husband's hands and placed herself between the boy and his raging father. From that day on, the older Strauss was gnawed by suspicions about his son's secret musical progress.

For some time, the Waltz King's business manager, Carl Friedrich Hirsch, a tall, wiry man with a long face, a hooked nose, and a manner of elegant lassitude, had been quietly making the rounds of Vienna's great ballrooms. He intimated, in a pleasantly roundabout way, that if that young whelp, Schani, were ever permitted to play at a given establishment, the Waltz King himself would boycott the place. This was tantamount to a threat of economic extinction.

As a result, the great luxurious ballrooms of the Inner City —Vienna's glittering pride—were closed to Schani. But out in the forest-ringed suburb of Hietzing, near the emperor's summer palace of Schönbrunn, where many pleasant coun-

try houses dotted the hillsides, stood Dommayer's Casino—
an elegant café with a large, tree-shaded garden that was the
frequent site of outdoor concerts.

Since Father Strauss confined most of his appearances to
the Inner City at that time, the suburban innkeeper of Dommayer's may not have felt concerned about the planned boycott. More likely, Hirsch had not yet traveled to the outlying
districts to deliver his threat. Messages of that sort would
hardly be entrusted to paper, and in the days before the
telephone, the only way to drop a discreet hint of blackmail
was in person. At any rate, Schani succeeded in signing up
Dommayer's for his debut.

The next problem was to recruit an orchestra and weld its
players into a cohesive group capable of interpreting the
boy's musical intentions. Such a task would be a challenge
even to experienced conductors with ample time. But Schani
was short of cash and could not pay for extended rehearsals.
He had to work in a hurry.

Fortunately, he knew where to find his men. He went to
The City of Belgrade, a rather disreputable inn frequented
by unemployed musicians. During days and nights of frantic
rehearsing, Schani hired, fired, and replaced musicians with
calm self-assurance and a seemingly innate judgment of a
player's capabilities. Within four weeks he had smoothed his
ragtag fifteen-man group into a reasonably polished ensemble.
The date was set. The posters went up.

Even before the public announcement, trade gossip carried
the news of Schani's rehearsals to the Waltz King. In a rage,
he announced that he would give a concert of his own on
the same night. That would show the young rascal!

No historic evidence exists that Father Strauss seriously
pursued his first impulsive threat of a competing concert.
According to one report, he abandoned the plan when he
heard that ticket scalpers, selling options on tickets yet to
be issued, were quoting higher prices for Schani's concert
than for his own.

Even if he had wanted to compete openly with his son, he would have been physically unable to do so. His fury had made him ill. Nearly paralyzed by frustration, he took to his bed. A deep depression settled over him. Two days before Schani's concert, he said to Tobias Haslinger, his publisher, "I hope to die before then."

Deeply worried about the Waltz King's health, the loyal Hirsch conceived a dramatic plan for cheering him up. He organized a group of rowdies and handed them tickets along with instructions to disrupt the concert when he gave the signal.

Hirsch was not alone in his enmity to young Johann. Many Viennese, learning of the stricken condition of their adored Waltz King, condemned the youngster's impertinence. Had this lad no respect for his father's greatness? Did he not know that his father's music had brought beauty and pleasure to countless listeners and added glory to Austria's name in the world? Why his ruthless insistence on grieving a man loved by everyone? And what could this boy gain by his defiance? Nothing but the humiliation due a stripling foolishly taking his measure against Europe's most idolized musician.

Others felt that the older Strauss was getting a well-deserved comeuppance from his mistreated family. They knew how brutally he had tried to stifle his son's musical talent. They knew that Anna had spent the last of her pittance to hire the orchestra for her son, and that young Johann, by the exercise of his musical talent, hoped to earn back for his mother some of the money the father had squandered on his mistress. In the music-mad city, nearly everyone took sides. The Strauss family quarrel exploded into a public issue.

Hours before the concert, the exodus began. Thousands set off on the four-mile journey to Hietzing, leaving behind Vienna's Inner City, still ringed by the massive walls that centuries before had thwarted the Turkish siege and saved Europe from Moslem conquest. Soon those walls were to be razed to make way for the Ringstrasse, that grand circular boulevard that was to become the world's most resplendent street. But in 1844, the walled city, surmounted by the gothic tower of St. Stephen's, still had an almost medieval aspect.

Through the majestic city gates the crowds poured onto the gardenlike meadows outside the walls, the Glacis, whose broad swath of green was by imperial edict to remain free of all encroachments. The Viennese penchant for making any occasion into a fashion show was abetted by a sunny day, quite warm for mid-October—just right for combining a concert with an outing. Prosperous top-hatted burghers with heavy watch chains dangling from their waistcoats, swinging silver-tipped walking sticks, looked almost as festive as their ladies, all feathers and lace.

Women were not yet cinched at the waist and confined to those voluminous walking tents that passed for skirts in the latter part of the nineteenth century. Their dresses still followed natural contours with delicacy and discretion, and though the hem of the skirt was still supposed to shield ankles from intrusive view, the demure collars of the earlier Biedermeier had given way to more generous décolletage.

The wealthier families rode in rakish landaus and cabriolets, driven by liveried coachmen. These fashionable carriages gleamed with the newly invented lacquer finishes that had just become the specialty of Viennese carriage builders, and some already had metal-leaf springs, which made Viennese cobblestones seem much less bumpy than the older leatherbelt carriage suspensions.

Others traveled less elegantly, though just as comfortably, in fiacres—those graceful horse cabs drawn by high-stepping pairs. The majority, however, came via *Zeiserlwagen*, that quaint precursor of the horse tram, consisting of a farm wagon fitted with rough benches into which lowlier citizens were piled.

Of the thousands who made the trek to Hietzing only a

fraction would come within earshot of the music. The box office had long been closed, even though extra tickets had been made available by selling standing room on the dance floor. This audience didn't want to dance. They had come to listen.

On the Hietzinger Platz, the spacious square outside Dommayer's, an impatient crowd milled about in vain hopes of gaining entrance. Coachmen tried to elbow a path through the crowd for their patrons. Doormen, trying to block the door to the inn, panicked under the pressure of a mob seemingly on the verge of riot. At last, mounted police, none too gently, parted the crowd and sealed off the café. Now the concert could begin.

Little of Vienna's usual *Gemütlichkeit* prevailed inside Dommayer's. What set people on edge, aside from nervous expectation, was the lack of the usual amenities. Unable to make their way through the aisles, the waiters soon abandoned their earlier attempts to serve food and wine—a privation not borne lightly in Vienna.

Not even the clear, cool evening air rolling in from the hillsides brought much comfort to the stifling crowd. And to make the mood even more ominous, rival factions of the audience glared at each other. In one corner, so to speak, sat Hirsch and Haslinger, the Waltz King's manager and publisher, surrounded by a loyalist following. Their studiously bored faces bespoke their expectations. They would hear some amateurish dance tunes gawkily conducted by an overbearing nineteen-year-old. Once the boy got this ridiculous charade out of his system, the tragic family rivalry would end.

Far in the background, in one of the trellised arcades abutting the open garden, sat Anna Strauss. She seemed to be praying.

The nervous murmur of the crowd quieted as the orchestra filed into the bandstand and began to tune up. Behind the scenes, young Johann stood before a mirror, fussing with his cravat. As if to conceal his youth, he had tried to grow a moustache, but little more than a tuft appeared on his lip. His hair, like that of his father, was jet black and curly, and his broad face with its high cheekbones and full lips held a dark intensity even in its smiles.

None of his new clothes had yet been paid for, but they were certainly in the latest fashion. A flowing blue coat with silver buttons, cut away at the waist and ending in the traditional tails, was draped over a silk waistcoat embroidered with tiny Alpine flowers. Uncreased gray trousers clung tightly to his legs, and their bottoms had loops to go under the soles of his buckled shoes. Floppy lace cuffs dangled from his sleeves to lend dash to his waving arms. And to heighten the effect of his gestures, Johann resorted to a trick he was to retain throughout the early years of his career: on his right wrist flashed a thin gold bracelet.

Yet all this finery could not bolster his confidence. As he admitted later, he was sick with stage fright, convinced of imminent failure. He half expected to be laughed off the stage. No amount of later acclaim would ever rid him of that fear, which stayed for the rest of his life.

Whatever doubts beset him, none showed as the lithe young man jumped nimbly to the podium and bowed briefly. But as he turned to the audience, Hirsch's hirelings swung into action. Their furious booing and catcalls mixed with the hurrahs of the opposing faction. Johann's fevered vision blurred. Quickly he sought refuge in the music.

The first selection was the overture to *The Mute of Portici* by the French composer François Auber. The piece was currently popular. Besides, it was with an Auber overture that the elder Strauss had opened his first Paris concert, so Schani was following a family custom.

It was not unusual at the time for a café concert to include a sprinkling of operatic and symphonic pieces. The Viennese made no sharp distinction between "serious" and "popular" music, and they liked something solid to listen to while catching their breath between dances.

Young Strauss, the newspaper critics agreed, did well enough with the overture, and if it failed to move the audience to anything but perfunctory applause, it was probably that the puny fifteen-man orchestra could not muster the requisite sonority. There was no sign from Hirsch, and his crew stayed quiet. The meager audience reaction was sufficient condemnation.

Johann was undismayed. He knew that the audience had come to judge him as a composer. They wanted to hear his own waltzes, to compare them with those of his father. The crucial moment would come with the next number, a waltz of his own. Originally, he had titled it *Das Mutterherz* (The Mother's Heart) as a tribute to the woman whose self-denying faith in him had made this evening possible. But the perceptive Anna Strauss had thought this dedicatory title too sentimental and had suggested an alternate: *Die Gunstwerber*, which translates rather clumsily as "Those Who Seek To Please."

The title was a coy bid for favor, but there was nothing coy about the music. The mesmerizing, willowy rhythm, the sweeping melody, and the bold, capricious accents that marked later works of Johann Strauss, Jr., were already evident.

Almost visibly, the spell of the music enraptured the crowd. Catcalls from the Hirsch contingent were drowned in overwhelming applause. Strauss had to repeat the waltz.

The second time, all constraint fell from him. Astonished, the orchestra responded to the new freedom and elasticity of his gestures, pouring out those swaying, lambent cadences that have since become the hallmark of Vienna's music.

An ovation followed. People climbed on their chairs, waving hats, shawls, and handkerchiefs. They wouldn't stop shouting until Strauss played the waltz again. And again.

After the fourth time, Strauss forestalled demand for another repetition. After the last chord of *Die Gunstwerber*,
he immediately signaled the start of a new polka: *Herzenslust*
(Heart's Delight)—another work of his own. He led with
demonic intensity. The orchestra, bewitched by the frenzied
audience as much as by the conductor, responded by playing
the sprightly polka with an effervescent lightness that seemed
to defy gravity itself.

The audience was jubilant. To the bewilderment of his
hirelings, Hirsch joined in the applause. True, he was a
friend of the father and he had a big financial stake in the
older man. But he had a greater loyalty: to music. He, a
former pupil of Beethoven, would not withhold approbation
from any artist who deserved it.

Next, another brand-new waltz by young Strauss: *Sinnge-
dichte*—"Poems of the Senses." The title says it all, and the
raving audience demanded and got nineteen repeats. Nothing
like that had ever happened before.

The hours passed. Vienna lay in darkness. Only the print-
shop windows were still lit. The morning papers couldn't be
put to bed without a report of the Strauss concert, and already it was past the deadline.

One by one, the reviewers left the concert, clattering back
to town in their fiacres to dictate last-minute notices directly
to the printers. Johann Nepomuk Vogt, the most influential
of the critics, complained in the *Osterreichisches Morgenblatt*
about being nearly suffocated, getting pushed and cuffed by
the crowd, and having nothing whatever to eat or drink. But
none of these rigors soured his judgment. In what was probably the fairest and most perceptive of all the comments, he
noted: "Talent is the monopoly of no single individual. This
young man is fully as melodious, as piquant, as effective in
his instrumentation as his father. . . . Nevertheless, he is no
slavish imitator of the latter's methods of composition."

Another reviewer, L. Wiest of the *Wanderer*, felt that
young Strauss's compositions were not superior to those of

his father, but pointed out that at the age of nineteen the elder Strauss had had nothing approaching the musical competence and aplomb of his son. And he ended his review with words that were to echo through Vienna for weeks: "Good evening, Father Strauss! Good morning to you, Strauss Junior!"

But long before the morning papers carried the news into the dawn, the crowd at Dommayer's knew that Vienna had a new Waltz King. In the midst of his triumph, young Johann—his face no longer pale but flushed and radiant— signaled for silence. Softly the orchestra began. This music had not been listed on the program. As the tremulous measures of the slow introduction floated into the night, listeners looked at each other in disbelief. Wasn't this *Lorelei-Rheinklänge*—the most famous of all the waltzes by the older Strauss? And how the boy conducted it! Into the lyric parts he infused something other than the customary sweetness. This went beyond the boundaries of a dance. Any waltz is a plea for love—a bid for romantic banter or an expression of yearning. But here the lyricism seemed transposed to a different emotional key. Gradually, as the music unfolded, the audience sensed the meaning of this interpretation. Young Strauss was playing his father's music not merely as a filial tribute of honor. He was playing it as a supplication—to beg his father's forgiveness.

There were tears in the audience, even among the men.

5

Elegy

Within the swirled patterns of history, beginnings and endings are lost in one another. That balmy concert in Dommayer's trellised garden marked the ascent of the man who would bring the Viennese waltz to its symphonic culmination. Yet it took place at a time when the social roots that had nourished the waltz in its early forms were already decaying.

The mental quarantine imposed by Metternich was no longer tight enough to isolate Vienna from time and the world. Though almost everyone crossing the border into Austria was tracked by the police to discover any contraband thoughts he might carry in his head, a handful of journeymen who had picked up socialist notions in France and Switzerland found their way into the Viennese working class. Occasionally even a member of the very proper bourgeoisie became infected by foreign intellectuals with subversive ideas about constitutionally guaranteed freedoms.

Those distant sounds of social reform would hardly have excited sympathetic resonance in Vienna's normally complacent atmosphere. Only a short time before, the German journalist Varnhagen von Ense reported that "daily life in Vienna is made of some special stuff that turns everything touching it into agreeable satisfaction." But by the mid-forties, that special stuff had begun to crumble, in its decay preparing a more receptive soil for the seeds of revolution.

Several circumstances combined to form eruptive pressures. One was the attitude of the police, who viewed every new idea as the product of organized conspiracy. By being needlessly ungentle in their search for presumed conspirators, they alienated segments of the bourgeoisie who normally would have supported the regime.

More significantly, the bourgeoisie itself was restive. The Napoleonic wars had been so costly that, forty years later, chronic inflation still pinched the middle class, caused a rash of bankruptcies, and made the stock exchange a haunt of unprincipled speculators. Even some old fortunes were shaved, and the Emperor himself was always borrowing from Rothschild, in return for which he made the Jew a baron—a mode of repayment that caused quiet head-shaking among the older and poorer Catholic nobility.

Though handicrafts practiced in small workshops still remained Vienna's dominant form of production, the first factories were already springing up. When some of these new enterprises succumbed to the pitfalls of over-imaginative financing, Vienna had its first taste of industrial unemployment. Of course, these blotches on the social fabric were still small enough to enable the good Viennese to look the other way, as the authorities expected them to.

As if all this weren't enough to nettle the Viennese, one kept hearing odd tales about the provinces. In the East, a tax rebellion by Galician landowners had to be squelched by the district governor, who expediently encouraged local farmhands to cut down their masters with their scythes. In the south, Venice protested a tariff on salt drawn from the sea. Lombardy also seemed disaffected. Good families in Milan no longer invited Austrian officers to dinner, and some people there muttered something about Italians forming a united country of their own. Up north, in Prague, Bohemian textile workers had to be dissuaded by bullets from wrecking the new automatic looms that threatened their jobs. And the Hungarians, a stubborn and impetuous breed, were always making a nuisance of themselves.

Metternich did his best to shield the people of his capital from such troublesome facts. Newspapers made no mention of them, and personal mail was censored. But little gossipy information pools formed here and there around returning travelers and homecoming soldiers, and an increasing number of Viennese burghers began to suspect that somewhere in the world there were alternatives to the complacent charm and cheerfulness that formed Vienna's spiritual core.

Of course, there was no possibility of questioning, no open inquiry or discussion, and on the surface Vienna remained merry and calm. The only intimation of doubt was to be found, paradoxically, in the most public of all places—onstage. In his popular comedies, Johann Nestroy presented mordant caricatures of the stock characters in Austrian society: peasant, landlord, artisan, shopkeeper, tradesman, merchant, and servant. Significantly, neither factory workers nor factory owners appeared in his plays, these social categories being yet too new for literary apprehension. Plays like *Einen Jux will er sich machen* (which re-emerged a century or so later in America adapted as *Hello, Dolly!*) came as close to genuine social criticism as the strictures of censorship permitted. Nestroy's satiric aim was unerring, but since his humor was homey and his thrust oblique, even the police laughed.

But if one listened closely to what Nestroy left unsaid, one sensed that by the time young Strauss made his debut at Dommayer's, the sweetly saturnine music of *Alt-Wien* belonged to an already fading time. The Biedermeier idyll, the dream of pleasured tranquillity, had begun to rot.

The revolution in Austria took its cue from France, a

country more practiced in such matters. In February 1848 Paris was exploding again. With its ample supply of students, artists, and visionaries of all kinds, Paris never lacked the elements needed to strike a spark; and the masses proved readily inflammable. The revolutionaries stormed the Tuileries, where they addressed themselves to the immediate challenge presented by the royal wine cellar. Thus fortified, they toppled the throne of France and shouted the republic from the barricades.

The object lesson was quickly learned by liberals throughout Europe: one way to power lies in the street, with the mob. Thus began the curious courtship of the masses by the liberals.

The unprecedented alliance of the educated and the illiterate, the discontented intellectuals and the desperate poor, promptly set fire to the continent. Within weeks of the French rebellion, a dozen principalities and countries flared up. But nowhere was the uprising as painful and prolonged as in Vienna, the foremost citadel of absolute monarchy.

In Vienna, even revolutions begin with proper decorum. On the morning of March 13, 1848, an orderly delegation of university students in their colorful fraternity costumes, led by frock-coated professors and top-hatted gentlemen from a liberal merchants' association, approached Metternich's palace to present a petition. They did not even mention the unspeakable word "Constitution." But they formally demanded freedom of the press, public accounting of state budgets, a municipal charter, and participation of the middle class in appointed councils.

All might have gone passably well, had not the middle-class liberals made one mistake. They invited a group of factory workers to come along to show their solidarity with the working class. Metternich might possibly have negotiated with properly dressed professors and businessmen. But the sight of the workers in their proletarian garb of blouse and cap—officially described in a state document as "brutal and

licentious trade and factory people"—had an unfortunate
effect on the fastidious prince. To him, they were *canaille*—
corrosive dregs. Remembering Robespierre's reign of terror,
he looked on them with loathing. Seeing them advance on
his palace in common, and therefore treacherous, cause with
proper burghers confounded Metternich's usual cool
judgment.

His reply to the petition was a volley fired into the waiting
assemblage—a strange response for a man renowned for
subtle statesmanship.

Metternich, one must remember, came from the Rhineland.
Germans, he knew, could be cowed by *Schrecklichkeit*—
calculated terror. Presumably he thought that the easy-going
Austrians would be even more readily subdued by such
means. What he didn't know about the Viennese temperament was that in the face of bald outrage, *Gemütlichkeit*
changes to stubborn courage. Within hours after the crack of
Metternich's muskets, the unthinkable happened: Austria's
capital rose in revolt, and from February to October 1848,
despite civil strife within, the rebels held the city.

Like Vienna itself, the Strauss family was now torn by
forces beyond its comprehension. Johann senior sided with
the royalists; Johann junior with the rebels. Already divided
by a broken marriage and bitter rivalry, father and son now
stood apart in politics.

Ironically, neither had strong political convictions. The
older man was a royalist mainly by force of habit. Like so
many Viennese then and since, he felt a civilized person's
loyalty to the past. Besides, royalism was convenient for a
musician who often played before kings.

Young Johann was a revolutionary for equally flimsy
reasons. Rigorous political analysis would have been totally
alien to his temper. Also, it was a discipline not yet in vogue.
As far as one can judge, his stand was based mainly on a
generous sympathy for his friends among the predominantly
liberal young artists and students.

Many rebels were far from radical. They did not object to monarchy as such. They merely hoped for the removal of Metternich and would have been happy to see the return of the Habsburgs in a new context of constitutional rule.

During the upheaval, the Strausses labored in support of opposing camps. Strauss senior bucked up the royalists with military marches so sprightly that, on the musical evidence alone, civil disorder seems a cheerful occasion. The crisis occasioned his most famous work, the *Radetzky March*. Among the generations of listeners enchanted by this sunniest of all marches, some would prefer to forget that it was written in honor of the Imperial Field Marshal who vanquished the insurgent democrats of Milan.

Young Strauss also switched from waltzes to marches. But his had revolutionary titles: *Freedom March, Songs of the Barricades*, and *March of the Students*. Later the authorities confiscated the sheet music of all these works and destroyed the printing plates. Posterity thus lost the only political mementos of the younger Strauss, and one surmises that the composer in his maturity was quite pleased at their eradication.

It may seem odd that both of Vienna's rival Waltz Kings so readily changed their musical idiom. Yet the emotional and stylistic gap between the waltz and the march was not as great in Vienna as one might suppose. The Viennese march, unlike its German counterpart, never proclaimed the cruel compulsions of military music that extinguish human feeling and help turn soldiers into mindless ranks of lethal robots. Far from being a goose-stepping Dance of Death, the Austrian march was an expression of graceful virility.

Even in instrumental technique, Viennese regimental bands differed from military styles elsewhere. Brass never blared and woodwinds never shrilled. The Viennese manner of playing these instruments produced a sweet, rounded tone with a distinctive *portamento*, gently yielding each note into the flow of the melody.

Such music made a review of Austrian troops more like a

ballet than a military parade. Responding to the winged measures, the soldiers intuitively lightened their gait. The whole aura of their motion was devoid of military abruptness and reflected the dancelike buoyancy of the melodies. Multi-colored uniforms, contrasting trousers, tunics, collars, and lapels in brilliant purples, browns, and blues, confirmed the impression that the sole function of Austria's army was ornamental.

In this context it does not seem incongruous for the two Waltz Kings to have held official positions as regimental composer-conductors. The gentle Lanner, before his early death in 1842, had held such a post. Even Beethoven, while he could still hear, did a stint as military bandmaster, and Schubert's *Marches Militaires* attest, with their charm and sprightliness, to the gay and festive spirit of Austrian military music.

Holding military rank while siding with the rebels did not seem to disturb young Johann. On one occasion he resolved a potential conflict in characteristic fashion. On August 22, while Strauss stood guard on the Karmeliterplatz in the Inner City, a courier warned him of a new workers' uprising in the Leopoldstadt, the district bordering on the Danube. If the mob marched on the Inner City, there might be skirmishes, and he certainly did not cherish the prospect of shooting or being shot by people who in better times had danced to his music. With eminent practicality, he simply left his post, went home to his mother, ate supper, and did a little compos-ing until all was quiet again. Elsewhere this is known as de-sertion. Strauss got away with it.

Between such occasional alarms, fighting in the city was rare, and during the long months of the revolution, the Viennese were often able to carry on a semblance of normal life. Metternich had fled to London, where he made long speeches to himself and played heaven-storming cadenzas on his violin to calm his nerves. The Emperor and his court had run off to the mountains of Tyrol, and in their absence, the revolutionary struggle became a political seesaw with more shouting than shooting.

All this time Vienna was without a government, and Eduard Bauernfeld, a prominent journalist, took the occasion to pat himself on his Austrian back. "Just try to leave Paris or London without authority for some days, and what scenes would ensue! Well, Vienna was in anarchy for seven months; but apart from caterwauling mock serenades, nothing happened that would have dishonored the city."

For most of the year, while public entertainments were curtailed, the Viennese slaked their musical appetite with private concerts and dances. The elder Strauss with his established entré to the great town houses was often the center of such evenings.

Neither had the revolution lessened Vienna's delight in elegant dress. A contemporary writer notes that "gentlemen, old and young, wore fashionable frock coats of various colors with light trousers, snowy linen, and kid gloves, while the ladies floated about in various costumes, some in pastels, others favoring deeper colors with trim in bright gold or rich bronze shades."

The splendor of bright occasions in these dark times was further enhanced by a new Viennese invention: the dripless candle. Unlike their wax and tallow predecessors, the new candles were nearly smoke-free, a fact permitting more chandeliers to be lit without polluting the air or blackening the ceiling. The new candles became the rage of Vienna, making their inventor one of Austria's richest commoners. Strauss, who spent most his working life by artificial light, promptly wrote his *Apollo Waltz* to celebrate the trademark of the new candles.

Vienna's plight did not halt the triumph of the waltz in other parts of the world. From Madrid came reports that the audience at Spanish theaters demanded Strauss compositions as intermission features, even at performances of serious drama. And in Paris and London, where Strauss himself had introduced his music, no popular concert or social gathering was complete without a group of waltzes.

Unlike the Viennese, the international public did not take sides in the family rivalry between father and son, simply enjoying the music of both. But the Viennese, being closer to this conflict, were quite shaken on discovering that young Strauss had secretly commissioned a series of articles in the *Pester Spiegel*, a leading Hungarian newspaper, attacking his father on both musical and personal grounds. Feeling affection for both men, the Viennese were also distressed when the younger Strauss so brazenly cheated his father in matters of exclusive performance rights that he was threatened by legal action. Only the intervention of young Johann's friends saved him from arrest.

In the latter part of 1848, the revolution seemed to gather momentum. A feeling spread through the city that matters were approaching some kind of culmination. This sense of urgency can hardly be credited to a still rather obscure visitor named Karl Marx, who came to Vienna in August to speak at the newly formed Workers' Association.

The year before, Marx had drawn up a kind of revolutionary Magna Carta in his *Communist Manifesto*. Yet despite its flashes of rhetoric, this document represented an intellectual departure as much as a political focus. As the first synoptic effort to define and confront the growing evils of exploitive industrialism, the *Manifesto* introduced a new system of analysis based on economic determinism. In his Viennese lectures, Marx spoke at length about labor, wages, and capital, drawing intricate connections between them. But his ideas of economic analysis were so new that nobody seemed able to follow his argument.

Another divisive point, one surmises, was Marx's view of history as progression and process—an idea he had distilled from the still freshly bubbling stew of Hegelian philosophy. Traditional historians tended to regard the past merely as chronicle, static and frozen. To Marx, history was a purposive design toward the idea of freedom that was just rousing the city in convulsive challenge. He spoke of history as growth and emergence, thinking of it almost as a living organism enveloping mankind and shaping the quality of human life. To him, history was a creature to be comprehended and tamed. Yet to his audience, accustomed to less dynamic modes of thought, Marx's intellectual bestriding the living body of history must have seemed too tempestuous a seduction of Clio.

Had they understood him, Marx might have given the revolutionary students of Vienna the conceptual cohesion they lacked, even though their aims reflected the rather rhapsodic liberalism of the French *philosophes* of the Enlightenment more than the rigidly systematic and deterministic spirit of Marx. Probably the students failed to respond to him just because their motivation was romantic rather than rational. And as for the workers, in whose name the whole uprising had begun, Marx's meticulous reasoning, far from inflaming them, tended to put them to sleep.

Yet it was Marx who in that fateful year gave the profoundly moral warning that any civilization inextricably linked to human debasement of any kind will induce a rage for its own destruction, and it was his metaphor of "the old age pregnant with the new one" that succinctly characterized the moment.

The birth of the new age, when it finally came, proved unexpectedly painful. All summer long, Count Windisch-Graetz, a Bohemian whose name and nobility were as ancient as Austria itself, had been massing troops in the provinces in behalf of the Emperor, who was virtually exiled in Innsbruck. At first, gentlemanly restraint kept Windisch-Graetz from deploying military force against the insurgent capital. But in October, an uncouth incident ended his forbearance.

A Viennese mob, with atypical passion and malice, murdered Count Latour, an imperial minister, and hung his corpse from a lamppost in unseemly display. Clearly this sort of thing was not to be tolerated by any commander with the power to prevent it. Windisch-Graetz promptly marched on Vienna, encircled the city, and invited the revolutionaries to negotiate.

At this delicate moment, some revolutionaries, in an access of sheer stupidity, played not merely the wrong card but the wrong game altogether. While delegates from both sides were conferring, radical students broke the truce and fired on the troops from the city gates.

Sniping from civilians is the kind of insult not even an Austrian army will endure. Windisch-Graetz promptly broke off all meetings, withdrew his men from exposed positions, pulled up his artillery, and during the night of October 30 ordered a cannonade of the city.

Where or how young Johann spent that night has not been reliably established. One suspects that he found a relatively safe and comfortable place. His brother Josef, a more ardent revolutionist, bravely stood on the barricades, ready to give battle to any imperial troops that might attempt to storm the city. Frau Anna Strauss and her youngest son Eduard watched in terror as fires spread through the city, lighting the sky so brightly that in the middle of the night they could read time from a nearby tower clock. Fearing that her home in the Hirschenhaus might fall victim to the conflagration, Anna took little Eduard and ran for shelter to a neighboring monastery, certain that sacred ground was safe from cannonball and firebrand.

In the early morning hours, the cannon fell silent, and at dawn the Viennese stared in stunned dismay into the hollowness of ruins. The loveliest of cities had been damaged. For a Viennese, no political issue could justify such eternal loss. Rather than risk further destruction, the liberals capitulated.

Yet the revolution was not truly lost. Metternich was gone. More importantly, the weak-minded Emperor Ferdinand was persuaded to relinquish his throne to his eighteen-year-old nephew, Franz Josef. As the boy kneeled before his feeble uncle to receive Europe's most venerable crown on December 2, 1848, the simple old Emperor was heard to whisper to him: "Just be good and all will be well."

Franz Josef seems to have heeded this plain advice. In his later years he grew into an uncommonly decent and honorable ruler, a man in whose personal qualities lay Austria's true strength. Under his benevolent sixty-eight-year reign, Austria saw the apogee of its distinctive civilization. In this period, Vienna became a veritable Parnassus of the human spirit, from which, until it was shattered by the brutal forces of the twentieth century, radiated a sunburst of achievements in the arts, in science, in literature, and in medicine.

But on the morning after the bombardment, few Viennese liberals could envision such a future. Defeated and scattered, they huddled in the gloom of approaching winter. They could not yet comprehend that they had been victorious in defeat, that they had dealt the fatal blow to absolute monarchy and that, for a few lucky generations, Europe would live through a brief golden age until 1914. None foresaw how soon tyranny would find new and harsher guises.

The Strauss family managed to get through the immediate aftermath of the revolution with only minor scrapes. Josef's revolutionary leanings had apparently been denounced to the occupation forces that kept order in the city. When Anna returned to her luckily undamaged dwelling, the maid ran toward her, screaming that five of Windisch-Graetz's Polish soldiers were already tearing open every closet and cupboard. Had they found the three rifles which Josef had hidden in the chimney, imprisonment and exile might have followed for the whole family. Fortunately, Anna had taken an emergency supply of money with her on her flight to the monastery. She reached for the cash in a pocket of her petticoat and kept pressing coins and bills into the hands of the soldiers, whose language she could not understand. The Polish soldiers understood well enough, took what money there was, and left without further search.

Young Johann got into trouble when he asked for it. On December 3, still unreconciled to the defeat of the liberals, he conducted the *Marseillaise* at a public concert. Playing this hymn of republicanism the day after the new Emperor's coronation was, at best, tactless. At worst, it was a call to insurrection. Predictably, the police asked Johann to explain his musical taste.

According to the protocol of his interrogation, he claimed that, as a musician, he was "quite naturally and of course" totally indifferent to the political associations of any piece and judged it only on musical merit.

Aesthetic argument rarely carries much weight in police courts. But at twenty-three, Johann was already far too famous to be jailed without causing further political uproar— the very thing the authorities dreaded. He signed a written promise henceforth to consider the political as well as the aesthetic aspects of music, and the charge against him was dismissed.

Some of Johann's musical friends did not come off so lightly. Two were shot for their part in the uprising. One was Alfred Julius Becher, a composer and critic whose harmonic audacity had impressed even Berlioz, and whose keen and incorruptible critical intellect earned the admiration of Wagner. The other was Hermann Jellinek, the musically promising twenty-five-year-old brother of Vienna's foremost rabbi. He was condemned for having written pamphlets supporting the revolution, and the manner of his death is a testimonial to the liberal's endearing faith in rational persuasion. Standing against the wall, he still reasoned calmly with the soldiers raising their rifles against him. He argued that it would be wrong to kill him "just because I wrote articles to enlighten the people about their rights and duties in a constitutional state."

PRECEDING PAGE: Once considered sinful and lewd, the waltz became respectable when Victoria, Queen of England, deigned to dance to the music of the elder Strauss. This lithograph (circa 1845) shows her waltzing with Albert, the Prince Consort, during the early years of their marriage.

BELOW: Johann Strauss, Sr., shown here at about the age of twenty-five, already was Waltz King of Vienna but had yet to gain his international fame.
From the Picture Archive of the Austrian National Library.

ABOVE: The portraitist Franz von Lenbach captured the moodiness and tortured intensity of Johann Strauss, Jr., in his mature years. *From the Picture Archive of the Austrian National Library.*

LEFT: Josef Lanner, partner in the early ventures of the elder Strauss. His gently lyrical melodies, no less than Strauss's more exuberant and passionate style, defined the aesthetic mold of the Viennese waltz.
From the Picture Archive of the Austrian National Library.

BELOW: The younger Johann Strauss, shown here at about the age of twenty, conducts at Dommayer's Casino in the Viennese suburb of Hietzing shortly after making his dramatic debut there in 1844.
From the Picture Archive of the Austrian National Library.

Johann Strauss Jr.'s trio of wives:

LEFT: Jetty Treffz-Strauss, his first wife, shown here some years before her marriage, at the time of her alliance with Baron Todesco.

LOWER LEFT: Angelika Diettrich-Strauss, the aspirant actress, projecting her notion of dramatic art.

LOWER RIGHT: Adele Strauss, the composer's final companion, solemnly holding still for the photographer's time exposure. *From the Picture Archive of the Austrian National Library.*

ABOVE: The *Ringstrasse* replaced Vienna's city wall in the 1860s. This steel engraving shows the residential section of the great boulevard with the elegant town houses of the *nouveaux riches*. This was the hub of Vienna's social and artistic life in the last era of the Habsburg Empire.
From the author's private print collection.

BELOW: Bernardo Bellotto painted this view of Vienna at the time the waltz was born at the end of the eighteenth century. The gothic spire of St. Stephen's Cathedral rises from the center of the city, with the Vienna Woods forming the background. In front, one sees the Belvedere Gardens, and a section of the old city wall is still visible behind the open space at the left.
From the Picture Collection of the New York Public Library.

ABOVE: The Grand Staircase and adjacent salons of the Vienna
Opera were the scene of fashionable encounters and conversations
during the traditionally long intermissions. Here Johann Strauss, Jr.,
celebrated some of his greatest musical triumphs with *Die
Fledermaus* and *The Gypsy Baron*, and in 1899 he conducted his
last performance in this house.
From the Simonson Collection; courtesy Opera News.

The waltz and the Waltz King in contemporary caricature:

LEFT: The younger Johann Strauss as seen by *Wiener Punsch,* an illustrated satirical newspaper.

LOWER LEFT: A somewhat cozier version of the waltz, as seen by a Viennese illustrator about the middle of the last century.

LOWER RIGHT: The "Waltz Dance" as practiced—at a safe distance between partners—in America. This copper engraving by Alexander Anderson (1775–1870) is now in the Worcester Art Museum, Worcester, Mass.

These were almost his last words. The few that followed were interrupted by the report of the guns. It took Vienna several years to recover from such lapses of *Gemütlichkeit*.

One who never recovered was the elder Johann Strauss. He couldn't quite understand why nobody really felt like dancing.

Neither could he understand the reason for the decline of his personal popularity. Many Viennese were angry at his support of the forces that vanquished their city and reproved him for having written that march in honor of Radetzky. It took a long time for this magnificent piece of music to live down its political provenance to become accepted the world over as a reliable tonic to lift the hearts of all who hear it. Meanwhile, quite a few Viennese sent threatening letters to their Waltz King.

Helpless in his confusion, Strauss brooded. Emilie was no help. In happier times, her personal dullness and the shabbiness of her ambiance gave Strauss a needed counterpoise to the pace and glitter of his professional life. What he now needed Emilie could not supply. Stupid and selfish, she had no inkling of the nature and dimensions of the tragedy that had engulfed her lover. There was no contact with Anna.

Desperate for reassurance, Strauss left Vienna in search of the only love he had ever known—public adoration. Whatever may have poisoned the Viennese against him, surely his loyal admirers would welcome him elsewhere.

Even that hope came to naught. In Prague, protesting students howled all night in front of his hotel. In Munich, Heilbronn, and Heidelberg, the composer of antirevolutionary marches found only resentment. In Frankfurt the audience shouted, "Berlioz! Berlioz!" demanding that he play the *Rakoczy March* recently written by Berlioz to celebrate the Hungarian rebel. Strauss refused and broke off the concert.

"What do I care about politics," he muttered to one of his players, "I only want to make music."

Almost like fugitives, Strauss and his orchestra traveled down the Rhine toward England, a country that had managed to sidestep the continent's turmoil. Here, at the scene of former triumphs, Strauss hoped to recover his shaken equilibrium.

On reaching London in April 1849, his first visit was to Prince Metternich. The exiled Chancellor received him in his garden with his wife and daughter. When Princess Metternich, who had so often enjoyed his music at home, saw Strauss approaching, she could utter only one syllable:

"*Wien!*" Then she broke into sobs.

Like Strauss himself, and like most exiles in any age, the old Chancellor had little comprehension of what had happened to him and why. "Thirty years of peace I gave the Austrians," he said bitterly. "And this is their gratitude!"

At first it seemed that Strauss's injured ego might heal in England. The Queen and her court received him, recalling the time he had played at Victoria's coronation. The aristocracy showered him with honors, and the Duchess of Gloucester personally sponsored a benefit concert at which Strauss was to appear. But often the halls remained half empty. The Liberals stayed away. Their sympathies were with the Austrian revolutionaries. Even in England, the mail brought threats and abuses. The whole world had become political. Strauss no longer felt at home in it. He did not feel well. This would perhaps be his last journey, he wrote to Emilie.

It is odd that London, that gray and curiously mirthless city, had always had an open heart for the music-makers of Vienna. Haydn had found a second home and his happiest love affairs among the British. The London Philharmonic, by donations and commissions, eased the financial burden of Beethoven's last year and enabled him to buy those cases of "good old hock" whose medicinal powers he never doubted. And the tubercular Carl Maria von Weber was to see his *Oberon* premiered at Covent Garden a few days before, at forty, he coughed out his life. And now this great and generous city softened all political discord to give Vienna's Waltz King what he most needed at the end of his troubled journey: an affectionate farewell.

As Strauss's ship pulled into the Thames, a whole flotilla of boats filled with well-wishers escorted him toward the estuary. As the Channel steamer headed for open water, leaving the smaller ships behind, the orchestra members stood on deck, softly singing Vienna's traditional leave-taking: *So leb denn wohl, du stilles Haus.*

Returning to Vienna, Strauss found the political situation less acerbic. The volatile Viennese don't bear grudges long, and they gave Strauss so warm a welcome that he promptly scheduled a public concert at Unger's Casino for July 15. Tickets sold briskly and the evening promised the mood of cheerful festivity Strauss had missed for so long.

In his usual manner of the *Stehgeiger*, Strauss alternately played the violin and conducted with his bow. But during the very first number, his bow snapped.

For a moment Strauss stood as in a trance. Then he reached for another bow handed him by a second fiddler and continued his part. But throughout the evening he was visibly disturbed. The broken bow seemed an ill omen.

All summer long, he was moody and withdrawn. The musician of laughter, the creator of eternally joyous domains, seemed overwhelmed by fears and doubts he could not express.

Perhaps he tried to come to terms with the issues of the revolution that had so profoundly altered public reaction to him. Perhaps he was trying to surmount those less obvious tendencies toward melancholy and self-defeat, even self-destruction, that have always lain beneath the cheerful surface of the Austrian character. Half a century later, another notable Viennese, Sigmund Freud, was to codify such matters. But Strauss and his contemporaries had neither the intellectual concepts nor the vocabulary to approach what they called "distracted" states of mind. Besides, a Waltz King must not speak of such perplexities. It would not be fitting.

From the intimations of death in his letter from London ("This may be my last journey. . . .") it appears that Strauss was suffering a severe depressive episode. Certainly, the tough, passionate energy devoted to the pursuit of his career, the flashing vivacity that mesmerized the audience, seemed suddenly drained from him.

His funereal forebodings were no doubt strengthened by a curious commission received from the executors of a devoted admirer. A suburban widow whose greatest joy had been the music of Strauss had expressed the testamentary wish to have Strauss and his orchestra play her favorite waltzes at her bier. She even set aside a generous sum for payment to the musicians. So firm were these directions that the executors, despite religious scruples, did not contest this clause, and Strauss and his orchestra were engaged to serenade the corpse.

One inclines to view such stories as apocryphal. Yet it is related by a reliable source, the music critic Eduard Hanslick, who claims to have heard it from Strauss himself.

The mental changes Strauss was apparently undergoing also altered his attitude toward young Johann. He had no personal contact with him or any other member of his legitimate family. Yet acquaintances noticed that the bitterness was gone. He no longer resented the "competition" of the young man's burgeoning career. On the contrary, he seemed secretly proud of his son's musical achievements and followed with evident concern the newspaper accounts of Johann's musical forays into Serbia and Rumania, regions where tribal chieftains still contended with nomadic brigands for the ancient right to rob unwary travelers. Strauss may even have wished for a reconciliation with his son, but in his stubborn pride he found no way to admit this even to himself. Thus the man whose music was the symbol of conviviality sank into inner desolation.

Toward the end of summer, a new prospect lifted Strauss from his melancholy. Field Marshal Radetzky was to return from Italy, and a great banquet in his honor was planned at the Redoutensaal, the huge ceremonial hall of the Hofburg. What could be more fitting than for Strauss to conduct his *Radetzky March* on that occasion?

A year earlier, that march had been a major political blunder. Perhaps Strauss's finest piece of music, it had nearly wrecked his career, But now most Viennese were trying to forget the revolution. Besides, Radetzky's reputation transcended partisan rancor. He was the great old man of the army; he had saved the Italian provinces for Austria—at least for a while—and few Viennese would begrudge him a hero's welcome. Strauss was delighted to play for the Field Marshal's homecoming. He brightened at the prospect and visibly regained some of his former élan.

The banquet was on September 22. But Strauss wasn't there. He lay in his mistress's flat in the Kumpfgasse, fighting the scarlet fever he had caught from one of his bastard children.

He had always liked to end his waltzes with a fast coda— a brief and unexpected febrile swirl. So also ended his life. Within four days, on September 25, 1849, in his forty-sixth year, the disease killed him.

Presumably Emilie had been with him at his death. She certainly wasn't there when the corpse was discovered. A delivery boy from a nearby grocery saw it and ran to the Hirschenhaus to bring Anna Strauss the news. Anna sent Josef to investigate.

Josef found his father's naked body on the floor, tumbled from a stripped bed, amidst a scene suggesting murder and robbery. Chests and drawers gaped open. All was in disarray. Emilie had packed up what she could, including the dead man's nightshirt and bedding, and scattered the rest. Then she gathered up her children and fled. That was her way of collecting final payment from her lover.

"Strauss died like a dog," wrote the essayist Hans Weigel, "but he was buried like a king."

On September 27, he was carried in his coffin from the dank Kumpfgasse to the gothic grandeur of St. Stephen's. A profusion of those new candles transformed the dusk of the cathedral into golden brightness, and the high-vaulted nave gleamed like the ballrooms at Sperl. A hundred thousand people, one-fifth of Vienna's population, filled the cathedral, crowded the Stefansplatz and Graben, and lined the funeral route to the city limits. The death of Strauss, more than the new Emperor's hopeful proclamations of unity, drew the divided capital together once again. It was with the funeral of the Waltz King that the revolution really ended.

The spirit of conciliation swept over remnant bitterness, and the Viennese were once again able to make contact with the essence of the gentle and cheerful tradition which Strauss had distilled into music. Once again they would tap the ineluctable wellspring, and the earth in which Johann Strauss was laid would sing again.

Slowly the cortege drew westward against the red autumn sky, traversing the city from St. Stephen's to the outlying vineyards. Hundreds of bells from all towers resounded in the air as if to join their sonority into the sum of all music. The bass in this concert rolled from the tower of St. Stephen's, where the Pummerin—the giant bell cast from the metal of Turkish cannon captured after the siege of 1683— slowly rocked its profound voice into the clangor. And beyond the sea of gabled roofs, in the suburb of Salmansdorf, a small bright bell in an onion-domed steeple pealed insistently as if to remind everyone that Johann Strauss had donated this bell to the little hill-hugging village where, during brief summer vacations, he spent the few restful days of his short life.

The cortege halted at the foothills of the Vienna Woods. The last part of the way Strauss did not ride in the tall, resplendent funeral coach drawn by four black horses. Instead, the grieving men of the orchestra took the coffin on their shoulders. So he reached the churchyard at Döbling, where he lies beneath the green slopes of the Kahlenberg, the mountain he had climbed as a runaway bookbinder's apprentice, determined to be a musician.

At the tomb, Anna and her children mourned the husband and father they had lost long before.

The other family was not to be seen. From that day on, they sank into obscurity. Only once more did Emilie attract notice. Years later, the police caught her stealing a bronze lantern from the grave of Johann Strauss.

6

The Successors

Johann Strauss the younger seized his patrimony in the spirit of Goethe's dictum that an inheritance must be earned to be truly possessed. As the dynastic successor to the kingdom of the waltz created by his father, he could not *gain* prominence, only justify it. Fame and fortune were not his to win; they were his birthright. His alternatives were failure by falling short of his father's standards, and transcendence through enlargement of his creative scope.

Johann may already have sensed that his musical destiny lay in going far beyond the traditional limits of dance music when he scheduled his first concert after his father's death. On October 11, as a memorial to his father, he conducted the dead man's orchestra and a group of vocalists in a performance of Mozart's *Requiem*.

For a young dance musician to direct Mozart's somber score would have been remarkable enough. But Johann's choice is all the more noteworthy because, at the time, Mozart was half forgotten. The romantic taste of the period preferred Beethoven, Schumann, Liszt, and their minor contemporaries. Not until Gustav Mahler, fifty years later, staged a Mozart revival did Austria's greatest composer re-enter the mainstream of musical awareness.

Aside from proving his musical scope, the memorial concert also gave Johann the opportunity to establish contact with his father's orchestra. After the years of rivalry, partisan resentment still rankled among the players. Now it was aggravated by fear that Johann would disband his father's group.

Johann avoided the trap of making enemies at the start. Rather, he combined his father's orchestra with his own, and though a dozen or so men were fired in the process, he handled the dismissals impartially on the basis of musical competence alone. As a result, the orchestra gained not only in size—now numbering nearly fifty—but also in quality. Franz Ammon, the concert master of the older Strauss's orchestra, who had secretly given Johann his first music lessons, now acted as his diplomatic emissary, helping him win the personal loyalty of the men who had formerly worked for his father.

Winning the loyalty of the Viennese public proved unexpectedly difficult. As long as Strauss was a young man defying a tyrannical father, he could count on widespread public sympathy. Now that his famous father was dead, the fickle public turned against him as a usurper. People were muttering that Johann's ruthlessness in pursuit of his own career had hastened his father's death. Feelings against him ran so strong that he felt impelled to publish a kind of *apologia* in a long advertisement in the prestigious *Wiener Zeitung:*

> Pitiable is every son who here below weeps at his father's grave; but still more pitiable is he whose divided home forces him to hear from the severely judging lips of his opponents a sentence passed on himself and those who have remained loyal to him; for him there remain no other weapons of defense than to make reference to a deserted mother and younger brothers and sisters. I decided to apply my simple talents to the support and nourishment of these. It was not my purpose, as hostile opponents believe, to brazenly challenge my father's superior gifts. May God be my witness, no!

My father died, and I now stand alone in the midst of my weeping dear ones. I intend to earn a portion, even though it be very small, of the favor that my deserving father so richly harvested. If I should succeed in showing myself not unworthy of my artistic profession and thus be enabled to fulfill my duty toward my mother and my brothers and sisters, I believe that my blessed father will be reconciled to me in his grave and this will give me the greatest possible happiness.

Such pretentious solemnity doesn't sound like Johann Strauss. But whoever wrote the notice knew the style and sentiment expected by the public of the period. He may also have known that the vulgar always enjoy a bit of public groveling by their betters. At any rate, this almost Asian ritual of self-abjection restored Strauss to public favor—a fact reminding one how far Vienna lies to the east and what curious and often cruel irrationalities lurk beneath its pleasant surface.

Still another reconciliation was due before Strauss could assume the royal succession in the realm of the waltz. He had to make peace with the Emperor of Austria, atoning for his revolutionary capers of 1848.

An excellent occasion for such a gesture presented itself in 1854 at the marriage of Franz Josef to Elisabeth von Wittelsbach, Princess of Bavaria. Elisabeth was sixteen when the young Emperor first saw her at Ischl, the little city at the center of the Salzkammergut. The setting alone was like a love potion. With deep-green lakes sprinkled among small Alps—all properly craggy but none tall enough to be the least bit grim—and with high-gabled toylike towns dotting the shores, the Salzkammergut landscape would make anyone fall in love with whatever girl happened to be within reach. But in the case of Elisabeth, no scenery was needed; and in her presence, no man would look at it, anyway.

The Princess of Bavaria was like those painted porcelain figurines made by the artisans of her land. Her tiny waist and graceful posture inspired comparisons with swans, lilies, and gazelles. Those fortunate enough to see her close would marvel at the ethereal fineness of her oval face with high forehead and straight brows framed by long, lustrous dark hair. Some of her portraits catch the amber fire in her gray eyes and a bit of that fey and sidelong glance one sometimes finds in women who are sure of their effect on others.

Franz Josef was too smitten, and perhaps himself too young, to perceive that this fairy Princess was but a child and that her spontaneous and sometimes willful nature—so charming in a girl—would make Elisabeth a tragic failure as an empress. He could not know that his love would doom her to a life of mounting futility, of incessant travel to escape the strictures of her court and her obligations as wife and regent, leading her at last to the boat dock at Geneva where an Italian anarchist would murder her with a rusty file.

No hint of this future clouded her radiant face as Elisabeth, at the age of seventeen, sailed down the Danube to Vienna to become the empress of Austria. Her ship was garlanded with roses from the royal park at Schönbrunn, and a great gilded coach drawn by twelve of Vienna's famous milk-white Lippizaner horses took her through the jubilant streets of her capital to the Hofburg.

On April 26, 1854, two days after the imperial marriage, a great court ball was to celebrate the event. An archduchess had expressed the wish to hear Strauss's *Annen-Polka*, a sprightly bit of melodic fluff that was the rage of Vienna. But Strauss, wanting to keep the popular polka exclusive for his orchestra, had refrained from publishing it. The result was a court crisis.

Obviously, the wish or whim of an archduchess can't be ignored. But Court Music Director Philip Fahrbach was unable to obtain the score of the *Annen-Polka*. The only solution was to invite Strauss himself to play the piece. Thus it happened that on the evening of the great coronation ball, the court musicians shared the flower-laden stage of the Ceremonial Hall in the Hofburg with young Strauss, and the beautiful Empress danced with her new husband to the music of the former revolutionary.

Pressing his advantage, Strauss shortly afterward sought to gain for himself the prestigious title of Imperial Court Ball Music Director, which his father had held before him. But the shadows of 1848 still clung to him and he met with a curt rebuff.

In the course of processing his bid for the exalted title, the Office of the Court Chamberlain conducted a character investigation of the applicant. After noting Strauss's role in the revolution and his friendships with radical students, the investigator added, "Since becoming a successful music director, he has adopted a prodigal and unseemly mode of life and has only recently shown any tendency toward a more orderly existence."

Presumably the Office of the Court Chamberlain was referring to the succession of girls passing through Strauss's life. Still in the possession of the Austrian State Archives, this document is one of two remaining clues to such private matters. The other is a note in the diary of Strauss's first wife, whom he apparently told about his earlier "connubials." She made an informal count of these affairs and puts their number at thirteen. With the marital tragedy of his parents etched in his mind, and with the abundance of his opportunities, it is not surprising that Strauss, until middle age, preferred his amours to remain casual.

Vienna in the nineteenth century tacitly permitted young people in certain segments of the upper bourgeoisie and in artistic circles a delightful and distinctive style of sexual accommodation that had nothing in common with the furtive and often sordid encounters by which Londoners, Muscovites, and even Parisians circumvented the mores of their times. Affection and sweetness was the expected essence of a Viennese *Liebelei*, and what was lightly given and lightly taken was not really expected to last longer than the bloom of a flower, yet not felt and cherished less deeply for all that.

Love? Not likely—for that takes time and leaves no out. And with parting implicit, there was also a little sadness in it all. Meanwhile, each was grateful to the other, and for glints of such happiness in the waltzes of Strauss, some of the credit belongs to those young ladies whose only trace now remains in the music.

The dominant woman in Strauss's life was still his mother. Her plan had worked. She wanted a Johann Strauss—a Waltz King—and now at last she had one. With his dark curly hair, intense gaze, generous moustache, and graceful movements, Johann recalled his father even in physical appearance, and Anna made her son the surrogate for her faithless husband.

How deeply her former rejection must have insulted this strong and perceptive woman can be guessed from the new vitality unfolding in her since her husband's death. She handled all of Johann's business arrangements, leaving him free for his artistic and personal pursuits. She saw to it that her younger son Josef, deeply fascinated by the new wonders of steam-driven engines, received an excellent engineering education at the *Technik*, where Professor Ressl had just invented a "propeller" to drive steamships much faster than a paddle-wheel, where bright *Konstrukteure* were struggling to build workable machines for sewing and for writing in type, and where everyone was wondering what practical uses there might be for electricity.

What is perhaps most remarkable about Anna is that, even in middle age, she never ceased to expand her own musical perception. Her purview extended far beyond entertainment music. In particular, she was captivated by the radically new harmony and orchestration that made Richard Wagner the most controversial musician of his time. His mesmeric sound textures, his almost lascivious freedom of chromatic modulation, no less than the conduct of his private affairs, made Wagner something of a permanent scandal in the artistic sphere of the nineteenth century. While Europe's most sophisticated ears still balked at such recent outrages as *Lohen-grin*, *Tannhäuser*, and *The Flying Dutchman*, Anna took these scores calmly in her musical stride, working her way patiently through piano arrangements for her personal study. It was through her that Johann's attention was first drawn to the chromatic marvels of Wagnerian harmony and the supple tonal shadings of orchestration. Thus she planted the seed in Johann's musical imagination that, long after her death, matured into the sonic opulence of his later works.

During the 1850s, the focus of Vienna's night life shifted from Sperl, the quondam emporium of the older Strauss, to the even more splendid *Sophien-Saal*, a creation of Franz Morawetz, a most unlikely promoter of elegant pleasures.

The son of a poor Jewish tailor in the Bohemian village of Raudnitz, little Franz never forgot the Russian colonel who had barged into his parents' house half dead after the battle of Kulm during the Napoleonic wars. What the colonel demanded was literally unheard of: he wanted a steambath.

The tailor failed to understand and was almost hysterical with terror of the fierce foreign officer. But little Franz, who had sometimes watched his father revive a tired suit of clothes by steaming, realized that the crumpled colonel craved the same sort of treatment. He persuaded his mother to arrange pots of steaming water all around the naked Russian. The colonel was delighted. "You are the first Austrians to understand about steam," he shouted, as he finally dashed out into the cold yard to shut his distended pores.

The next morning, the colonel, refreshed and resplendent in his cleaned and pressed uniform, presented Franz with a gold watch—taken from a corpse on the battlefield—and some business advice. "If you ever go to the great city of Vienna," he told the boy, "you will make your fortune there with steambaths."

So Franz, at the age of seventeen, set off on foot to Vienna and ascertained that, as the colonel had implied, the city was indeed lacking steambaths. The Russian and Turkish custom of parboiling people had not yet penetrated that far west.

After this initial market survey Franz extemporized by taking a job as cloth-cutter until, ten years later, he managed to get the necessary capital for his venture by marrying the boss's daughter, who brought him a generous dowry.

Now the building of the bath could begin. He sold stock in the venture, called upon the architects Siccardsburg and Van der Nüll, who later were to design Vienna's famous Opera, and specified a huge indoor pool where customers would cool off after their steaming. Taking a technical cue from the great iron girders that had lately been employed as roof supports for big railroad stations, the architects projected a wide ceiling span over the pool that was a marvel in its day.

The building authorities, taken aback by such daring, promptly denied their approval. But Morawetz's tiny frame harbored unmeasured amounts of gall. He managed to gain audience with the Emperor himself and convinced him that steambathing was essential to the national health. At the first hint of the Emperor's personal interest, the building authorities concluded that the roof would hold up, after all, and the bold construction finally took shape. In gratitude for the imperial intervention, Morawetz named his ornate steambath the Sofien-Bad, after Archduchess Sophie, the Emperor's mother.

But the architectural success turned out a commercial failure. The Viennese just couldn't stand the steam. A few came to swim in the big pool, but they did so only in summer, believing winter swimming to be unhealthy, even indoors. Most of the year, the great hall stood empty.

To satisfy his creditors, Morawetz had to think of a more profitable use for his edifice. He knew what the Viennese liked to do regardless of the season. They liked to dance. So Morawetz let out the water, put in parquet, and the Sophien-Bad became the Sophien-Saal, Vienna's most famous enter-

tainment palace. Tiers of loggias, like those of a Renaissance
courtyard, surrounded the glittering dance floor and could
be used as private boxes where elegant spectators would dine
in brocaded splendor amidst palm fronds while watching the
dancing throng below. The great vaulting roof that had so
perturbed the building inspectors turned out to be an acoustic
wonder that made any singer or orchestra sound bigger and
better—a quality that a century later was to make the
Sophien-Saal a favorite location for recording sessions.

It was in this transmogrified swimming pool that Strauss
enraptured the Viennese with countless compositions deftly
turned out for special occasions. He would oblige professional associations and prominent clubs with pieces named in
their honor. The Engineers' Club, for example, would dance
the *Electromagnetic Polka*, the *Motor Quadrille*, or the
Soundwave Waltz. Jurists would be set in motion with the
Due Process Polka, *Torts Dances*, and *Five Paragraphs from
the Waltz Code*, while the men of the Medical Association
and their ladies responded nicely to *Heightened Pulses* and
even the *Paroxysm Waltz*.

Luckily, the titles bear no relation to the music. The
Transaction Waltz, written for stockbrokers, would not
sound substantially different from a waltz written for the
Waschermadlball, the traditional reunion of Vienna's laundry
girls, which at the height of each Carnival season gave the
young gentlemen of Vienna opportunities to broaden their
range of acquaintance.

In short, the names of these dances are about as meaningful
as the names of race horses. Nestroy alludes to this in one of
his plays where a young man asks a girl to dance with him:

He (eagerly): "They're playing the *Irresistible Waltz*.
Shall we?"

She (primly): "Though it is a modest title, I resist. No,
thank you."

One notable exception to this rule is the still-popular *Accelerations Waltz*, dedicated to the students of the *Technik*. The violins swirl faster and faster in a fantasy of limitless speed as the quivering bows half-mockingly suggest the frantic shuttling of pistons, connecting rods, and other such prosaic appurtenances of reciprocating engines. It is perhaps the only composition ever to have captured the mechanical concepts and images of the period.

Nearly three hundred such occasional pieces came into existence during the twenty-year span between Strauss's debut and his retirement as a regular dance-hall conductor. This works out to a production rate of about one new composition per month. "The melodies gush out like water," Strauss wrote to his friend, the critic Max Kalbeck. (The aqueous simile recalls Mozart's earthy claim, "I compose music as naturally as a sow pisses.")

Every hour Strauss could spare from rehearsing and performing was devoted to composition. The incessant flow of invention filled stacks of notebooks, which Strauss regarded as a hoard on which to draw if his imagination ever ran dry. As it happened, a mere fraction of the melodic raw material in the notebooks was ever worked into finished products.

Such mass production, one expects, would yield shoddy goods. Yet if Strauss's music of this period lacks anything, it is not quality but distinctiveness. His works were almost uniformly good, marked by verve, sweetness, and sometimes by haunting sensuality. If they are rarely played today, it is only because they are overshadowed by the surpassing creations of his later years.

Accelerations and *Morning Papers* (Morgenblätter)—the latter dedicated to the Concordia, a famous club of writers and journalists—mark the culmination of Strauss's work during this period. Up to that time, most of his waltzes were, as the critic Franz Grasberger puts it, "a game of changes in which folk idiom alternates with artful device in the service of the dance." Unlike his father, who clung to the folk idiom as his aesthetic anchor, Strauss gradually cut loose from the concept of the waltz as folk-based dance-hall music. In *Morning Papers*, for the first time, he achieves the free inventive range of a concert piece. The melodic phrases grow longer, arching sweetly over the support of the three-quarter beat. At times, the beat itself is implied rather than explicit—a daring refinement that pays tribute to the musical sensibility of Vienna's sophisticated audiences. A rising expressiveness gives this waltz the controlled shape of a serious composition, and the listener senses that Strauss—perhaps without conscious intent—had now fixed the course that would ultimately take him from the dance hall to the concert hall.

The creative intensity of these formative years, added to the physical strain of daily rehearsals and performances, finally took its toll. At the age of twenty-eight, Strauss fell unconscious at his door after returning from a concert in the early morning.

The doctors spoke of *Nervenerschütterung*, a typically vague yet graphic nineteenth-century diagnosis that translates literally into the current vernacular of "shook-up nerves." Recommended treatment: a rest cure in southern Styria.

A sanatorium bed is a good place for stock-taking, for which Strauss had hitherto lacked time and inclination. Here, in the quiet of the Styrian Alps, he sorted out his dual functions of composer and performer. Up to then he had considered the two inseparable, uncritically accepting the popular image of the composer-conductor as his own essential identity. Now he was not sure that the two functions were necessarily linked, and it occurred to him that he might prefer to devote himself to composition exclusively. Unlike his father, who was at his best before the public, he didn't really like crowds. He was not an entertainer by temperament. He liked solitude and the inner silence from which all music springs.

Yet to abandon public performances would be economic suicide. He was, after all, the head of a family business. His concerts were the main support for Anna, Josef, Eduard, and his sister Therese. His present illness proved their dependence on him, what with no money coming in and fifty musicians on salary.

The trouble was that the Waltz King had no Viceroy. What the dynasty needed was a working prince to assume some of Johann's burden. Brother Josef would have to be drafted into musical service as substitute conductor.

Like all of Anna's children, Josef was musically literate. He played piano with the kind of phrasing and rhythmic justness that is the proof of innate talent. Johann spoke to his mother about his plan. As head of the family, Anna was to prevail upon Josef to abandon his engineering work and devote himself to the family business of making music.

Josef dismissed the suggestion outright. Once before he had defied his parents in a similar matter. His father had wanted him to become an army officer.

"Let me be what I am," Josef had written to his father in a formal refusal. "Do not force me into that crude occupation of soldiering that destroys all feeling for humanity, a calling for which I am not fit and to which I was not born. I do not want to learn how to kill people, and I do not want to be rewarded with high rank for having hunted human beings. I want to be useful to mankind. . . ."

Josef's idea of usefulness was engineering. With the naïve optimism shared by many of his contemporaries in the age of steam, he looked on the emergent technology as the main road to human happiness. Perfectability lay within his grasp on the drawing board. Humanism and technology had not yet been divorced, and a young man whose gentle, life-affirming nature made him shun the military could still love machines. Viennese mechanics, faced with some recalcitrant device, were apt to remark, "Well, after all a machine's only human."

Two years younger than Johann, Josef had already distinguished himself by supervising a dam construction, publishing a "Collection of Formulas, Problems, and Tables in

Mathematics, Mechanics, Geometry, Physics, *et cetera*," and, above all, by inventing the first mechanical street sweeper, which was the pride of Vienna's sanitation department. He had no intention of trading his excellent professional prospects, nor his bourgeois respectability, for the chancy, semi-itinerant life of a musician.

"I'm too ugly," he said. That was a simple and sufficient reason for refusal and better than trying to explain everything else.

True, Josef looked different from his natty brother. His face lacked Johann's compelling vividness; in fact, his usual expression was a bit glum. His movements were often clumsy and leaden, a severe handicap for the prospective conductor of the world's most evanescent music.

Johann listened from his bed as Josef itemized his shortcomings. Then he turned on his pillow, looked at his brother, and said without smiling:

"But you have the most talent of us all. You would be a greater musician than either myself or our father."

It never occurred to the good-hearted Josef that his brother might say this to gain personal convenience from his assent. He believed that Johann spoke the truth as he saw it. Johann probably believed the same thing.

Overcome by Johann's faith in him, Josef permitted himself to be torn from his accustomed life. With his customary diligence and the systematic approach of a good engineer, he now enlarged his musical competence. Under the tutorship of the now-ancient Herr Ammon, Johann's former teacher, he soon achieved a passable conducting technique.

Josef's self-conscious awkwardness presented a striking contrast to his brother's fluid, impassioned conducting style. But his manner did not repel the audience. Public affection lavished on Johann seemed to include Josef simply by virtue of his family membership. Besides, his shyness, along with the invariant melancholy of his face, appealed to the protective instincts of lady listeners.

From a purely musical point of view, Josef's conducting influenced the development of the waltz to a marked degree. He lacked the incisiveness, the tension and thrust by which his brother let musical phrases spring into the air like a lariat. His music-making held none of the delicious threat of withheld passion. But Josef's performances had distinction of their own. They projected an aura of sweetness and voluptuous lassitude—an elegiac repose that lies as deep within the essence of the Viennese waltz as the counterbalancing elements for fire and spark.

Josef slowed the tempo, trading propulsive exuberance for an almost hypnotic, insinuating songfulness that revealed new expressive possibilities within the structure of the dance. In short, his influence tended toward the broad, pliant performance style that, among conductors, is known as the Viennese tradition. Josef's affinity for the more reflective aspects of the waltz, in turn, influenced Johann's musical imagination, turning it increasingly toward a mellowed lyricism.

When Johann returned fully recovered from his Styrian cure, Josef briefly considered resuming his engineering career, especially since Eduard, the youngest of the three Strauss brothers, was already being groomed as a substitute conductor. But the engineer had fallen irrevocably under the spell of music, and Josef remained with the orchestra for the rest of his brief life.

His self-effacing temperament, always deferring to Johann, forestalled any rivalry between the brothers, even after Josef edged further into Johann's preserves by becoming a composer.

The stimulus of conducting unshackled Josef's musical creativity and emboldened him to play a work of his own, titled with typical diffidence *The First and Last Waltzes of Josef Strauss*. Deserved success made it impossible to keep the promise implied in the title, and his next composition was called *The First Waltz After the Last*.

As if driven by a compulsion to live up to the fullest possible extent to his brother's faith in him, Josef devoted himself to his new career with fierce concentration. He led the orchestra whenever Johann went on tour or, as happened more and more often, simply wanted time off. Posters announced concerts by "J. Strauss," leaving it to the convenience of the moment which "J" was to direct them.

By 1857 Josef felt confident enough in his prospects as a musician to marry his childhood sweetheart, Karoline Pruckmayr—his beloved "Lintscherl"—a quiet, gentle girl who shunned public appearances and gave her husband a treasured retreat of domestic tranquillity.

But Josef did not know the meaning of leisure. Every moment he could spare from the orchestra, he labored over his scores, completing no less than 283 compositions in the seventeen years remaining to him after his musical debut. Aside from music, Josef poured his energies into an amazing range of activities. He maintained an informed interest in science and engineering, became an accomplished amateur painter, wrote passable poetry, and completed a tragic drama entitled *Manfred Rober,* based on the adventurous life of a supposed maternal ancestor. He slept little, rarely allowed himself any relaxation—not even a walk—and smoked twenty cigars a day.

His health, never robust, eroded rapidly under this regimen. He began to suffer fainting spells. Mounting nervous tension impaired his dealings with the orchestra. Wrangling during rehearsals left him exhausted, though he never vented his irritation. He had none of the innate coolness and authoritarian aplomb that enabled Johann to lead an orchestra with a minimum of emotional friction. He also suffered deeply from being away from his wife during concert tours. Almost every day they were apart he wrote to his Lintscherl deceptively cheerful letters full of affectionate longing for her and their small daughter Lina.

On one of these tours, in April, 1870, he was to conduct a series of concerts in Warsaw, opening with a gala concert in the presence of the Russian Czarevitch. At rehearsal he discovered that, due to faulty travel plans, seven of his key players had failed to arrive. The chairs were filled with local substitutes, who proved less than satisfactory. The leading violinist kept muffing a difficult passage. Josef told him to skip it. His pride hurt, the fiddler attempted to play it anyway during the performance, thereby throwing the orchestra into confusion.

For endless seconds, Josef signaled frantically, trying to pull the orchestra together again, but with swift and sickening inevitability, discord mounted into chaos. The shock triggered one of Josef's fainting spells. He tumbled from the podium. For a moment he lay on the stage. Then, before anyone could reach out to grasp and hold him, he rolled off the high platform, his head crashing against the floor.

Blood running from his ears indicated the possibility of a skull fracture and of brain damage, though this diagnosis was not confirmed. In 1870, rest was the only available therapy for injuries of this kind. By the time Karoline and Johann arrived from Vienna, Josef was fully conscious again, which inspired hope for his possible recovery.

From April to July, Karoline sat at her husband's bedside in the strange city, putting ice bags on his wounded head, while Johann, often in tears, conducted the orchestra to fulfill contractual obligations. The considerable proceeds of fourteen thousand *Gulden* he immediately put at Karoline's disposal.

By July, Josef began to deteriorate. Yet despite frequent lapses of consciousness and increasingly spasmodic breathing, he kept asking to be taken to Vienna so that he could once more see his little daughter.

It would have been easier to bring Lina to Warsaw, but Karoline, placing her sinking hope in the superior skill of Viennese doctors, arranged for Josef's return home. Rattling for two days in a hard-spring coach over the jolting rails of still primitive railroads may have mercifully shortened Josef's sufferings, and he died a few days after his homecoming, at the age of forty-three.

Three eminent Viennese doctors had examined Josef immediately on his arrival and ventured the opinion that his fainting spells may have been symptoms of a brain tumor. This presumed tumor, rather than the fall from the podium, might have been the primary cause of death. They asked for an autopsy, but Karoline could not bring herself to grant permission.

Such medical concerns may seem rather academic under the circumstances, yet Karoline's refusal sparked a bevy of strange rumors among the gullible and sensation-hungry Viennese. Russian officers on occupation duty in Warsaw had killed Josef with their sabers for declining a request to play a chauvinistic Russian tune. With political animosities running fairly high between Russia and Austria at the time, this story was widely believed and elaborated. One tabloid insisted that, instead of the corpse, the Russians had shipped a big wax doll to Vienna. Karoline had been bribed into secrecy by the government. That was why she had forestalled an autopsy.

To prevent popular indignation from becoming a political issue in the strained Austro-Russian relations, Karoline asked the priest who had given the last rites to Josef to make a public declaration that Josef was still alive when extreme unction was administered to him after his arrival in Vienna.

Even that did not still the rumors. They kept going for years, growing more fanciful with time. One version, pointing to the fact that Josef left no posthumous works, accused Johann of having stolen his deceased brother's notebooks when he, as executor of Josef's will, sifted his papers. Johann's later works, the rumor insisted, were really purloined from Josef. Even Johann's generosity was twisted to suit this sordid fiction. Why, asked his detractors, would Johann have given such large sums to his widowed sister-in-law except to soothe his own conscience?

In the tight, gossipy world of Vienna's music-makers, it was impossible to shield Johann from hearing such talk. He was deeply and lastingly embittered, and his later tendency to personal withdrawal—aside from occasional public appearances—may have been a reaction to the sheer malice of these attacks. He never uttered a single word on the subject. He had the innate nobility to know that some things are beneath comment.

As if to moot such spurious questions of authorship, time itself has melded the music of the two brothers. Over the years, the identity of Josef dissolved into that of his longer-lived brother, and listeners delighting in their work no longer bother to tell them apart.

It is a measure of Josef's talent that his works are almost invariably confused with those of Johann. Anyone hearing such enduring masterpieces as *Village Swallows, Music of the Spheres,* or *Mein Lebenslauf ist Lieb und Lust* (in hobbled translation: My Life Is One of Love and Joy) would find it hard to believe that anyone but the Waltz King himself could have been inspired with such melody. Yet Josef was not just an apt imitator. A certain sweet gravity distinguishes Josef's melodies from those of his brother, and his harmonies, often heavily underlined in cellos and horns, paint a darker background for the ecstasy of the dance.

One lasting favorite, the *Pizzicato Polka,* bears the signature of both Johann and Josef, who collaborated in its composition. The polka remains one of those rare moments of pure laughter transmuted into music. It is well that the two brothers share in these moments of transfixed joy a common monument.

7

Russian Interlude

Ever since footsore troubadours trudged among the castles of Provence, musicians have been at the mercy of transportation. But until the age of steam, there had been few basic advances in the technology of travel. All this changed in Johann Strauss's time. By the middle of the nineteenth century, rails stretched all across Europe, and the ease and speed of steam-powered travel created a new internationalism in the arts. With the new mobility of artists, tastes grew more eclectic and sophisticated as audiences were exposed to a greater variety of musical styles. Concert tours, still considered exceptional adventures in the day of the older Strauss, were now an expected routine.

This was no comfort to Johann, who had a horror of trains. "Going on the railroad is for me like going to be hanged," he complained.

He had a point. Austria's Alpine topography tended to bring out the worst in trains. The air brake, capable of slowing all cars at a uniform rate of deceleration, was yet to be invented by that ingenious Pennsylvania mechanic, George Westinghouse. Meanwhile, on Austria's sloping tracks, brakemen in each car frantically pulled at their cranks to keep trains under control. If they slipped up on their coordination, trains would come apart with far from reassuring results.

Strauss was haunted by the idea of a wreck. When traveling, he never looked at the landscape. The scenery moved— a fact that only underlined his fright. The blinds of his compartment were always drawn, and most of the journey he spent stretched out under the seat, which he considered the safest position. He also carried with him ample supplies of champagne to loosen the rigor of his fear.

In this peculiar manner Strauss reached Bad Gastein in the Salzburgian Alps in the summer of 1854. The railroad had just been extended westward from Vienna into the mountain regions of Salzburg and the Tyrol, and it had become the fashion of prosperous Viennese to seek Alpine tranquillity in plush hotels built in quiet valleys just off the track. In the parlance of his day, Strauss had come to "take the air," unsuspecting that his sojourn at Bad Gastein would get him more than ever involved with railroads.

As he sat on the terrace of his hotel, a tall man with an enormous beard approached him. In fluent French he introduced himself as the Director General of the Czarskoje-Selo Railway Company, a Russian line going from St. Petersburg to apparently nowhere. To induce people to travel on its trains, the company was developing an elegant resort at Pavlovsk, within easy reach of excursion trains from the Russian capital. A splendid music pavilion had been erected, and it only remained for Monsieur Strauss to please come and play there.

The white nights of the northern summer, the Russian gentleman assured Strauss, yearned for the magic of his music —music that would melt the Russian soul with Viennese warmth—and in any case, the board of directors felt that only Strauss could fill up those trains. Of course, in Russia one understood that persons of fine artistic sensitivities would be spiritually jolted by staying in public accommodations. No, Strauss would not be expected to live at the great hotel the railroad company had just built. A private villa, fully staffed, and with suitable grounds, would be at his disposal. And, oh yes, if M Strauss cared to discuss the more mundane arrangements, his stipend would be. . . . The Russian named a sum beyond the fondest dreams of greed.

Strauss, never averse to a rapid ruble, signed a contract to play at Pavlovsk for several summers. Actually, it was not his musicianship alone that made him so attractive to the railroaders and their high-placed government backers. Political considerations were involved also. The British were blocking the Baltic. In the Crimea, the French had landed with the English, and the Turks and Italians laid siege to Sebastopol. The Crimean war had been a profound embarrassment to Russia, and it seemed advisable to keep the population of the capital pleasantly entertained. But with nearly every European country arrayed against Russia at Britain's behest, the choice of talent was limited. A Viennese, the Russians felt, would be sufficiently neutral and politically innocuous. Thus the *Pax Britannica*, in its more warlike extensions, was responsible for the importation of the waltz to Russia, and its echoes ring through Russian music from Tchaikovsky to Shostakovich.

Russia, the variable enigma that separates East from West, happened to be in one of its westward phases. St. Petersburg was aping Paris in dress, decor, and entertainments. But the Russians, like most ardent imitators, exaggerated their model and falsified it by mistaking style for substance. The great balls at the Winter Palace and in the houses of the Russian aristocracy outshone all else in such splendors as lace, jewels, and boot polish can bestow. But the spirit of Paris—that exacting calculus of nuanced pleasure and humane sensibility— withered near the Arctic Circle.

Dancing was the favorite diversion because one didn't have to talk much. Talking was always risky in Russia, and, since the upper classes disdained their native language and insisted on speaking French in public, it was also difficult for some.

Fortunately, conversation rarely extended beyond a formal exchange of pleasantries (or a formal exchange of insults), and even fractured French served well enough for that.

Outside the gate, beyond the glow of the candles, Russia lay in the dark, sealed against the luminance that had been flickering in the West since the Renaissance. In this vast land, dominated by a closed system of organized superstition, there simply was no place for western European modes of thought and feeling. Those endlessly talking Russian intellectuals, the poetic doctors of Chekov, the educated Jews, and the brilliantly bitter nihilists with their bombs and apocalyptic longings for redemptive violence were yet to spring, several years later, from the growing urbanization of Russia. At the time of Strauss's visit, the country, with its feudal fiefdoms, its serfs and icons, still lay in Byzantine torpor. Over the endless plains, mired or frozen, the Dark Ages still held sway. Aside from a small stratum of semiliterate officials, few could read and write in the shabby little towns; and where no letter civilizes the mind, life is inevitably brutal, each man driven by the intensity of his own alternately cruel or exuberant passions.

It was an incongrous country for a Waltz King, far from Vienna's pliant amiability. Within his sybaritic setting at Pavlovsk, Strauss was comfortably insulated from the harshness, the paralyzing diminution of life, that permeated Russia. But his very first experience on Russian soil provided him with a less sheltered view of Russian conditions.

No sooner had Strauss and his musicans crossed the Russian border from Silesia than some questions arose as to the validity of their travel documents. At a sign from the border guard, Russian soldiers swarmed aboard the train, rudely pulled Strauss and his men out of the cars, herded them like cattle across open fields, and locked them overnight in a freezing barn.

The local commander, offering no explanation, might have kept them there indefinitely, but something in Strauss's self-assured manner intimidated him, and he thought it wiser to rid himself of his prisoners. Hoping to salvage some credit from a potential embarrassment, he dispatched Strauss and his entourage to General Abramovich, the Russian commandant of occupied Warsaw, with the standard explanation that they were suspected spies. Like a good military man, Abramovich accepted this at face value. As an occupation officer, he was obsessed with fear of conspirators and revolutionaries, and operated on the precept, "When in doubt shoot them dead." Or at least lock them up.

A local friend of Strauss's, the music dealer Friedlein, heard of his predicament and attempted to intercede with Abramovich. After persistent effort he succeeded in gaining audience with the commandant. He explained that he knew Strauss and would vouch for him with his own person and his fortune.

Abramovich listened with his back turned. Suddenly he wheeled around:

"You what!" he snorted, rudely using the familiar address. "You vouch! You try to bargain with me! Just for that I'll have you sent to Siberia. In chains!"

Only after abasing himself before the fuming general was Friedlein permitted to leave the building.

Even the Austrian consul was no help. He expressed doubt that the consulate could provide effective protection against the whim of a Russian officer, and took no action.

Abandoned by his consul, Strauss was forced to take initiative in his own behalf. If the Russian authorities could not be bothered to check his credentials, he had other ways of showing them who he was. He and the orchestra offered to play a private concert for Abramovich as proof of their identity. No other orchestra could play like his. His music would be his passport.

Intrigued by this proposal, the general agreed, and the concert was arranged at police headquarters. Later Strauss recalled: "It was one of the best concerts we ever played. Every man did his best."

Abramovich was equally appreciative. His eyes and mouth narrowed into the slitted grimace that passes for a smile in men of his type.

"Very well done," he said. "Truly well done."

Strauss later recalled the nasty edge in the general's voice as he mouthed his praise. Then, suddenly, the voice changed to a bellow: "But it is a fraud! Everything can be faked! A deliberate trick! Spies!! Robbers!!"

Strauss and the orchestra were packed off to a dingy hotel, held under arrest there, and told to surrender their clothes.

At this juncture, the faithful Friedlein once more risked his liberty, and possibly his life, to help Strauss. He knew that the Czarina was visiting Castle Laschenski near Warsaw, and though communications to and from the city were controlled by Abramovich's censors, he managed to get word of Strauss's predicament to the Czarina's chief chamberlain.

The reply was an imperial command: Strauss was to give a gala concert before her Majesty the following week at the Théâtre-Paré, the city's most prestigious showplace. Among the guests of honor, attending in full regalia, was General Abramovich. After the concert, he felt it advisable to pay his respects to Strauss in his dressing room.

Strauss asked Abramovich if he had liked the playing as much as at the police station. The general managed an urbane answer: "You must forgive me, dear Master. It is my duty to be exceedingly cautious. We are living here between two revolutions, one past and one future. You and your men might have been political conspirators. And if that had been the case, I might have been banished to Siberia. You must not take it amiss that with this possibility before me, I would rather have had *you* deported."

In its bland way, the general's apology was the classic credo of authority resting upon terror.

Pavlovsk offered a friendlier welcome. The ovations of the audience often lasted until the early hours of the morning. People simply refused to leave after concerts, demanding encore after encore.

No music like this had ever been heard in Russia. Its frenzied acceptance clearly betokened something more fundamental than the appeal of novelty. The Viennese waltz—amiable, expansive without being emotional, sensuous without passion, and filled with delight and spontaneity—gave many listeners their first inkling of a whole climate of feeling quite different from the stern, passionate cast of the Russian temper. In listening, the Russian discovered a hunger for such music; and a few of the most perceptive may even have sensed that this hunger was not for the music alone but for the qualities of life articulated through it.

In Strauss, Russia encountered another, more volatile world. The atmosphere of this encounter was one of unrelenting festivity. Six days a week, those trains from St. Petersburg were packed with excursionists whose day in the country would be topped off by a Strauss concert in the evening. And if the audience, clamoring for more, refused to leave the music hall on time, the trains just had to be kept waiting at the station. All summer long, they trooped out by the thousands, the starched and crinolined families of those resoundingly titled clerks and officials who formed the social core of the capital.

Going to Pavlovsk was simply the thing to do, but for a good many visitors the attraction was not purely musical. In a country that proscribed the arts and frowned on personal intellectual pursuits, the middle class often found itself at a loss for serious interests. Routine work was done for them by their servants, sports had not yet become a popular diversion, and about the only areas available to absorb the more dedicated energies of "good families" were snobbery and social pretense. Not to be seen at Pavlovsk was a social lapse. Besides, with their elevated mood, long intermissions, and champagne and caviar served at tables in all the boxes, the Strauss concerts provided an advantageous atmosphere for showing off one's unmarried daughters.

Best of all, the summer festival at Pavlovsk offered untitled Russians a rare opportunity to enter the presence of princes. Ever since the Czarina had rescued Strauss in Warsaw, he seemed to enjoy the special favor of the court. Often those profitable trains to Pavlovsk pulled private salon cars filled with Grand Dukes, Grand Duchesses, and lesser nobles, whom ordinary Russians regarded as mystic relatives of the Divinity. To be in the same room with such personages, breathing the same air, and hearing the same sounds, was in itself worth the trip.

The Czar himself attended often and would honor Strauss with a nod of his luxuriantly bewhiskered head. At his side in the imperial box, the teen-age girl with the fragile features and the shining hair was, as everyone knew, Princess Katherine Dolgoruky. The Czar had fallen in love with her when she was still a child, arranged for her to go to school at St. Petersburg, and made her his constant companion while the Czarina retired almost permanently to her apartments in the Winter Palace.

By far the most ardent of Strauss's royal admirers was the Czar's brother, Grand Duke Konstantin. An avid musical amateur and a passable cellist, Konstantin was so taken with the Viennese music that he asked Strauss for permission to play within the ranks of the orchestra.

For the Czar's brother to join a group of paid entertainers was, in imperial Russia, something more shattering than an earthquake. St. Petersburg was quietly scandalized, unable to grasp the full dimension of an outrage combining elements of class treason and lèse majesté. The specter of revolution was always hanging in the European air in the nineteenth century. But this was worse: it was revolution in reverse, from the top down. Minds boggled, but it all had to be borne in silence. In the first place, one mustn't say anything adverse about the brother of the Czar. Besides, there were no words for such occurrences.

None of this troubled either Strauss or Konstantin. The Grand Duke fitted himself into the cello section of the orchestra with the casual ease that comes from unshakable self-assurance; and though he was not as polished a musician as his professionl colleagues, he and the orchestra seemed to enjoy each other's company.

Such liberality, rare among Romanoffs, seemed altogether fitting for the brother of Russia's remarkable ruler. The reign of Alexander II was a uniquely humane interlude in Russia's harsh history, and to adherents of traditional autocracy, Alexander's rule seemed even more subversive than Konstantin's stint as a cellist. Alexander voluntarily limited his own power by giving Russia its first constitution. He relaxed censorship, instituted legal and economic reforms, and ended the ubiquitous practice of legal torture and flogging.

As a boy, Alexander had put away his pocket money, and when he had saved enough, he would give it to his tutor to buy the freedom of a serf. Now that he wore Russia's crown, he was able to exercise his innate conscience on a grander scale. On March 4, 1861—the very day Abraham Lincoln took office—Alexander decreed freedom for the serfs. More than twenty-five million human beings gained their humanity that day. It was history's greatest single act of liberation, accomplished without bloodshed by the conviction and good will of a single man. It casts a curious light on human affairs that the liberator was soon afterward to be murdered in the name of liberty.

Alexander died some hours after he, along with twenty bystanders, was mangled by a homemade bomb. His killers were idealistic radicals, uncomprehending in their youthful naïveté that the Czar's reforms, vitalized by the moral thrust of his convictions, held the only hope for the realization of their own dreams.

As usual, the paradox of idealistic violence bore tragic fruit. After the murder, the tide turned. The constitution Alexander had granted was revoked, and Russia froze again into the cruel mold of repressive despotism.

As these events lay nascent in the womb of time, Strauss staked out a small preserve of charm and cheerfulness in this grim land. His music blended with the scent of jasmine in the great park at Pavlovsk, and the Viennese airs floated out into the silvery paleness of the northern summer night. It is hardly surprising that quite a few women in his audience discovered within themselves special feelings for the handsome and palpably virile creator of this entranced atmosphere.

This could be inconvenient, since in Russia dueling was frequently an adjunct of love. One morning a pair of formally dressed gentlemen presented themselves at Strauss's villa with a challenge. An officer of the Czar's army found out that his wife had left a standing order with the florist to send a dozen roses to Strauss each day. He demanded satisfaction.

Strauss was disinclined by temperament to settle affairs of the heart by means of bullets, the more so in this case since he didn't even know the lady. He led the two gentlemen into a suite of three otherwise empty rooms filled to overflowing with the daily consignment of flowers sent by various admirers. "Would you pick out the ones you mean?" he said airily to his visitors, who looked at each other, clicked their heels, and departed without pressing the matter any further.

On another occasion, Strauss escaped romantic consequences only by allowing himself to be kidnapped. He had been flirting, perhaps a little too openly, with the daughter of a prominent St. Petersburg merchant, a girl still in her teens.

Like most well-brought-up girls of her time, she had been carefully protected from reality in almost all its forms and therefore may have relied too much on her imagination.

Russian women of the upper class, having little else to do, generally dwelt in a world of their own fancies, which may account for what happened to Strauss.

History does not record the progress or ultimate degree of this acquaintance. But at one point, the girl's father felt himself compelled to introduce Strauss formally as his daughter's fiancé at a large gathering.

Strauss, who had had no inkling of all this, showed great presence of mind and accepted everyone's congratulations as bravely as he did the radiant girl's engagement kiss. But when the family announced a wedding date, the perplexed Strauss sought advice from the Austrian ambassador, who arranged to have Strauss "kidnapped" at his fiancée's house. Several members of the embassy staff came to the door, demanded to see him, and carried him off at full tilt in a troika. For several days Strauss, like a political refugee, found asylum at the embassy while the Austrian diplomat, aided by some highly placed Russians, persuaded the girl and her father to desist from their planned ensnarement of Johann Strauss.

Now in his mid-thirties, Strauss was still staying loose. He picked women—mostly very young ones—for charm and looks. Superficiality reassured him. For all his romantic éclat, he was too innocent to realize that by shying away from those elements that lend substance to a sexual attraction, he was setting a trap for himself. Her name was Olga.

He called her "l'Espiègle"—imp—and indeed there was something enchantingly spectral in the iridescent black eyes that enlivened her slim, intense face. To Strauss, this sprightly and capricious girl, just turned twenty, may have seemed like one of his own more ephemeral melodies. To her, Strauss was by far the most intriguing of her toys, and it was easy for her to play with him, for Strauss was for the first time helplessly, pathetically in love.

For all her girlish volatility, Olga was not flimsy. She had read enough novels, if nothing else, to stretch her emotional range beyond the usual boundaries of a Russian *jeune fille*.

She spoke French with a fine expressive flair, and it was through her that Strauss for the first time experienced the delights of open and precise communication with another person. Under her influence, his own mode of expression grew richer and more adequate to his thoughts. This, in turn, provided him with new avenues of self-discovery, and released in him a new freedom of feeling evident in long letters he wrote to Olga during the early morning hours of lovesick insomnia:

"Have you noticed how sad I was during the concert? I was causelessly enveloped in melancholy increased to a supreme pitch by the music of Schumann, so filled with agonized harmonies. . . . Why can I not be like others? Olga, how unhappy I am! I have never wept for inner pain before, but today—I would confess this to no one but you— it happened. . . ."

True, the style and the maudlin sentimentality are those of a schoolboy. But for Strauss, who never before had been able to verbalize any feeling at all, this was a crucial point of departure; his first and only approach to expressing emotional experience.

The transformation left him overwrought. To every whim of hers he reacted with intense and unaccustomed pathos. After a trivial spat, Strauss—who never before even acknowledged his own inner realities, or anyone else's—suddenly ascended to harrowing levels of emotional candor: "Let me know your selfishness, your pride, and the demon within you —so that I too may regain the balance of wholeness."

Olga was enchanted with her new power. A man had put himself in her keeping. With the fatal innocence of a cat playing with its prey, she turned him into an exercise ground for her young femininity. She tantalized him with her moods. Strauss was defenseless. "If you see me suffer," he wrote in his anguish, "why not tear my heart completely with just one scornful glance?"

But the kaleidoscope of her moods also held moments of

radiant happiness. She lit his world with her smile, warmed it with hints of that ultimate generosity a woman can bestow on a man—letting him sense her acceptance of his being. His life now had a face—hers; and all music was now to him but the reflection of her voice.

June was an idyll. Olga and "Jean" lived their courtship like characters out of Turgenev, taking long garden walks and, during those unendurable separations between secret rendezvous, depositing letters for each other in the hollow of a tree.

On July 31, 1859, the tree held this note: "I am more and more convinced that you are being destined for me by God, and there is no space within me that could harbor the thought of living without you.—Jean."

This complicated matters. Olga's toy unexpectedly turned out to have a heart. It was breakable. And so, ultimately, was she. Now one had to be careful.

Even if she had requited the passionate earnest of Strauss's love, there would have been obstacles. Olga Smirnitzki belonged to a family with aristocratic connections, and it was unthinkable for her to marry a man whose name appeared on public placards and whose autograph was hawked in the streets for ten kopeks. Olga understood this. For all her romantic fancy, she had, like so many proper young ladies, a sure intuition and a tough sense of reality about her social milieu. She took refuge behind her family.

Strauss received an invitation to the Smirnitzki *palais*. Greatly pleased to be asked to Olga's home for the first time, he was in no way prepared for the reception awaiting him. To his surprise Olga was not there to greet him. On his arrival, he was ushered by servants into the formidable presence of Olga's mother, who awaited him with a prepared speech designed to discredit Olga in his eyes.

But she could not shake Strauss's devotion to her daughter. As soon as he left the house, he reported her mother's action to Olga, characteristically unsuspecting that Olga herself may have initiated it. "When [your mother] said to me that I was not to believe a word you said, that all you did was designed to bring me to the point of madness, that all your wishes were inspired by the devil within you, then I conceived a positive hatred against your mother . . . who could say such insulting things against her own child."

Madame Smirnitzki demanded that Strauss hand over Olga's letters. Strauss refused—"For I need these letters to preserve my own life and I cannot do without them."

It is a mark of Olga's basic kindness—quite rare in a woman so young—that after this contretemps she permitted Strauss to go on believing that she loved him. She even put a few more letters in the hollow tree, hinting that only the surveillance of her parents prevented her from seeing him. Strauss tried to console her: "Do not let your parents' obstinacy burden your heart. I only want to know that you are not sad. Not a single moment should be shadowed for you. . . ."

The Russian summer was short. Darkness fell early by September and the evenings grew cold. The gardens at Pavlovsk lay still and the music hall was locked.

Johann Strauss braced himself for the ordeal of the long railroad trip back to Vienna. He had no opportunity to take leave of Olga.

A few more letters passed between them, but their correspondence ceased soon after when Olga allowed herself to be married to a man chosen by her parents.

Strauss sought solace in work, but for almost a whole year he seemed distracted, going through his daily routine like a somnambulist. Gradually the fire that transfigured his remembrance of Olga died down, and he found deliverance from the hazards of happiness.

8

Turning Points

The Vienna of the 1860s that welcomed Strauss after his Russian adventures was a city far different from the one in which he had spent his youth. Urban growth altered the very face of Vienna as the city spilled over its walls, and the old fortifications were finally razed to be replaced by sumptuous thoroughfares. The rise of industrial capitalism poured into Vienna new people with new money, contending for influence and prestige with an older, less vital aristocracy. New attitudes, tastes, and ways of feeling pervaded Vienna in the wake of these social shifts; and since music mirrors its time, even the Viennese waltz took on a different mood.

It was an era when all of Austria drifted into a new climate of existence. Outwardly it was an era of opulence, but beneath its gloss Austria's fundamental premise had begun to dissolve. For almost a millennium, Austria had been a family of many nationalities sheltered under the paternal roof of monarchy. The mystic idea of the crown unified and validated the existence and self-image of Magyars, Serbs, Croats, Slovenes, Lombards, Poles, Slovaks, Czechs, Ruthenians, Montenegrins, and Germanic Austrians. Beneath its sheltering majesty they fitted into the pattern of the realm without loss of individuality like patches in a quilt, and their diverse temperaments formed the spectrum of Austrian character.

But by the century's midpoint, the basic glue joining the parts of this structure had cracked. The crown no longer inspired mystic faith, and without this kind of secular piety, the harmonious subjection of the parts to the whole could no longer function as an idea of order. The concept of a supra-national community, derived from the Catholic universalism of the Middle Ages, had lost its hold. Other thoughts were in the air.

The revolution of 1848, though technically squelched, had given legitimacy to libertarian ideas. Independence and self-determination were the new watchwords as Austria's national-ities now aspired to become nations, pulling apart the mosaic of the monarchy.

Had this trend toward national self-determination been merely a striving for political power or economic advantage, Vienna could have dealt with it politically. But the new divi-sive forces within Austria did not spring from such rational motives alone. They were subtler and therefore stronger.

The yearning for separate national identities among Aus-tria's ethnic segments was, in essence, a spiritual quest. Slavs and Magyars in particular were convinced that within the framework of the Habsburg monarchy they could never achieve independent control of what they felt to be their communal destiny. To them, secession from Austria appeared as a necessary prelude to a basic self-realization. Rousseau's idea of popular sovereignty, of government by consent of the governed, had at last reached eastward—not with the brazen proclamations once heard in France, but with whispers in the wind. Yet tides turn with such whispers. And now the tide ran against Austria.

Vienna reacted to the growing tension within the empire like a woman putting on her loveliest dress to quell her fear of some half-perceived danger. A great circling boulevard, the Ringstrasse, was built around the Inner City. Nearly two

hundred feet wide, it had three separate roadways—a broad
center for wheeled traffic flanked by two tree-shaded lanes
for gentlemen riders—and ample sidewalks for leisurely
promenading under additional double rows of trees.

Magnificent buildings adjoined "the Ring," many of them
set back in spacious parks and plazas, framed between the
festive jets of high-spouting fountains. The Opera, the first
great edifice to be completed along the Ring, was soon followed by the Parliament, the City Hall, the Stock Exchange,
the Imperial Theater, and a vast art museum facing an equally
grandiose science museum. The most renowned architects of
the time—Semper, Hansen, Hasenauer, Siccardsburg, and Van
der Nüll—vied for the opportunity to let their neo-Renais-
sance and neo-Gothic visions take shape in the great new
street. Emperor Franz Josef himself had commanded the Ring
project—a virtual transformation of the city—and his edict
gave the architects virtually limitless access to the state treas-
ury. For once, lack of money did not get in the way of the
builders' imagination. The result was far more than a great
boulevard. The Ring represented a total concept of urban
landscape, so grand that even Baron Haussmann's stone
dreams of Paris paled before its harmonious splendor.

Squandering national treasure for beauty's sake may, to
rational economists, seem frivolous. But frivolity was foreign
to Franz Josef's nature. What inspired him to the extrava-
gance of the Ring was neither a vain urge for self-glorifica-
tion nor aesthetic abandonment. It was sound political
intuition. Austria needed a spiritual binding force to
strengthen the fading faith in the crown, and the only power
competent for such a task was that of beauty.

Almost certainly Franz Josef, a man of limited intellect,
did not elucidate the situation to himself in such explicit
terms. But his instinct harked back to the Habsburg rulers
who, as shapers of architectural environments, had long relied
on aesthetic delight as a humanizing influence and political
stabilizer. By transforming Austria's capital into a palpable
expression of generosity, dignity, and exaltation, Franz Josef

was asserting and validating the ideal of monarchic rule. Architecture in its grandest sense was the metaphor through which the Emperor spoke to his people—a metaphor transcending the divisions of language within his realm, reaching the mind through eyes and heart.

The Ringstrasse was his way of countering the challenge flung at his crown by the divisive forces of the new nationalism. Against an idea he posed a symbol. It was an appropriate answer.

East of the Opera, the character of the Ring changed. The massive monumentality of public edifices yielded to the more intimate scale of private mansions—the new homes of Vienna's *nouveaux riches*. Behind their elaborately stuccoed façades, new forms of social life developed in Vienna. The "Ring Millionaires," as the old aristocracy contemptuously called the fashionable residents of the new street, were an emerging class—the creatures of industry. Their wealth was not inherited land; it was new money, often made by one man's enterprise in a single lifetime. It flowed into Vienna from the textile mills and machine shops of Bohemia, the Styrian mines and ironworks, from Moravia's sugar refineries, and from the private and discreet investment banks springing up everywhere to finance the belated burgeoning of industry in Austria.

In outlook and life-style, the Ring Millionaires differed greatly from the rigid, land-owning establishment. As creative businessmen they had to be adaptable and responsive, open to ideas. And something of this intellectual openness spilled over into their mores and social attitudes. Vienna's creative brilliance during the later nineteenth century had its roots in their salons. For it was in the houses of the Ring Millionaires that, for the first time, Vienna's intellectual and social worlds mingled on equal footing.

Jews played a germinal part in this development. Emancipated and given civil rights litle more than two generations before, an educated elite of Austrian Jews availed themselves of the new opportunities created by rapid industrialization. While the older land-owning aristocracy remained disdainfully aloof from commerce, a bright and sophisticated Jewish minority spearheaded Austria's industrial development, establishing factories, inventing new technology, and creating the needed capital flow.

Rich Jewish families—the Arnsteins, Wertheimsteins, Konigswarters, and others—soon added flair, elegance, and manners to their traditional respect for learning, thus creating a new *haut monde* in which fashion joined intellect. Unlike the old aristocracy, which had meanwhile become stultified, they provided the aura of liberality necessary for the flourishing of artistic and literary life. In short, they were the catalyst for the iridescent coming together of mind and money.

It was among the Ring Millionaires that Johann Strauss—by now fairly wealthy himself—found his new social milieu. He moved in their circles with the assurance of a seasoned habitué. After all, he was a second-generation King, no more parvenu than his hosts, and the smell of the tavern where his father had been born had long been masked by the perfume of international fame.

Even so, the old aristocrats of the Inner City would never have allowed a musician on their guest lists. But Baron Moritz Todesco, whose Ring mansion abounded with artists, literateurs, and an attractive sprinking of bright debutantes, evidently had no such scruples. In fact, the charming, urbane woman who was the Baron's constant companion and a gracious hostess to his guests was herself a famous singer.

Jetty Treffz was remarkable in many ways. Being able, as Todesco's mistress, to assemble one of Vienna's most fashionable social circles in itself attests to her courage and charisma. For all its relative emancipation, even the new Viennese society did not condone the flaunting of marital irregularities. But Jetty's personality surmounted all possible objections.

Years on stage had given her the assurance of a woman who sets a scene by her mere presence. Though no longer young, she had retained a figure conforming to prevailing standards of feminine beauty. Lustrous dark hair framed her expressive face. Above all, she had the kind of alert vitality that immunizes against age. It was Jetty who saw to it that Strauss came to her house often.

Only a few years earlier, music critics had compared her to Jenny Lind, the Swedish Nightingale who had enchanted Europe. Mendelssohn and Berlioz had dedicated songs to her. But at the age of forty, she abandoned her career for the companionship of Moritz Todesco.

The Baron could not marry her. He had promised his dying father never to abandon the Jewish faith. Jetty felt that she could not give up her Catholicism. Austria recognized no civil marriage between persons of different religious beliefs. So, even after the birth of their two daughters, the union between Moritz and Jetty remained unhallowed.

In the baronial mansion on the Ring, Jetty led a fairly sheltered existence. Only in conversation with Strauss could she recapture the stimulus of her former life as a musician. Through him, this middle-aged woman revisited her youth; through him she was revitalized.

Strauss, left emotionally undernourished by his earlier ephemeral attachments and still smarting from Olga's rebuff, responded to Jetty's warmth and the quiet, assured dignity gained from her wide and deeply sympathetic experience of human nature. It didn't matter to Strauss that Jetty was ten years older than he. To him, youth was no longer a celebration. Love lay deeper.

When the relationship between Strauss and Jetty could no longer be maintained within the bounds of discretion, Jetty asked the Baron for her release.

Moritz Todesco let her go without a word of reproach. He must have loved her greatly. He settled on her a sizable fortune as a parting present, and he kept their two daughters to give them the advantage of his title.

It was a quiet wedding, almost furtive. Aside from Jean and Jetty—she preferred the French version of his name—

only two witnesses were present at St. Stephen's at eight in the morning on August 27, 1862. One was Carl Haslinger, Strauss's publisher. The other was his mother. Neither was altogether pleased.

Haslinger worried about Jetty's money. Todesco's generosity had made her financially independent. With all economic pressure removed, would Strauss remain productive? He was, after all, Haslinger's best "property," and any cutback of his output would affect Haslinger's profits.

Anna Strauss had other reservations. Carrying off somebody else's mistress was not her kind of marital premise. For all her artistic bent, she retained the outlook of a middle-class housewife. Her own husband's defection had narrowed her tolerance, and Vienna's new society in their Ring mansions must have seemed to her incomprehensible and threatening. To her, Jetty was a "fallen woman" who had beguiled her dearest son into some alien world of ingrained wickedness and ultimate perdition.

Yet if Strauss's marital prospects seemed doubtful, it was not for the reasons imagined by Anna. The real danger lay in the temper of the times and its effect on creative artists.

Artists, dependent on inner tension and perpetual unfulfillment to spur their creativity, have always had greater exposure to the risks, though perhaps also the felicities, of marriage. But the age of romanticism, then near its apex, multiplied the hazards for the artist in love.

Within the romantic purview, love is not a household item. To the artist, it is the transcendent vehicle of yearning in which to pursue the impossible. To him, it is the strenuous exercise of the soul, the oblique career of spiritual ambition.

That's hard on women. Within the heady mash of sex and spirit created by the romantic attitude, the woman is not really the object of love, only its instrument. Transcendence lies not within her but through her. She is not the destination; only the way.

The romantic artist-lover is so involved in this supernal quest for what lies beyond woman that he really pays little attention to her; nor, in a deeper sense, has he any appreciative capacity for her. As a result, his loneliness is intensified by his love. What he gains from her is not sharing, but, on the contrary, the bitter though inwardly desired proof of his essential solitude. This he translates into the febrile intensification of self which forms the wellspring of romantic art.

From this pattern arises the disembodied ardor of romantic music. The courtly, never intrusive, persuasions of the Strauss waltz no less than the convoluted erotic futilities of Tristan are essentially love-songs *manqué*. Their yearnings focus on the feminine but aim at the infinite.

Given such psychological premises, it is hardly surprising that in the latter decades of the century, Vienna's artistic and intellectual community turned into the emotional pressure cooker that yielded the steamy literature and fervid art of post-romanticism and from which Freud later tapped his particular potion. The final distillate was drawn in the writings of Wedekind, Schnitzler, Hofmannsthal, and early Zweig and Werfel, in the paintings of Klimt and Schiele, the graphic design of Mucha, and the architecture of the Viennese *Jugendstil*. A desperate fire, a vibrant inwardness, lies in all these elite expressions, and the smile that is the last self-knowing gesture of a wounded culture sensing its own end.

It was Jetty's influence that enabled Strauss to escape the subtle morbidity of this atmosphere which, like a darkly glowing haze, slowly wrapped itself around Vienna's spirit. Strauss's own personality had undergone certain changes that made him more susceptible to the melancholy and introspective aspects of the romantic attitude. After the time in limbo, following the break with Olga, he suffered occasional spells of moodiness during which he would spend whole days just staring out the window. Yet with the resolute emotional realism forced on her by her socially unorthodox past, Jetty was just the woman to give Strauss the support he needed at this point in his life.

Deliberately, one suspects, she bypassed the prevalent risks of romanticism, avoiding emotional intensification through searching encounter, and steered her marriage with Strauss into the safer and undemanding channel of cozy domesticity. She saw to it that their lives were basically routine, keyed to an even note of sustained tranquillity. For Strauss, this was a novelty as well as a need. With the unsentimental clearsightedness that often passes for "feminine wisdom," Jetty knew this. The home she created was a refuge, shielded from all intrusions. None but intimate friends came, and Strauss had few of those. His way of entertaining those rare visitors was a quiet game of billiards. For the most part, Jetty had Strauss to herself, and the mood of their being together was one of unbroken repose. Their marriage was not a romance—it was an idyll.

Even the setting was bucolic. With the money given her by Todesco, Jetty bought a mansion in Hietzing at the western outskirts of Vienna, adjoining the great park of Schönbrunn palace. It was a two-story building of golden-yellow sandstone, its base slanting to the rise of the Maxing-strasse as it ascends a low hill with the typically Viennese name of Küniglberg. The northward view from its rounded top scans the entire city, with Schönbrunn in the foreground, the spire of St. Stephen's in the middle distance, and the Danube as backdrop. Toward the west one sees the gentle range of the Vienna Woods enfolding their vineyards between arborate ridges, and far to the south the eye meets the gleam of the first Alpine peaks.

A double gate, large enough to admit a carriage into the cobbled entrance hall, brought the visitor to the bottom of a stone staircase with ornate balustrades leading up to the main floor.

Jetty furnished the house in the latest fashion. The walls were covered with brocaded silk. Strauss's study, for example, was lined in emerald-green with wine-red stripes to match the velvet upholstery of sofas and chairs. Near a window opening onto the garden stood a large rosewood writing desk with two great candelabra and a special circular file to hold large sheets of score paper.

The walls of most other rooms were brocaded in deep red, a favorite color in this period of sated opulence. But in her choice of furniture Jetty resisted the late Victorian trend toward the massive with its dark, elaborately carved chests and tables, reminiscent of the Italian Renaissance. She preferred the lighter materials and more graceful lines of the Biedermeier, and throughout the house the light from the crystal chandeliers coaxed a pale reddish glow from waxed cherry wood and raised golden reflections in vermeil.

As an environment, the house had aesthetic integrity. Its luxury never declined to ostentation, and the interiors hung together in a cohesion of spirit recalling Robert Musil's description of a Viennese patrician household: "It was evident that these were things that someone believed in before they came into existence."

For Strauss, the house became a shell. He rarely went out. By 1864, at the age of thirty-nine, he had fulfilled his contractual obligations as a conductor, and his wife's wealth enabled him to retire from regular appearances and devote himself entirely to composition. The Strauss orchestra, still the pride of Vienna and the mainstay of his family, was now wholly in the hands of his brothers Josef and Eduard, and after Josef's fatal accident in 1870, Eduard alone carried on as conductor and administrative head of the orchestra.

Unlike his brothers, Eduard was ordinary. A competent musician, he yet lacked true musicality, and the lack was less of talent than of character. A true musician spends his life courting Music, pervaded and enchanted by her essence, but knowing she can never be possessed and that all his hope and all his attainment lies in his longing. It is this unending supplication that makes the playing of great musicians forever spontaneous, with the glint of ecstasy always beneath the surface. But Eduard was too proud for that and too narrow.

As a conductor, he was able to ape Johann's style. He had the Straussian manner if not the substance. For the audiences thronging to his concerts, that was good enough. It wasn't good enough for Eduard. He knew the difference, sensed his lack, and grew into a bitter, shallow man who cared more for good tailoring than anything else.

In his foppish way, "Edi" Strauss became one of Vienna's most fashionable personages, always seen in the right places and at the right parties, a man recognized in the street. He was box office.

Edi also fancied himself a composer and introduced his own works along with those of his brothers. His personal popularity assured the success of his waltzes and polkas, and, to be sure, they were neat, well-crafted music that required no excuse. But Edi had no illusions. His were occasional pieces. Johann's work was timeless. Edi was not strong enough to live with this knowledge. Gradually the poison sank into his relationship with Johann.

Johann tried to bridge the widening gap. "You see everything too darkly," he wrote to Edi. "You always suspect that I want to do you harm. I wish you would rid yourself of such foolish notions. When will you grow up enough to realize that your brother is not your foe?"

But Edi rejected every conciliatory approach. He envied not only Johann's gifts but also his aristocratic seclusion with Jetty while he himself was left amid the tensions and annoyances of the musical marketplace. Johann, on his part, may have felt resentful of Edi's prominence now that he himself rarely stepped into the limelight. Though Johann's own name remained as lustrous as ever, he would sometimes mockingly identify himself by saying, "I'm Edi's brother." Still, throughout his life Johann treated Edi with openness and largesse, while Edi seemed to be shrinking under the burden of his ill-concealed envy.

Only after Johann's death could Edi vent his hate. In a macabre gesture of posthumous murder, he set a great fire, feeding it for two full days by burning all of Johann's un-published manuscripts. No one knows what beauty and de-light was sacrified to Edi's fratricidal lust, and it is the measure of the man that he would turn music to ashes.

Yet Edi's anger, so reminiscent of that earlier rift between Johann and his father, cast no shadow on Johann's life. Freed from the pressures and obligations of public performances, he settled into a routine that released in him new areas of crea-tive potential. Dressed in his red velvet smoking jacket, he would sit at his desk almost every night until the small hours, filling sheet after sheet of music paper. Occasionally he would jump up to stand by the window awhile, looking out into the nocturnal garden, or try a few chords on the piano—very softly so as not to wake Jetty.

In the morning, after a late breakfast and a romp in the courtyard with his two Great Danes, he would go walking in the still rural hills of Hietzing, and after lunch he would play for Jetty the music composed on the previous evening. At times, Jetty suggested revisions, and Strauss trusted her advice.

As a singer, she had sufficient theoretical training to under-stand the technicalities of composition, and her stage experi-ence had left her with a keen sense for an effective phrase or modulation. Her background in operatic and symphonic music encouraged Strauss to follow more boldly his own leanings toward increasingly symphonic structures.

All his life, as if drawn by some constant and invincible seduction, Strauss tended toward more generous concepts of music than the dance hall could accommodate. But it had been a hesitant yielding. Always he had held back, distrust-fully shackling his own creativity to keep within conven-tional limits of entertainment music. He needed the protection of the customary, the knowledge that he was turning out salable products.

Now at last the emotional security, no less than the economic freedom, he had gained through Jetty released him from this need for self-confirmation in the market. He was inwardly free to grow. And Jetty's competent, knowing participation in this growth gave their marriage a workable content, a shared substance.

This was the germinal period in Strauss' life that prepared the ground for his great symphonic waltzes: *The Blue Danube, Wine, Women, and Song, Tales from the Vienna Woods, Voices of Spring, Artist's Life,* and the *Emperor Waltz,* to name but the finest. In these works Strauss achieved the apotheosis of dance music, because the music is liberated from subservience to the dance. It exists and attains validity in musical terms alone as an unfettered creation in the realm of ideas, thus elevating the dance to its own level of freedom.

Long before his symphonic proclivities gained predominance in his own music, Strauss had made his mark as a symphonic conductor. As early as 1856 he performed Liszt's *Mazeppa* in the composer's presence to his explicit approval, and throughout his life he had interspersed symphonic selections and operatic overtures among the dance numbers at his concerts. But his greatest coup as a symphonic conductor was the Viennese premiere of excerpts from *Tristan und Isolde,* the most controversial and radically advanced score of its time.

The work had been scheduled at the Vienna Opera in 1861, but plans for the performance were dropped when the orchestra declared the music to be "unplayable." Strauss was incensed. An ardent Wagnerian, he considered the cancellation a dereliction of artistic responsibility on the part of Vienna's ranking musical institution. He firmly believed in the new musical language embodied in *Tristan,* and if the famous Vienna Opera lacked the skill and courage to perform the work, he would do so on his own. He asked Wagner for permission to play orchestral excerpts from the score. Surprisingly, Wagner assented and furnished orchestral versions of the great Love Duet from Act II and of Isolde's impassioned *Liebestod.*

It was not merely chagrin at being snubbed by the august Opera that prompted Wagner to entrust Strauss with this difficult music. Rather it was Wagner's belief in Strauss's essential musicality, in his ability to perceive and realize in performance the specific musical attitude and aesthetic of *Tristan*. Wagner characterized Strauss as "the most musical mind in Europe." Apparently he really meant it.

Thus, on August 31, 1861, at an outdoor concert in the *Volksgarten*—the spacious park extending along the Ring between the *Hofburg* and the City Hall—Vienna witnessed one of the strangest paradoxes in the history of music: the most profound score of an era being introduced by the Waltz King.

Was it really so strange for Strauss to conduct *Tristan?* Not if one sees to the bottom of music as into a well where the true ground of the art appears beneath its liquid shimmer. There Wagner and Strauss converge. For in the deepest fount of their inspiration both saw music the same way: not as an art but as a spell. To both, music was transfiguration to the level of ardor, and there are parallels between the hypnotism of Wagner and the raptures of the waltz. That is what Wagner and Strauss sensed and appreciated in each other. Both were dealers in sonorous mesmerism.

Wagner's influence on Strauss became increasingly evident, not only in the supple orchestration of his later waltzes, but also in their melodic conception. Wagner espoused the idea of the "endless melody," a mystic concept of song filling the world at all times. From this eternal *melos* the composer renders audible the portion filtering through his mind. Thus all music is ideally a weaving of sound to the cadence of timelessness, and only human and other earthly imperfections deprive all music from becoming a single, endless unity in a Platonic realm of ideal song.

Within the limits of his *métier*, Strauss managed to capture something of the characteristic mood of such concepts. He abandoned the earlier form of stringing together sharply contrasting waltz tunes like a multicolored garland. Instead, he now created endlessly flowing waltz streams of related themes in a kind of seamless continuity.

These long lines of sustained songfulness—wholly new in popular music—were supported by the fluid harmonies pioneered by Wagner, gliding freely from key to key. Particularly the introductory measures of the later waltzes often float off on harmonic side trips to far-off tonalities.

Audiences responded readily to the surpassing beauty of these later waltzes, but some found them puzzling. "They can no longer be called dance music," maintained Eduard Hanslick, the dean of Viennese critics. And in Paris, where Strauss was played almost as much as Offenbach, Alexandre Dumas père observed in his journal: "It often happened that my partner and I, dancing to the magical music of Johann Strauss, would stop in order to follow into the infinite this inspired dreaming. It almost seemed to us a desecration to allow such melodies to be resolved into a physical pleasure."

Dumas clearly perceived the psychological premise of Strauss's new style: it is sublimatory, and in this it reflects the deepest precepts of romanticism. As the music of amorous attention, the waltz in its later forms portrayed Eros in Victorian mask. The common idea of the Victorian era as antisexual is as absurd as it is glib. Culture cannot suspend biology, and on the evidence of Balzac, Stendhal, and even Trollope, the nineteenth century was probably subtler and more sentient in its sexual perceptions than the more unbuttoned centuries preceding and following. It is the mode of expression that misleads. What now appears as innocence is merely a stylistic preference of mood over matter. And seeming innocence is by no means an allergy to experience.

It was, to be sure, an age of prudery. Sensual acts were placed in a category often insurmountably separate from emotional rapport between men and women. As a result, the possible dimensions of romance, as well as the need for romantic relationships, became enormously augmented.

But even romance, the acceptable framework of ostensibly

chaste appreciation between men and women, cannot deny Eros. Romantic relationships—unless resolved, or ended, in marriage—thus presented Victorians with an ultimate choice between aridity and dissolution; and many stereotypes of Victorian fiction derive essentially from this impasse.

One function of the waltz was to amend this Victorian dilemma. It is music that is always "in love" but never erotic. It is tender but shy, and in tune with that Catholic fear of women that, in its happier manifestations, changes lust to adoration. In the embrace of the waltz which is not an embrace, the Victorian dualism of body and spirit is both affirmed and resolved, and as a man and a woman look at each other so steadily during the swirling dance, the ache of yearning melts in their eyes.

The later symphonic waltz style formed the musical terrain suited to these intricate maneuvers of the soul. Without changing the basic elements of the dance, Strauss gave the waltz a new psychological cast fitted to the needs of the romantic era.

The old, simpler waltz implied a feeling of happy, uncomplicated togetherness. To each couple, the music said: "WE." The new waltz, far more subtly differentiated, admits more complex encounters. To each couple the music says: "YOU AND I," and the lasting separateness is the root of romance.

The new waltz adumbrates the core of romance in yet another way: it eternalizes the moment. Other dances may have many steps. The waltz has but one. Always repeated, always renewed, each step regenerates the essence of the dance at each turn, intimating but never attaining fulfillment in endless self-renewal.

Endlessness is inherent in three-quarter time. It lacks the final beat to close the measure. It remains open, leading into the next circle, and the next, in stylized infinity. Time flows into itself, and limits lift in the convergence of time.

For the dancers, there is no release. Only sustained tension, illuminating for each couple the fact of existence by an enfolding emphasis to each of the other. Such music, perhaps, is a spelling of love.

That is why waltzes cannot end. Stopping such music is not a finish but a fracture.

"The waltz will not cease," writes the essayist Hans Weigel. "The odd number *three* cannot be resolved. Unlike music in 2/2 or 4/4 time, the circling of the waltz dictates autonomous motion that cannot be broken. The end of the waltz is a trauma, a precipitous fall into a world where two times two equals four."

Without the music, the dancers are again imprisoned in time and self. But then perhaps it no longer matters; for, as Eliot says, "you are the music while the music lasts."

9

The Blue Danube

The universe of the waltz can be epitomized in about fifteen minutes simply by playing *The Blue Danube*. More eloquently, more concisely than any other work, it embodies the essence of the waltz in form and spirit.

The Blue Danube has suffered the perils of popularity. Subjected to countless arrangements and abridgments, assaulted by unfeeling incompetence in myriad indifferent performances, it has often been stripped of its gentle, smiling poesy and reduced to a tawdry cliché. But when its softly mysterious opening stirs the air with the rich, vibrant pianissimo that only a great orchestra can achieve, if the conductor keeps the tempo a little hesitant and pensive and retains a touch of lassitude even in the more exuberant phases, then the music takes subtle hold of the listener and makes him a living part of a vanished world.

Paradoxically, the waltz that was to become Vienna's musical hallmark was one of Strauss's rare flops when it was first heard in February 1867. After the initial rebuff, Strauss had been ready to withdraw the piece and stuff the score somewhere among his papers, perhaps to be forgotten and eventually burned in the malicious holocaust set by brother Edi.

But a fortunate chain of events, involving high diplomacy, a scheming woman, and the Emperor of France, saved *The Blue Danube* from possible oblivion.

A line by the now obscure poet Karl Isidor Beck served as Strauss's inspiration for *The Blue Danube* and suggested the title. In his day Beck had been hailed as "the German Byron." The only way to account for this appellation is to assume that Byron lost something in German translation. Beck, however, has little to lose, even when translated into English:

> And I saw thee, gracious, youthful,
> Bearing yet a world of pain,
> Where our hearts are ever truthful,
> Where our gold has ever lain,
> By the Danube, beautiful blue Danube.

This, for all one can tell, may have been intended as a love song, addressed perhaps to one of those charming young ladies of Vienna who usually managed to avoid emotional honesty toward their admirers by being everlastingly bittersweet. It was their style, so one must make allowances for the poor poet.

At any rate, the fluid sound and aquatic image of the phrase "by the Danube, beautiful blue Danube" captivated Strauss. He chose it as the title of a new waltz and transmuted the phrase into the opening D-major theme, which suggests the gliding flow of the great river.

Shortly after completing the score during the first weeks of 1867, Strauss turned it over to Johann Herbeck, the conductor of the Viennese Men's Choral Association. Always in search of new material for his excellent choir, Herbeck had asked Strauss to write something for his group, not considering that the Waltz King was unaccustomed to write for voice but that his melodic imagination had been conditioned by the flowing continuity of sound attainable on the violin.

That was the first portent of disaster. The second was the need for a singable text. Beck's poem about the "beautiful blue Danube" had served only as a general inspiration to Strauss. He had not actually set the words to music. What Herbeck needed was a wordsmith, and he happened to have one within convenient reach. He handed the score to one Josef Weyl, a police clerk who sang in the chorus. Weyl occasionally fabricated verses and therefore ranked as a poet among his friends.

This time Weyl drew his inspiration from the new electric arc lights that had just been introduced as experimental street lanterns at some of Vienna's busier corners. The subject was indubitably brilliant, but unfortunately those early arc lamps proved highly unreliable and would sputter out into darkness whenever the carbon electrodes broke off or the spark gap was improperly adjusted. Weyl's literal police poetry duly reflected these circumstances in the opening lines of *The Blue Danube:*

> *Wiener seid froh!*
> *Oho, wieso?*
> *Ein Schimmer des Lichts!*
> *Wir sehn noch nichts.*

Without undue liberty, this may be rendered as follows:

> Vienna, be gay!
> And what for, pray?
> The light of the arc!
> Here it's still dark!

Some commentators argue that the provenance of this poem should not be too closely tied to the street lamps. Rather they feel that the poet was celebrating the coming of the light (Ein Schimmer des Lichts) in a more metaphoric and philosophic sense. But this hardly improves matters. On the contrary.

It speaks well for the collective intelligence of the chorus that its members nearly rioted when they were obliged to sing out these inanities in antiphonal dialogue, one side exclaiming "The light of the arc!" and the other responding "Here it's still dark!" But rebellion in the ranks seldom availed anything in absolutist Austria, and on February 13, 1867, at the height of the carnival season, a massed chorus of 1200 men bellowed forth this doubtful hymn to electric street lights.

The concert took place in the baroque hall of the Imperial Riding School, usually reserved for showing off the elegant capers of Vienna's famed white Lippizaner horses. Judging by the lukewarm response, the audience might have preferred to see the horses. They certainly would have been more graceful than the huffing of a small army of men gasping for breath in an attempt to span the flowing melodies conceived in Strauss's mind for the bowed continuity of string sound.

Strauss received the news of the disaster quite nonchalantly. It had been a good season for him. Only the night before, his new waltz, *Cabled Dispatches*, had been loudly acclaimed at its premiere at the ball of the Vienna Press Club, and just five days earlier, the public had cheered the first performance of *Artist's Life*, a composition Strauss rightfully considered as one of his most beautiful. What did it matter then if *The Blue Danube* was a flop? He just shrugged, reportedly muttering, "Well, the hell with it."

The Blue Danube might well have been forgotten, lying unremarked among Strauss's papers, if he had not soon afterward received a letter from the Comte d'Osmont, a well-known French patron of music, inviting him to Paris for the World's Fair to be held that spring. Apparently the count had been in touch with the Austrian ambassador to France, Prince Richard Metternich—the son of the former Chancellor against whom Strauss as a young man wrote his revolutionary marches.

An astute diplomat, Richard Metternich not only forgave

Strauss's agitation against his father, he let himself be persuaded that having Strauss visit Paris at this time would be a smart political move. If Strauss succeeded in captivating the Parisians, he might create an atmosphere favorable to the ambassador's own schemes, which aimed at nothing less than the reshuffling of the European balance of power, allying France and Austria to check Germany's arrogant rise under the leadership of Bismarck.

Just a year before, Bismarck had given Austria a taste of his statesmanship. He provoked a trivial border dispute, insolently pushed it to the point of war, and in just three weeks, by the first application of *blitz* tactics, his Prussian-drilled troops trounced Austria's brave but bumbling forces.

Bismarck claimed no spoils in his victory. All he had wanted to do was to give the world a German lesson. He had created a modern monster—the militarized industrial state—and wanted to show it off on its first outing.

Stunned by this prophetic encounter with German *Realpolitik*, Austria reached for the hand of France. In terms of military prowess, Austria had little to offer to a potential ally. Comparing Austria's attitude toward its army—a kind of permanent costume ball for its aristocracy—with the professionalism of the French officer corps, Metternich quipped: "The Austrians make generals of their dukes; the French make dukes of their generals." But even in its impotence, Austria could offer France a vital security factor: strategic location. With Austria in the east and south and France in the west, a restraining ring might be forged against the unpleasantly stirring German monster.

To make Johann Strauss an instrument of such diplomacy had been the lucky inspiration of Richard Metternich's wife, Princess Pauline. This vital and perceptive woman saw that the situation called for a pied piper who could make everyone dance to his tune. Common denominators were needed, and music might be the most persuasive. It would show that Paris and Vienna had more in common than just an enemy.

Music, better than anything else, might point up the natural affinity of the two great cities that, in many ways, were creatures of the same spirit. Even outwardly Paris and Vienna resembled each other. The harmonious urban vistas of the Ringstrasse had their parallel in the Place de la Concorde; Schönbrunn had its counterpart at Versailles; and the Prater with its glens and lagoons might be compared to the Bois de Bologne. Both Paris and Vienna offer aspects that do not seem like cities at all. From their vistas springs a suddenness of sky. It does not appear in strips and patches of blue, nor in broken shards glimpsed between buildings, but in great open expanses, a horizon ringed at the edges by the silhouettes of distant domes and towers. The long views along the Seine, like those near the outer Hofburg, seem not so much architectural vision than a natural landscape formation—fantastic yet harmonious outgrowths of an abundant earth. Yet Paris and Vienna are never forbidding in their grandeur. Despite the vastness of proportions, the eye beholds everything on a human scale. Both are truly capital cities, but they bear their majesty with a smile.

Even more important, the maze of unremarkable little streets whose names hardly anyone remembers, narrow and crooked and full of surprises to the delighted eye, bespeaks yet other similarities between Paris and Vienna. Countless fleeting impressions spell out the character of an environment that projects the collective experience of its people, the sum total of conditions and influences affecting their lives. The city is the stage set for living, and the scenery partly shapes the action. Space and structure are formed in accordance with half-conscious dreams, and in turn the physical setting creates visual, emotional, and sensual reality—the temperament of existence.

Seen in those terms, Paris and Vienna reveal their kinship: two cities devoted to the affirmation of the fundamental joy of living, agreed on the surpassing importance of art, cooking, and the less strenuous modes of philosophy, not to mention wine and women. To the astute Austrian ambassador, what could seem more natural than to confirm such basic sympathies with political accord? And with Johann Strauss at the Paris Fair, the letter of a treaty might later follow the lead of the music.

If this scheme sounds like the plot of a Viennese operetta, it was, after all, in the best tradition of Austrian statecraft. The Habsburg Empire had been gained through marriage rather than might, so foreign relations had always been more or less a family affair; music had always been Austria's main export, and the national purpose, if such a formidable concept could ever be applied to Austria, was simply to continue in this amiable vein. And in its own way, France of the Second Empire was no less a projection of sybaritic fantasy. Fey, febrile, and frivolous, its civilization was sustained as much by style as by substance.

Paris under Napoleon III was a city drunk with the worship of the Bourse. The uncontrolled stock exchange was like a great roulette wheel tossing fortunes from hand to hand. Financial caprice also enlivened the gigantic real estate schemes that pushed the bright new boulevards out into the *banlieu* and put vast sums into the eager grasp of promoters. Speculation was a way of life. Reaching deep into the middle class, the aura of gaming undercut the traditional morality. Life itself was a stock issue, a quick capital turnover—a bubble.

Gem-laden denizens of this ephemeral world rolled through their days in glittering equipages from matinee to fête to theater. Music sounded ceaselessly from a hundred stages. The galop and the cancan, the wildest of dances, created a contagious *folie des jambes* setting the keynote for the compulsive sexuality that passed for pleasure until, some decades later, *la belle époque* gentled this fevered thirst toward more temperate modes of sensuous delight.

Like the Bourse, Woman became an obsession of the bourgeosie, and the two concepts were joined in the fashionable understanding that love was to be bought and sold. It was the era of the elegant courtesans—famous actresses with a lucrative sideline or simply women of beauty, wit, and intelligence who, like their rich clients invested their assets for maximum returns. Names like those of Hortense Schneider, Thérèse Lachmann, Anna Desilons, and Leonide Leblanc represent an aristocracy of sorts, whose boudoirs were perhaps the essential locus of the Parisian spirit during the reign of Napoleon III. In the later stages of French romanticism, the erotic mythology of Paris found its ideal in the frail, gentle, and generous little *grisette* who had made a present of herself—the poignant archetype of all the Mimis in all *Les Bohèmes,* wherever they might be. But in the robust years of the Second Empire, the sex myth centered on the feisty, cash-counting *horizontales* as the ultimate enshrinement of the vision of life as a trade.

Paris of the 1860s was the city of the bourgeoisie. Not the keen and mordant bourgeoisie of Diderot's time, which a century before had prepared the moral and intellectual ground for liberal enlightenment, but a fat gaslight bourgeoisie bursting with gross vitality.

Society was a pyramid of parvenu opportunists, topped by a matching monarch. He claimed to be a nephew of Napoleon I, but may have been illegitimate. By trading on his official family link, Louis-Napoleon styled himself a pretender to the French throne. To legitimize his claim, he sometimes went to considerable lengths. On one public occasion he reportedly signified his royalty by keeping a tame eagle flapping about his head. The eagle was attracted to the royalist cause by a piece of bacon tucked into Louis-Napoleon's hatband.

His mental resources were somewhat limited, but he had others. His most notable asset was a slim-waisted, exquisitely beautiful blond English girl in her early twenties who called herself Miss Harriet Howard so as not to embarrass her estimable family. She had been endowed with a vast sum of money by one of her former lovers, a certain Major Martyn.

When Harriet became infatuated with Louis-Napoleon, she abandoned the generous major and, along with herself, placed her fortune at the disposal of the French pretender. Louis-Napoleon quite casually accepted these conveniences. Unfortunately, the throne of France was not for sale at the time because the country, after 1848, happened to be a Republic. So the best job Louis-Napoleon could get through the influence wielded by Miss Howard's money was that of President.

But for a man of Louis-Napoleon's enormous vanity, being President was only a technical setback that could be overcome. It probably took just another dip into Miss Howard's coffers for the bribes necessary to assure the success of the coup d'état—disguised as a plebiscite—in which the President of France overthrew his own government in 1852 to proclaim himself Napoleon III, Emperor of the French.

For a while, Miss Howard was allowed to share some of her lover's glory—at a distance. Disguised as a peasant woman, she was sometimes trundled about inconspicuously in a plain cart to watch the Emperor's public appearances. But Napoleon soon put her entirely out of sight. He banished her to a castle near Paris where he could visit her at his convenience while, on other occasions, devoting himself to the pursuit of Eugénie de Montijo, whose dark beauty provided him with a suitable aesthetic complement to Miss Howard's British pallor. Eugénie has been described as "a lady of exquisite posture with the curved mouth of a coquette and the eyes of a *pietà* downswept in dolorous sensitivity." Notwithstanding her Spanish name, she was the granddaughter of a Scottish wine merchant and her mother was said to have personally served wine in the back room of the shop until she inveigled a Spanish grandee into marrying her. Unlike Miss Howard, who had given Napoleon her fortune and herself without a moment's hesitation, Eugénie had better sense. She never offered or advanced anything, and when the smitten Napoleon asked her to tell him the way to her heart, she coyly replied: "Through the chapel, Sir." Eugénie evidently understood the *Zeitgeist* of speculative trading, and she had her own notions of fair value and equitable exchange: she claimed France as her price.

Throughout his life, Napoleon was a man haunted by relentless lusts which were the projections of his vanity. His political ambition, his countless intrigues and conspiracies no doubt fit within the same psychological framework as his interminable lechery. Besides, he was short-legged and stumpy, and his face was undistinguished. Braided and bemedaled in his tight-laced uniforms, he looked, according to one account, "like a barber dressed up as a lion tamer." Men combining an unprepossessing appearance with an overweening ego often find it difficult to take no for an answer, especially from a woman. When such men are ensnared by desire, they find no way out. Eugénie sensed this. The game was tricky, perhaps dangerous. But she played it with cool confidence.

Being Emperor, Napoleon found it fairly easy to resolve matters in regard to Miss Howard. Under the pretext of sending her on a secret state mission, Napoleon tricked Miss Howard into leaving for England. During her absence, he ransacked her castle and broke open her secretaire to retrieve his letters. He then announced his engagement to Eugénie in the throne room of the Tuileries. A few months later Eugénie achieved her goal: she was crowned Empress of France at Notre Dame. Josephine's diamond and sapphire coronet was placed on her head, and on her breast reposed the Sacred Talisman of Charlemagne.

But even Napoleon III, not normally given to the weighing of values, must have felt that he had overpaid Eugénie, and he revenged himself upon her by flaunting his countless peccadillos before the court and even the public. Eugénie, in retaliation, locked her bedroom.

It was to this royal pair that Johan Strauss was presented at a splendid fête arranged by Princess Pauline at the Austrian embassy in the rue de Grenelle. She launched her diplomatic offensive with typical aplomb. Wheedling a fortune of 167,000 francs from the Austrian government for just this evening, she decked out the great hall of the embassy in green and pink satin and stuck gold arabesques to the ivory-colored ceiling. Conniving with the director of the municipal utilities, Pauline managed to get a special pipe laid to the embassy to carry sufficient water for a great artificial cascade which, flanked by thousands of fresh roses, faced the great staircase on which Napoleon and Eugénie were to make their entrance. Her greatest feat, possibly, was to borrow Baron de Rothschild's personal cook—a legendary kitchen-master who had never before been permitted to feed anyone outside the Rothschild domain.

Strauss could not have asked for a more auspicious introduction, for Princess Pauline was the darling of the Parisian *haut monde* and the personal confidante of Empress Eugénie. Pauline's lack of conventional beauty was a blessing to her; it kept other women from being too envious of her other attributes, which included charm, cheerfulness, wit, and independence of spirit. Her pixie face—the kind the French call *belle-laide*—was her license: it allowed her to be mildly scandalous. She was the first socially prominent woman in Paris to eat in a public restaurant. She disdained the private cage of the crinoline that transformed women of her day into bulky bales of fabric, obstructing streets and doorways, spilling over chairs, and occasionally catching fire. Pauline usually sported a straight skirt that showed off her trim and agile figure, conditioned by her accomplishments as an *equestrienne*. At home, she smoked an occasional cigar. But when one gentleman, perhaps to test her reaction, asked her if she would mind if he smoked, she answered icily: "I don't know, sir. No one has ever dared smoke in my presence."

With Pauline being the inexhaustible topic of Parisian gossip, her party for Johann Strauss was easily the most prominent event of a social season ablaze with festivities occasioned by the Fair. Appearing arm in arm at the top of the grand staircase, Napoleon and Eugénie managed a fairly convincing pose of regal serenity, Eugénie temporarily deposing her pout in favor of a smile, and Napoleon, with his wide moustache and long goatee jutting from his face, looking almost as majestic as Buffalo Bill. There was a moment's consternation when the Prussian Crown Prince, in town for the Fair, managed to crash the party, assuring the hostess how happy he was to be there. Pauline, with her customary tact, somehow kept the impudent Prussian from intruding on the happily developing *entente* between the numerous French and Austrian dignitaries and diplomats.

It might also have been a little embarrassing that Johann Strauss, having as good an ear for language as music—and thanks to extensive practice with Olga—spoke better French than the Emperor, who, raised in German exile, still was apt to say *Zil fous blait* instead of *S'il vous plaît* and called his wife 'Ugenie. But such delicate concerns ceased to trouble the Princess as soon as Strauss, taking his place before the orchestra, launched into the first waltz.

It had been thirty years since Strauss's father had played at the Tuileries before Louis-Philippe, that civilized monarch who would have hardly recognized the *arriviste* court of France or the ebullient Paris of this later generation. Not since then had Paris heard that authentic Viennese lilt.

At first the floor was crowded. But gradually the dancers withdrew to the sides. With music of such subtle charm, just listening seemed even better than dancing.

That evening saw Strauss in his prime. At forty-two, with the casual assurance of a man who takes his rank for granted, the Waltz King was at ease among other royalty. His twirled moustache, augmented by short, wiry whiskers ringing his cheeks, were in the latest fashion. Fastidious tailoring and an erect but graceful carriage made up for his lack of stature. With beady eyes and a bulbous nose, he was not handsome;

but his swarthy skin and black hair gave him an aura of dark masculinity that was by no means unappreciated. In turn, Strauss's responsiveness to women had not noticeably diminished since his marriage—a circumstance that definitely enhanced his social cachet among the French.

If Strauss had proved himself at the embassy to be indeed Austria's greatest diplomatic asset, it yet remained for him to win over the wider Parisian public, to create a general atmosphere of sympathy for Austria conducive to a possible alliance. It was his good fortune to find the man who would provide as good an introduction to the Parisian *tout le monde* as Princess Pauline had given him to the social elite. That man was Jean Hippolyte Cartier de Villemessant.

A fire-eating journalist, Villemessant was the prototype of such latter-day presslords as Pulitzer and Hearst. "A story that doesn't cause a duel or a lawsuit can't be any good," he instructed his editors. He had launched half a dozen sensational newspapers, and they all had fallen victim to his own flamboyance. As a last resort, Villemessant turned to respectability and competent reporting as the premise for his final journalistic venture—*Le Figaro*, which has flourished ever since as a mainstay of the French press.

Metternich had invited Villemessant to the party at the Austrian embassy. Always a canny promoter, Villemessant immediately made common cause with Strauss. He would provide the publicity. In turn some Strauss glamour might rub off the message onto the medium and establish *Le Figaro* as an arbiter of arts and fashion.

Villemessant promptly routed memos about Strauss among his staff; and since few newsmen ignore hints from their publisher, stories in praise of the Viennese visitor soon found their way into print under various bylines. Villemessant also arranged a dinner in honor of Strauss and included among the guests such influential littérateurs as Gustave Flaubert,

Theophile Gautier, Alexandre Dumas fils, and Ivan Turgenev, who, like several Russian writers since, preferred living abroad.

Repaying his social debt, Strauss in turn invited the whole editorial staff of *Le Figaro* to another dinner the following week. Happily accepting the invitation, Villemessant asked only to be permitted to choose the wines. A typical Frenchman, he would trust no foreigner's judgment in such a vital matter. During the evening, the talk turned to Strauss's forthcoming concert at the Fair. Someone suggested that a new waltz, never before heard in Paris, would add special interest to the occasion.

Strauss liked the idea but had nothing new ready. Then he remembered *The Blue Danube*. He would give the waltz another chance, this time in purely orchestral performance, unhampered by vocal limitations. The next morning he telegraphed to Vienna for the score.

Thanks to *Le Figaro's* relentless promotion, and with other papers picking up the story, the French premiere of *Le Beau Danube Bleu* was anticipated as a major event among the musical offerings of the Fair.

The Fair itself was like festive music. This was the year that Paris earned its name as the City of Light. Gas jets flared from pipelines stretched along the iron railings of those endless rows of Parisian balconies. A million spots of flame illuminated the length of the great boulevards, bringing to life every sculptured detail of the elaborate façades against the soft sky of the Paris night. In an era when street lighting was still in its dim beginnings, the effect was hypnotic. It turned the whole city into a luminous fairground.

Across the Seine from the fountain-studded Place de la Concorde, the exhibition halls themselves stood as marvels for their time. Built of vaulted steel and glass, they contrasted with Paris's predominant masonry and foreshadowed the future of architecture. Within, the new wonders of the age stood on display: puffing steam engines, chattering looms, the shining brass microscopes whose improved optics had just helped M Pasteur to discover such interesting things about microbes, and whirling dynamos humming a promise of the dawning era of electricity.

To a Danish visitor, Hans Christian Andersen, the Fair was a fairy tale: "It's like a great Christmas display," he wrote back home to Copenhagen, "with toys for grownups. The marvelous gifts of industry, of art and affluence are surrounded by delightful tokens from all countries. In this world-bazaar each nation displays smiling memories of home."

Near the center of the Fair stood the Cercle International, the great auditorium for special events. Here, along the westward-running Seine, Johann Strauss now set forth his apotheosis of the Danube, that great eastward river that is Europe's vein toward the Orient. Unwittingly, he had formed a symbolic link across the watershed between East and West, thus sounding the deeper theme of a world's fair.

The audience, numbering thousands, had already heard Strauss in earlier concerts, playing such tuneful gems as *Morning Papers* and *Vienna Bonbons*. Would the new waltz stand up to these standards?

The answer unfolded slowly. It rose from a long, misty introduction that sounded more like the opening of a symphony than the beginning of a dance. Then suddenly from the preludial haze sprang the sweeping surge of the theme that was soon to become a byword in the language of music.

Like the river itself, *The Blue Danube* flows on, swirling with exuberant melody, vibrant with orchestral color. The tuneful flood gains momentum, its pulsing zest mounts; yet before it can dash itself against a brash climax, Strauss stems the onrush. Once more the waltz subsides into pastoral serenity, reverts to the fine-spun strands of the opening, and a formal coda consigns the music to silence.

For a moment before the jubilant applause, the audience remained still. They may have sensed that what they had heard was more than the premiere of yet another waltz—that they had been the sharers of a great gift.

Time and again Strauss had to repeat *The Blue Danube*. Every orchestra in Paris took up the tune, though the symphonic scoring was sadly reduced for the countless little café ensembles that suffused the city with music, but the sheer melodic genius of Strauss survived even in the simplest version. Despite the melody's obduracy to the human voice, Parisians insisted on singing it. One of Villemessant's facile hacks provided a text just slightly more digestible than the Viennese doggerel about the street lights:

> *Fleuve d'azur*
> *Sur ton flot pur*
> *Glisse la voile*
> *Comme une étoile.*

The new waltz became the musical motif of the Fair. Foreign visitors returning to their own countries couldn't get it out of their heads. Edward, Prince of Wales, went home humming. So obsessed was he with the new melody that he asked Strauss to come to London, where Strauss later gave six highly acclaimed concerts at Covent Garden. When he conducted the new waltz as the main feature of the series, even the formidable Queen Victoria nodded her pleasure, as she had once nodded to Strauss's father at her coronation.

Back in Vienna, a crisis developed at the printing plant of Strauss's publisher. The relatively soft copper plates then used for printing music wore out after ten thousand copies. Photo-engraving had not yet been invented, and with the slow hand-engraving methods in use at the time, printing plates wore out faster than they could be replaced. Just about every available music engraver was busily punching *The Blue Danube* into metal. Before the first printing was over, a hundred sets of plates had been worn down, and *The Blue Danube* had become the most profitable "property" in the history of music.

Only in one sense was *The Blue Danube* a tragic failure. It wasn't Strauss's fault, of course, but all plans for a French-Austrian alliance which Strauss was to help promote suddenly collapsed. On June 19, 1867, hardly two months after Princess Pauline's magnificent party in the rue de Grenelle, Austria and France were torn apart by a salvo of shots in distant Mexico. Juarez and his revolutionaries had killed Emperor Maximilian, the brother of Austria's Franz Josef.

The news traveled slowly at first, riding with couriers across the desert toward Texas. At Laredo it reached the nearest outpost of the electrical communications network that was just then beginning to span the world, and an American telegrapher tapped it into the wire to Washington. Twelve days after the event, the tragic message finally flashed to Europe on Cyrus Field's new undersea cable.

Paris and Vienna were stunned. In an era in which the dynastic concept, despite the rise of constitutionalism and the broadening of the franchise, still retained some of its magic in the minds of men, the murder of royalty evoked a particular horror. Empress Eugénie was at the Fair handing out medals when she received the message. She fainted. All festivities were promptly canceled.

Hopes of an alliance between Austria and France now lay shattered; for it was the French who had persuaded the Austrian Archduke Maximilian to accept the crown of Mexico, to act essentially as Napoleon's puppet for the protection of French interests in Central America. The French had pledged him their military support; then they abandoned him to his enemies amidst the turmoils of a strange land. No music could heal the wound left by the broken promise.

Slowly, like wrought-up soil after a landslide, Europe settled into a new shape. Cut off from France, Austria drifted uneasily into Germany's sphere, giving Bismarck his chance for the cruel assault on France in 1870.

Princess Pauline and her husband fled back to Vienna. What they, with the aid of Johann Strauss, had hoped to prevent had become reality. France and England were now on one side, Germany and Austria on the other. Europe was split along the Rhine. With central Europe as a solid bloc bolstering Germany's aggressive imperialism, the stage was now set for the two great wars which, in our own century, were to disfigure the face and break the heart of the Old World.

Art has been defined as the lie that makes us see the truth. It rescues us from the merely real by providing a vision beyond what is. Poets, Paul Valéry observes, *"ne parlent jamais que de choses absents."* But art is no illusion. Rather it is a commitment to what might be, to what remains forever a possibility in our fancy and our longing. It mediates between actuality and potentiality, between appearance and essence. It is the beginning of other worlds latent within us.

This is especially true of music, whose realm lies beyond word or matter. Anyone who has ever seen the Danube knows that it is gray-green, with an unromantic predisposition to muddiness. It is the measure of Strauss's genius that his music has turned the river forever blue.

10

The Perils of the Stage

An unforeseen byproduct of Strauss's sojourn in France was the eventual adaptation of French operetta into a Viennese art form, a process accomplished partly by the substitution of Viennese *schmalz* for Parisian flair. Strauss was by no means a willing transfer agent for grafting this patch of Paris onto the Viennese stage. It took a conspiracy between his wife and an enterprising promoter to inveigle Strauss into composing for the theater—a step that was to lift him to the exultant heights of *Die Fledermaus,* but which also led him to the despondent awareness of fundamental failure.

The term operetta, the Italian diminutive for opera, provides no salient clue to this musical form, for it places this genre in quantitative contrast to grand opera. The real difference, however, lies in spirit, not size. Grand opera is epic; operetta is parody. It clearly proclaims its intention not to be taken seriously. Romantic operetta flaunts its sentimentality as a joke, while the jokes of satirical operetta often ring with mordantly serious undertones. In either case, the internal contradiction puts the tongue firmly in cheek.

The ancestry of operetta lies in the comic operas which in the later eighteenth century marked the rise of bourgeois theater in contrast to the older, distinctly aristocratic forms of musical stage works. One example, Mozart's *Marriage of Figaro,* actually seems more operetta than opera, being sprightly, cool, and full of irony. Even its book, based on Beaumarchais's biting farce about prerevolutionary *vie en château,* presages many later operettas in its barely disguised political persiflage.

Mozart's *Magic Flute* is a precursor of operetta in a similar sense. Unlike most operas of its period, it was conceived as a popular entertainment rather than as an aristocratic pastime, and as a projection of social attitudes and ideas rather than as drama solely in terms of individual character. One may regard *The Magic Flute* as perhaps the first deliberate and successful attempt at a "theater of ideas." For in *The Magic Flute,* both the critical spirit and the humane values of the Enlightenment find enduring expression in terms of musical allegory. In Mozart opera and operetta are contained in each other at the level of sublimity.

The generic split between opera and operetta, and the emergence of operetta as a distinct form, came later as reaction to the rise of romanticism. Under the influence of romanticism, opera became increasingly bloated by sheer incontinence of feeling. Striving for the grandiose and monumental, romantic opera by the middle of the nineteenth century severed its links with social and emotional reality. With the coming of the industrial age, the ideal of chivalric heroism vanished. Yet opera, heroic both in concept and tradition, became even more so.

The growth of the orchestra, with the addition of more brass, winds, and percussion, supported this trend. The sheer sonority dictated that outsize concepts of human character be presented on stage. The drama had to match the excessive gesture of the sound.

Opera composers from Meyerbeer onward, yielding to the temptations of their enriched orchestral palette, became victims of their own orchestral technology. Their musical accounts of human sentiment became tonally intensified to the point of untruth. The very term "operatic" acquired the ring of falsity.

It is true, of course, that great operatic masterpieces, notably those of Wagner and Verdi, were cast in this mold and are marked by the sonic and emotional enlargements of the romantic tradition. But like most great works of art, they were exceptions to the norm of their time, attaining their greatness as much in spite of their style as because of it. The nineteenth century may well have been the golden age of opera, and like such periods in any art, it also produced a preponderance of dross.

The inevitable reaction to the fustian and fatuity of standard operatic fare came through the work of Jacques Offenbach, who combined two qualities rarely found together: creative genius and market sense. He saw that Paris needed a small-scaled, lighthearted alternative to the dreary bombast dispensed at the *Opéra*. Designing a product to meet this demand, he created the prototype of modern operetta. It dominated the boulevards of Paris during the Second Empire, migrated to Vienna via Strauss and Lehár, and nearly a century later metamorphosed in America into the Broadway musical.

Offenbach traced his musical background to the synagogue at Cologne, where his father had been cantor. But nothing of Hebraic plaint survived in the pulsing, exultant tunes of his Paris period, which more than any other music caught the scent of *la ville lumière*, the dry spark of its brash delights, and that singularly French blend of cynicism and sentiment.

Offenbach's music had a voluptuous iridescence, a kind of sunshine sensuality that infuriated some people as much as it delighted others, and the most revealing, if inadvertent, tributes to his work came from those who detested it. Wagner, for example, always the moralist in art if not in life, expressed himself with Lutheran-Germanic forthrightness: "Offenbach's music is like a dungheap in which all the swine of

Europe wallow." Some years later, George Bernard Shaw, always an Irish puritan at heart, betrayed his rather uneasy relations with the "Life Force" that so preoccupied him by making an essentially similar observation: "I warn . . . solemnly that Offenbach's music is wicked. It is abandoned stuff: every accent is a snap of the fingers in the face of moral responsibility." No wonder Paris loved every note of it.

The freedom of spirit, the basic shamelessness of Offenbach's music, is matched by his daring use of the musical stage as a launching platform for cheerful and disingenuous sallies of social subversion. In such works as *Orphée aux Enfers* (1858) and *La Belle Hélène* (1864) he pokes savage fun at the gods of Olympus. But the clear implication, conveyed by the twinkling insouciance of the music, is that the irony was aimed at more terrestrial wielders of power. The plot was a ploy—social criticism disguised as romantic comedy. During the politically repressive Second Empire, Offenbach's operettas served as expressions of bourgeois resentment against remaining aristocratic privilege. Irreverence toward institutions and persons of authority, though safely camouflaged by mythological settings, marked these operettas as an art form that could have come into being only after the French revolution and before the ultimate demise of French aristocratic power in the upheavals of 1870–71.

Yet the social meaning of a style is rarely apparent at the time of its emergence, and it is doubtful that Johann Strauss was able to appreciate Offenbach's work in those terms. Rather, he responded to the singular amalgam of wit and sensuality in both the music and the plots, and freely expressed his admiration. Offenbach in turn greatly admired Strauss, and on the occasion of a personal meeting said to him, "You ought to write operettas."

Most likely, Offenbach tossed out this remark merely as a casual pleasantry. After all, to offer Strauss serious advice would have been presumptuous. Besides, not even a man of Offenbach's stature would invite competition from a genius.

At any rate, Strauss shrugged off Offenbach's suggestion without giving it further thought. He had no ambition to write for the theater. To him, the stage was linked to the world of literature. That alone was enough to frighten him away. His experience with *The Blue Danube* in its original choral version had convinced him that his music could not properly unfold within the cage of text. In musical theater, music must make allowance not only for the sound of words but for the whole restrictive aura of linear linguistic concepts and constructions. Relating music to concepts and ideas was the essence of Offenbach's wit. Strauss sensed that such linking of music and language was basically alien to him.

A man who never read a book and rarely even a newspaper, Strauss had the distrust of a functional illiterate of anything connected with words. Even among friends, he rarely said anything but standard social phrases and commonplaces. His charm resided in his manner, not his conversation. The only person in his life to whom he ever talked at length had been Olga. But that Russian summer was long gone.

Strauss himself was fully aware that language failed him. When he was asked by a publisher to write down some of his reminiscences, he declined. "This has to do with words," says his letter. "For me words have always been tough and intractable stuff."

Strauss also realized that he had no sense of theater. In Vienna, where theater formed the central point of the cultural pattern, Strauss almost never went to see a play. In this respect, Strauss stood in complete contrast to most Viennese, for whom the stage was a paradigm of life—the metaphor through which they perceived their own existence.

The idea of theater penetrated to the core of the Viennese personality. In a city envisioned as stage set for an empire, the typical Viennese viewed life as a scenario and formed his self-definition in terms of a role. Seeing himself as an actor gave the Viennese his characteristic freedom. To be sure, within the scenario of his rigidly stratified society he had little choice as to the part assigned to him. But as an actor, he had various options in the interpretation of his role. This accounts for the characteristic spontaneity of the Viennese within the framework of their tradition, the freedom of manners and the sense of personal spaciousness that so enriched and vitalized the Viennese atmosphere. Quite likely, it is this view of life as theater that, more than anything else, set apart the Viennese from the German, who tended to be bound by more rigid ways of looking at himself.

Vienna's penchant for the stage accounts for the almost riotous welcome Offenbach's works received when they were first heard in the Austrian capital. Immediately, theatrical promoters began searching for ways to grow a local crop of operettas. One talented Austrian composer, Franz von Suppé, made the first start in this direction with *Poet and Peasant*, *Light Cavalry*, and a few other works whose overtures occasionally still fill the summer air at outdoor concerts. But it remained for Strauss, chiefly through his creation of *Die Fledermaus*, to give Viennese operetta its distinctive stamp.

It was Maximilian Steiner, the impresario of the Theater an der Wien, who finally managed to overcome Strauss's steadfast refusal to have anything to do with the inimical world of words, scripts, actors, and the stage. He called on Jetty Strauss, whose former career as a singer apparently still left her approachable and predisposed toward theater managers even if they made outrageous suggestions. What Steiner proposed might well have raised an eyebrow and some questions on the part of anyone less inured to backstage ethics than Jetty. Steiner asked her to steal some of her husband's manuscripts. Then, he said, he would have a text set to the tunes, and if Strauss liked the result, maybe something could be worked out with him after all.

Steiner, no doubt, did everything in his considerable thespian power to play on Jetty's nostalgia for the stage. And in Jetty, the aging, isolated woman longing to enter once more the milieu of her youth, he found a receptive audience. She may also have hoped that a theatrical venture might somehow bring her closer to Johann, who, after the first happy years of their marriage, had been paying little attention to her and had resumed his habit of making brief acquaintances with young ladies. At any rate, she agreed to commit the theft.

One morning a group of Steiner's singers appeared at Strauss's house in Hietzing. On being admitted by Jetty, they grouped themselves around the piano, and the nonplussed Strauss found himself listening to his own unpublished melodies melded with words he never dreamed of. The element of surprise gave Steiner and Jetty a tactical advantage over Strauss, who wavered between being intrigued and annoyed. Besides, as Jetty and Steiner probably knew, the outcome of this confrontation disguised as a musical surprise was a foregone conclusion; for Strauss generally permitted himself to be manipulated by Jetty in business matters, knowing that in the private sphere he had his own ways of asserting his independence of her. Yielding to her persuasion, he agreed to compose an operetta for Steiner's theater.

Steiner supplied Strauss with a barely competent hack, one Josef Braun, to cook up a libretto. Both Braun and his work were disastrous. Anyone who has glanced at the synopsis of *The Merry Wives of Vienna* readily understands why Strauss, for the first time in his life, wrote some thoroughly uninspired music. Besides, the libretto wasn't the only plot Braun provided. He insisted that his inamorata, an actress named Josefine Gallmayer, should play the leading role. Fräulein Gallmayer was talented enough but happened to be under contract to another theater. Braun felt that true love should rise above such legal impediments. But to engage Frl. Gallmayer for the performance would involve Strauss in liability for the breach of her contract. Hence his consent was needed.

Strauss, who valued nothing more than his privacy, found

himself constantly beleaguered by Braun, Steiner, Gallmayer, and their garrulous retinue, who proposed an endless stream of frauds, evasions, and subterfuges to circumvent Gallmayer's contract. Too stolidly decent to feel anything but disgust at these machinations, Strauss took the only recourse that would keep his new theatrical associates out of his house: he withdrew the score.

But Strauss was too naïve to measure the full extent of Steiner's gall. The dauntless impresario promptly presented Strauss with another libretto—this one presumably of his own manufacture. Yet Steiner himself was sufficiently embarrassed by his evident plagiarisms to attribute *Indigo und die vierzig Räuber* to "Max Steiner, as arranged from an older story." The oily and vulgar plot failed to inspire Strauss, and his score ran considerably below par. But since it was impossible for any work of Strauss's to fail in Vienna, *Indigo*'s brief run at the Theater an der Wien in 1871 may be counted as a *succès d'estime.*

Only Jetty was unreservedly delighted. She had achieved her purpose. Under the burden of Johann's infidelities and continued neglect of her, she had become a little drab and despondent. But now the smell of theater air in her nostrils revitalized her. To her it was the regained fragrance of youth. All her influence was now bent on involving Johann more inextricably with the stage.

Despite the lukewarm reception of *Indigo,* Jetty and Steiner promptly informed Strauss that they expected another operetta from him. Strauss received this dictum with the air of indifferent submission that at this period characterized his attitude toward Jetty in most practical matters. He did not even object when Josef Braun, the intrigant wordsmith, was once again hauled in to hammer the text together. *Carnival in Rome,* the abortive result of this collaboration, was a quickly forgotten exercise in sentimental trivia.

With three failures in a row, Strauss was more than ever convinced that his music was miscast on the stage. His genius lay in the circular, self-renewing repetitions of the waltz, not the linear progression of dramatic dialogue. For Jetty's sake and against his inclinations, he had committed himself to the theater, and, in consequence, enmeshed himself in a creative crisis. It seemed that the man whose music spanned the world, whose name was in the minds of millions synonymous with sheer joy, would now subside into the mediocrity of theatrical hackwork mainly to keep his wife in tolerably good humor.

Then, abruptly and unpredictably, the descent into failure reversed itself. With a sudden rekindling of his creative fire, Strauss achieved the singular peak among his stage works: *Die Fledermaus.* The man who believed that he couldn't write music for the stage produced the one operetta ever to transcend its own genre to become the most joyful classic in the total realm of musical theater.

For once he had a libretto to match the spark of his music. *Die Fledermaus* was based on a play that had already proved its theatrical merit on the legitimate stage. Written by a German playwright with the unlikely name of Roderich Benedix, it ran in Berlin under the title *Das Gafängnis* (The Jail). Later, two popular Parisian writers, Henri Meilhac and Ludovic Halévy, adapted the German comedy for the French theater, and in 1872 it played at the Palais Royal under the name of *Le Réveillon.* Through the French authors' agent, who was peddling foreign rights, the piece came to the attention of the Viennese publisher Gustav Lewy, a personal acquaintance of Strauss's. Lewy sensed that this brash, bubbling comedy had just the ingredients that Strauss's previous librettos had so notably lacked: believable characters and situations, genuine wit, and some not-so-gentle satiric bite— not enough to draw blood, but enough to leave a mark.

The final title, *Die Fledermaus* (literally: The Bat) gives no clue to the story. It simply refers to the fact that one of the characters attends a ball costumed as an oversize flying squirrel. The plot was a preposterous mélange of intricate masquerades, mistaken identities, husbands inadvertently flirting with their own unrecognized wives, chambermaids posing as ladies of fashion, devious lawyers, and sybaritic princes. All this is beside the point. What matters is that within the mantle of ostensible absurdity resided an evident kernel of human reality. Beneath its zaniness and spoof, *Die Fledermaus* conveys a tough, unblinking vision of a social milieu. Behind the screen of theatrical hyperbole, the script shows a recognizable portrait of Vienna's *nouveaux riches* with their aristocratic pretensions, the fashionable ambiguity of their sexual mores and stratagems, and their insouciant attitude toward authority and law. In short, it shows an upper middle class no longer really containable within the absolutist framework of the Austrian monarchy. As a farce, *Die Fledermaus* makes no claim to any factual truth. But as essential truth, it comes as close as any work of art to capturing the spirit of Vienna's *haute bourgeoisie* in the late afternoon of the empire.

Strauss, whose social intuition was apparently far sharper than he could ever verbally express, immediately responded to these qualities in the script with all the genius and energy at his command. He composed in a frenzy, barricading his room against interruptions, working day and night with only sporadic meals and sleep. It was as if this aging man, now close to fifty, mired in an increasingly meaningless marriage and perhaps with a sense of his own decline, were challenging fate and circumstance by the determined exertion of his creative will. Only a condition bordering on mania could sustain his effort. Jetty, the only person to come near him during this period, later told friends that Strauss was sometimes weeping with the joyful ecstasy of work. In forty-three incandescent days and nights he wrought his miracle—music that perhaps more than any other reaches toward the essence of laughter.

But on the evening of April 5, 1874, when *Die Fledermaus* was first heard at the Theater an der Wien, Vienna could not laugh. The very stratum of the population that formed both the subject of *Die Fledermaus* as well as its most likely audience—the elegant, pleasure-seeking theater buffs—had been cast into despondency by the great stock-market collapse of the preceding year.

Vienna had reaped a spectacular windfall when the Franco-Prussian war of 1870 immobilized the Paris Bourse. By France's default, Vienna had become the financial hub of the continent. The sudden influx of capital fleeing the defunct financial institutions of France loosened an orgy of speculation not only among the rich but also among the wage-earning citizens of Vienna. The stock exchange took on the atmosphere of a perpetual carnival, a mood entirely congenial to the Viennese temperament. In this aura of irrational glee, stock prices soon lost touch with economic reality. For a couple of years, the sheer buoyancy of the Viennese spirit supported these financial fictions. For entire segments of the population the stock market was a kind of secular religion that set the tone of daily existence. The champagne-doused life-style both celebrated and satirized in *Die Fledermaus* is largely the result of another kind of intoxication: the illusory removal of all travail that comes from unbelievable paper profits.

Reality can be flouted in many aspects of life, but economics is not one of them. The sudden reckoning came on Black Friday—May 9, 1873. Stocks supported by nothing more substantial than cheerful temperatment dropped almost one hundred percent. Thousands of Viennese families waking in the morning to accustomed affluence were impoverished by nightfall.

Some Viennese took the disaster with typical sang-froid. A former millionaire reduced to cooking his own meals would still pull on the bell before bringing his food to the table. "It's not so bad," he explained. "I get prompt service. I ring —and I come." Another incident of that era illustrates the quality of Viennese ethics, which always derived more from sentiment than from reason. When a crash victim implored the help of the Baron Rothschild, the great banker instructed a servant: "Throw the man out. He breaks my heart."

Since every disaster must have a plausible explanation, most Viennese blamed the Jews. Indeed, the peculiar viciousness of Viennese anti-Semitism, which was to reach its full bloody flower in a later era, had its most poisonous roots in the convenient assumption that Jewish brokers had manipulated the exchange to defraud Christian investors.

It took nearly a decade for the Austrian middle class to recoup its solvency and psychological composure. After all, the bourgeois, far more than the rich man, is defined by his money. His attitudes and even his feelings are to a considerable extent a function of property. So are his entertainments and his capacity to respond to entertainment. European theater of the nineteenth century was largely a reflection of the urban middle class. It is understandable, therefore, that in the wake of the stock-market debacle the Viennese public was rather constrained in its response to the lighthearted fluff of *Die Fledermaus*. The economic basis for the life pictured on the stage had just been demolished. What had been conceived as contemporary satire on Viennese society had been transformed into nostalgic shadows of the past. Instead of liberating laughter, Strauss's masterpiece evoked rueful reminiscence. It closed after only sixteen performances.

Time, which paints all human events with a patina of irony, usually puts on a extra layer in Austria. Like so many other things in Austrian life and art, *Die Fledermaus* at its premiere represented something already lost—a still vital present that had already ceased to exist. Austria traditionally suffers from this congenital confusion of Now and Once. Perhaps that is the key to the Austrian soul and its fatal incest with history.

Die Fledermaus went into exile. Like *The Blue Danube*, it finally won the world's heart not in Vienna but in Paris, where some years later it enchanted the French as *La Chauve-Souris* and flew off triumphantly to more than two hundred theaters throughout Europe, North America, India, and Australia. Twenty years later, a young firebrand musician, Gustav Mahler, presented *Die Fledermaus* for the first time on the operatic stage, symbolically transplanting the work from the ephemeral precincts of operetta to a setting fit for enduring classics. His conducting of *Die Fledermaus* at the Vienna Opera has remained one of the legends in the history of musical performance.

It may seem odd that Mahler, the most profoundly tragic of composers, had such effervescent ways with this light-hearted score. But at a deeper level, one sees a causal linkage. Mahler's musicality was demonic—aflame with the unspeakable and the supernal. So perhaps it is not surprising that a sensitivity so haunted, so steeped in tragic consciousness, would embrace in kindred sympathy its complementary opposite, the music of laughter.

Strauss went on to write a total of sixteen stage works. But aside from *Die Fledermaus* only *Der Ziguenerbaron* (The Gypsy Baron), first produced in 1885, proved viable. Even so, it is flawed by a plot so static that not even Strauss's abundant melodies can enliven it. Besides, in telling a story of Hungarian village life, the libretto is unpleasantly patronizing, reflecting an attitude of colonial condescension on the part of the Viennese toward the Slavic and Magyar provinces.

In his theatrical work, Strauss seemed under a curious compulsion to prove that he was not really a dramatic composer. With the consistency of some deeply motivated self-obstruction, he rendered such proof fifteen times. Only *Die Fledermaus* remains as the one redeeming exception.

For Strauss, the perils of the stage were not merely artistic. There were also young actresses. For the most part, they provided only fleeting encounters and thus did not in themselves disrupt Strauss's marriage which, in any case, had ceased to be functional. But by their ephemeral nature, these liaisons left Strauss without real companionship, and he slowly descended into a vortex of deepening loneliness.

In Jetty, who was about ten years older than he, he had sought and found a mother-surrogate. It is characteristic of Jetty's attitude toward her husband that in her letters she refers to him as "my Jeany-Boy." While Strauss was still emotionally attached to his real mother, this was altogether satisfactory. But over the years, his requirements changed and the relationship grew unworkable. Like most nineteenth-century men, Strauss was disinclined to examine his own emotional needs, much less those of his wife. And Jetty, judging by her letters, also lacked the self-awareness requisite to cope with the deterioration of her marriage. The result was a silent rift.

This atmosphere no longer allowed Jetty to offer Johann advice on his work. The collaborative spirit, the shared substance of their early years together thus vanished. Jetty and Johann occupied separate apartments in their house. She continued to look after him in a concerned, motherly fashion. They did not quarrel, and, at least in the presence of others, their relations were considerate and polite.

The situation was resolved by Jetty's death. In the fall of 1876 a young man presented himself at the Strauss mansion. To everyone's embarrassment he addressed Jetty as "mother" and asked for money.

Strauss did not know that Jetty had children other than the two girls by Baron Todesco, and Jetty didn't interfere when Strauss ordered that the young man be thrown out. But later she allowed herself to be blackmailed by her son, whose demands grew increasingly unreasonable. On April 9, 1877, while Johann was away, Jetty received a particularly threatening message from the extortionist. When Johann returned in the evening he stumbled over something in the dark. It was Jetty's corpse. Presumably she had died of a stroke induced by her agitation.

To come suddenly upon one's wife's cadaver might be un-
nerving to anyone. For Strauss it was a terror beyond comprehension. His was an unproblematic world. Death had no
place in it. In his lack of literacy he had not encountered that
perennial motif of reflective awareness: the encompassing of
death within one's thought so that one can learn how to live.
Innocent of all philosophy, he was unequipped for the tragic.
Consequently, his response was irrational. It was as if, in the
fact of death, Strauss had suddenly glimpsed the face of his
own murderer. Like a panicked animal he took headlong
flight. He rushed to the railroad terminal: To Italy! Toward
the sun!

Eduard, the younger brother, was left to arrange for the
funeral which Johann did not attend. Eduard's feelings
toward Johann ranged from ambivalent to hostile, and he
made no secret of what he thought of Johann's abdication of
responsibility.

It was months before Strauss found the courage to return
to Vienna. Even then he avoided his house, and took an
apartment at the Hotel Viktoria in the Kärntnerstrasse. The
fear of death still clung to him like a contagion. And since
love, the standard antidote to such existential malaise, was not
readily available to him anywhere, he settled for sex.

It was only natural that Strauss, now adrift, would veer in
this direction. As the creator of music that drove men and
women into each other's arms, he was suffused with imma-
nent sensuality. His music had only one referent, that of the
senses. And he himself had nothing—no words, concepts, no
critical framework of thought—by which to mediate his
own sensuality. Therefore he became its victim.

Too driven to sense the depredations of shallowness and
falsity in his casual affairs, he did not realize that, at this
moment in his life, he lacked the exploitive ruthlessness that
would allow him to remain unscathed by such liaisons. Had
he, as in his younger years, engaged himself in passing affairs
purely for companionship and sensual pleasure, he would not

have been vulnerable in the way he was now. During his final years with Jetty, certain tendencies in him had become intensified. In his reminiscence of Strauss, the playwright Ignatz Schnitzer describes how Strauss's former charm and sociability slowly gave way to an air of remoteness and long spans of brooding silence.

It was at this period that Strauss, once a fiery and charismatic fiddler, stopped playing the violin. He never played it again. Without any specific event to mark the turn, Strauss seemed to have taken an inner direction against himself. Photographs of this period, as well as a famous portrait by Lenbach, show the changes in his face, the tension about the corners of his mouth, and something close to panic in his eyes. Hans Weigel offers a terrifying interpretation. These pictures, along with the banal cheerfulness of most of his operettas, seem to him the mask of a man secretly enraged at himself. He views Strauss's entire period of theatrical composition as "an artistic suicide attempt lasting almost thirty years."

Strauss had always suffered morbid fears. His obsessive preoccupation with railroad accidents, his refusal to enter a cemetery or to make a will for the disposition of his wealth, and a fit of hysteria at the sight of a mummy shown at an exhibition in Vienna, are all facets in a mosaic of *Angst*. After Jetty's death, the syndrome intensified.

At the time, there was no psychiatry in the modern sense to help him and, since he was neither religious nor philosophical, the conventional modes of facing the human condition were not available to him either. Eros, the primal remedy, was his only recourse.

Thus his affairs, more than being physical, became metaphysical. Such relationships are nearly always untenable because they involve not people but abstractions. Given his particular set of psychological coordinates, Strauss could not recognize and enjoy the *person* in the women he encountered; in his situation, women had to be symbols. They were magic totems against his fears, counterpoise to his terror, and depersonalized pawns in a strangely rigged version of the archetypal game of love and death.

To possess a woman, by the unspoken definition residing in any man, is an assertion against mortality. Like the Italian sun to which Strauss fled from his haunted house, she is the location of warmth, the focus of the courage that wrests meaning from existence and the way to the recovery of laughter. Such perspective lends a certain pathetic dignity to Strauss's relentless philandering and provides some basis for understanding his second marriage to a girl named Angelika. To the man whose music is a single love song, Angelika was the lyric sensuous presence of life singing on.

Angelika Dittrich had come to Vienna from Cologne in search of a theatrical career. No one ever remarked her talent, but she was pretty enough to get along without. Besides, in Vienna, she derived a certain advantage from being pale blond with light-blue eyes. Like all ethnic melting pots, Vienna had a population with predominantly dark hair and dark eyes. But in myth and fantasy the Viennese worshipped those recessive traits of blue-eyed blondness that had been submerged in the genetic mix. Living at the southern edge of the Germanic region, breathing the soft air that streamed across the Alps from the Mediterranean, the Viennese almost perversely adored the Nordic. A few decades later, this romantic and basically innocent penchant for the exotic was cynically exploited by the politics of racism that led Vienna to its darkest hour. Meanwhile, Viennese men dreamed of blond girls and wrote songs about them. (The women wrote no songs, so it is not known what *they* dreamed.)

It may have been something of this archetypal yearning that drew the fifty-three-year-old Strauss to the twenty-six-year-old Angelika when they first met in the lobby of his hotel. Angelika, who had been drifting somewhat aimlessly in theatrical circles, was not about to discourage the atten-

tions of Vienna's most famous composer. She permitted herself to be made the object of the kind of intense and impatient
courtship that older men, with a sense of time running out,
bestow on young women. On the evidence of acquaintances,
there seems to have been little joy or spontaneity between
Johann and Angelika, no gradual ripening of affection. The
adventure and delight of sharing eluded them. Each used the
other for private purposes, but blinded by their respective
needs, neither realized this. On May 27, 1878, their mutual
delusions culminated in marriage.

Strauss could not bring himself to return to the house in
Hietzing where he had once lived so happily with Jetty. Instead, the couple took residence in the Inner City at the
elegant town house in the Iglgasse which Strauss had built
shortly before with the money earned by the belated success
of *Die Fledermaus*.

There must have been moments of private happiness for
Johann and Angelika—at least one hopes so—but no letters
remain, no notes, no descriptions by acquaintances, to give
any clue to the nature of their life together. At any rate,
whatever happiness they may have shared at the outset vanished soon.

At first, Strauss took obvious pleasure in being seen with
his lovely young wife, who dressed well and had the kind of
animal grace that in someone still young can mask a fundamental commonness. For a while, he and Angelika were the
focal point of countless soirées in the bright whirl along the
Ringstrasse, whose sybaritic denizens were gradually recov-
ering from the vicissitudes of the stock market. Some years
earlier, the Habsburg Court, realizing that it could no longer
withhold some kind of official recognition from the most
famous man in the empire, had forgiven Strauss his youthful
role in the revolution of 1848 and bestowed on him the resounding title of *Kaiser- und Königlicher Hofball-Musikdi-
rektor* (Imperial and Royal Director of Court Ball Music).
His functions in this capacity were largely ceremonial, but
he occasionally conducted a few of his waltzes at the splendid

gatherings at the Hofburg or at Schönbrunn. It was thus that Angelika, the little parvenue from Cologne, entered into the presence of royalty.

If Johann and Angelika projected a public image of assurance and success compounded into a kind of happiness, it had no counterpart at home. Having abandoned even the pretense of seeking a theatrical career, Angelika soon fell victim to her vacuity. Childless and lacking both taste and capacity for meaningful work, she fell into chronic boredom. In her own lack of self-fulfillment, she grew envious of Johann's talent. His genius seemed to her a reproach of her own insignificance, and she mistook his sustained concentration on his work for deliberate inattention to her. While Strauss spent his days in creative solitude, Angelika grew exhausted and embittered by her idleness.

She had no friends to enliven her time, for Strauss avoided the more intimate kind of friendships. He and Angelika seldom entertained; and when they went out, it was to large formal gatherings, which gave her little communicative opportunity. She had none of the imagination, openness, and self-assurance needed to reach out to others on her own. She was a small-minded person drawn to the theater because she needed somebody else to give her a role; Johann could not give her one. Always nonverbal, he could not spell out for Angelika any perception of herself, himself, or anything. Thus the two walked around each other in impenetrable spheres of mutual isolation.

Angelika was not the sort of woman to endure this kind of solitude. She began to seek diversion elsewhere, mostly backstage at the Theater an der Wien, where Johann's operettas were produced. This prompted Maximilian Steiner, the impresario who had induced Jetty to steal Johann's manuscripts and thus launched Strauss's theatrical career, to involve himself once more in Strauss's private life.

Glib, glossy, and full of the inauthentic charm one often finds among actors, Steiner seemed to Angelika the very image of the brittle glamour she had come to Vienna to find.

His facile gossip filled her days with a semblance of meaning. Steiner could give her a context made to her measure. Strauss could not. The situation was both clear and convenient. Nothing in the character of either Steiner or Angelika prevented them from following their inclination toward each other.

Angelika's liaison with Steiner provided the conversational spice by which fashionable circles of society manage to maintain interest in themselves. Vienna, always avid for scandal, made the most of this one. Strauss himself uttered not a single word about the matter, at least not before witnesses. He, if no one else, knew the meaning of discretion.

Twenty years before, Olga's rejection had perhaps permanently damaged some aspects of his self-assurance. Very likely that was the reason he had chosen an older woman, who would present less of a challege to his essential masculinity, as his first wife. Then, in diametric reversal of this pattern, he submitted to the enchantment a young woman casts on a man no longer young. Each course had led to disaster. No doubt Angelika's defection was to him another of those grievous puzzles in life that he could meet only with patient and pathetic incomprehension.

The one quality in himself that saved him under these circumstances was his deep kindness. He rarely came close enough to people to show it, and only a few isolated acts bear witness to it, such as his generous care for little Lina, the orphaned daughter of his brother Josef. Now his kindness became his last possible gift to Angelika. Whatever pain he endured because of her, he would inflict none of it on others—not even her. As far as is known, he did not reproach her and they did not quarrel. She quietly left his house. And Strauss was too much a man of the world to break off his cordial association with Steiner. He may not have understood what had happened and why, but he had the largesse of spirit to accept it with exemplary grace.

11

New Worlds

For Strauss, the 1870s were a time of transition. At the beginning of the decade he was still mainly a composer of waltzes, still sanguine in temperament, and still passably content in his first marriage. The end of this period found him almost exclusively composing for the stage, rather pensive in his mood, and looking for a third wife.

Among the adventures and misadventures that marked this passage, none was more picturesque and incongruous than his journey to the United States. If his earlier sojourn in Paris symbolized the cultural bond between Austria and France, his visit to Boston and New York revealed the chasm between the Austria of Franz Josef and the America of Ulysses S. Grant.

Civic rivalry between Boston and New York provided the occasion for his transatlantic jaunt. By the later nineteenth century, Boston had been eclipsed as the country's foremost city by the rapid ascendance of New York. Bostonians, proper and otherwise, felt somewhat miffed about this. With New England's literary renaissance barely past its Emersonian peak, Bostonians still regarded their city as America's artistic and intellectual hub and looked upon burgeoning New York as the crass citadel of upstart commercialism.

The Boston Peace Festival of 1872 was one of the more doubtful attempts to bolster Boston's claim to cultural glory. Conceived as a festive tribute to music as a symbol of world peace, the event degenerated in the hands of over-enthusiastic promoters into a crude spectacle.

The Blue Danube had made the name of Johann Strauss a household word even in America, and the management of the Peace Festival invited the composer to come and conduct his music in Massachusetts. Fearful of transportation in any form, Strauss was terrified at the prospect of an ocean crossing. True, by that time steam-powered ships had become fairly reliable. Exploding boilers no longer scattered ships and their passengers upon the sea as often as they had done in earlier decades. The hulls were now made of iron, the better to withstand the forces of Atlantic storms, and thanks to these technical advances intercontinental travelers at last had an excellent chance of arriving at their destination. Even so, the very thought of an ocean voyage so unsettled Strauss that at first he declined the invitation. What finally changed his mind was the offer of an unprecedented fee: $100,000— certainly one of the most persuasive inducements ever dangled before a musician. In equivalent Austrian purchasing power the amount must have seemed closer to a million—enough at any rate to conquer Strauss's fear of the water.

However, Strauss still had other reservations. Strange tales of American business ethics during the period of reconstruction following the Civil War had reached as far as Vienna, and Strauss would not budge until the City of Boston had deposited the full amount in advance to Strauss's account at the Vienna Anglo-Bank. Even then he made yet another demand: the Bostonians were to pay all travel expenses for himself, for Jetty, for his valet, his maid, and his dog. All of which may explain why the Peace Festival ended with the near-bankruptcy of its sponsors.

Contrary to expectations, Strauss greatly enjoyed the sea voyage. Of all the passengers aboard the S.S. *Rhein,* he alone never was seasick during the entire thirteen-day crossing from Bremerhaven. In rough weather, he was almost the only guest in the dining room, his appetite enhanced by the sea air. After meals he would watch with childlike amusement as his brandy snifter slid about on the swaying table.

The New York he saw on his arrival on June 13 presented a far different aspect than at present. Steel construction and elevators, preconditions for the skyscrapers, had not yet come into widespread use. New York was not yet what Louis-Ferdinand Céline later described as "a city standing up." Like most European cities, New York was still "lying down." The graceful little spire of Trinity Church at the head of Wall Street marked the highest point on its horizon.

But if New York in 1872 did not seem architecturally strange, other aspects of America induced in Strauss an acute case of culture shock. Immediately on arrival, he found himself encircled by reporters, concert agents, promoters, and curiosity seekers who fired unintelligible questions at him in English and would not be silenced by the wave of his hand.

In Europe, at that time, a gentleman of distinction could assure his quiet and privacy simply by saying that he wished to be left alone. But in the boisterous United States of the reconstruction period, such deference and even ordinary politeness were considered undemocratic. Voices were loud and manners insistent. Word had got around that Strauss was a bigger sensation than General Tom Thumb, the Siamese Twins, or anything else in Barnum and Bailey's circus. Naturally, the tabloids and the theatrical demimonde wanted their share of him, and apparently nothing had been done to protect Strauss from their onslaught. The importunities to which he was subjected were gleefully noted as a sign of his popularity.

Nothing in the quiet mannerliness of Strauss's central-European background had prepared him for the kind of noisy cameraderie by which Americans of the nineteenth century expressed the dominant myth of Jacksonian egalitarianism.

He was appalled at the gross familiarity with which strangers addressed him, at the probing rudeness of their questions, and at their obtrusiveness in suggesting all kinds of business propositions and schemes to him after only a few minutes' acquaintance.

Strauss reacted predictably. Always inclined toward solitude and withdrawal, he simply locked himself in his hotel suites both in New York and in Boston and never went out except to his rehearsals and concerts.

Had he been better informed or more literate, he might have been prepared for the cultural differences that so offended him. Even if his lack of English made the writings of Franklin, Jefferson, Lincoln, Emerson, and Thoreau inaccessible to him (most of them had not yet appeared in translation), he might have read de Tocqueville in French to gain an understanding of America. He could then have sensed the openness and generosity of spirit behind the rough-hewn manners. Unable to see beneath the surface, he remained at the mercy of his first impressions.

Had he been more curious and apperceptive, he might have explored American musical idioms and found in Stephen Foster a melodic imagination in many ways akin to his own. Or he might have sensed in the rhythmic exuberance of American banjo tunes something related to the propulsive force of his own waltzes and polkas. But throughout his American sojourn, his predominant reaction was one of discomfort and alarm, and he did everything he could to isolate himself from his surroundings.

The Boston Peace Festival confirmed his impression of America as a land of grotesque improbability. Appearing for the first rehearsal, he faced a truly staggering musical assemblage. His waltzes were attacked by a task force of nearly two thousand orchestra players and a chorus of twenty thousand. These were augmented by anvils, firebells, "chimes" consisting of odd lengths of railroad track freely suspended on wooden frames for convenient whacking, and a "Monster Bass Drum, 18 Feet in Diameter."

This musical monstrosity had been perpetrated by P. S. Gilmore, a famous bandmaster who evidently shared the prevalent America notion that bigger is better. At the helm of this musical army, Strauss was stationed in a sort of look-out tower, watched by dozens of subconductors who followed his movements with binoculars and relayed them to the players. Strauss, always stressing subtlety of phrase, was in despair at being unable to convey any feeling of musical nuance through such a relay of conductors, especially since the downbeat—to get everyone started at the same time— was to be the belch of a cannon.

Strauss's first impulse was to cancel his appearance. But somebody had warned him about lynchings, pointing out that Americans have been known to react violently to an acute disappointment. "A refusal to conduct would have cost me my life," he wrote back to Vienna. From then on, he simply regarded the whole matter as a farce and conducted no less than fourteen concerts at the Boston Peace Festival in an enormous wooden shed that held an audience of a hundred thousand.

On one occasion, the cannon marking the downbeat went off prematurely, and Strauss described the ensuing performance as "an unholy row such as I shall never forget." But the audience loved it, and for the remainder of his brief stay in America, Strauss was the hero of the day. Women besieged him for locks of his hair, and his valet obligingly handed out scented envelopes, each containing a black curl snipped from the shaggy pelt of Strauss's Newfoundland dog.

After the Boston series, Strauss still found the courage to conduct three concerts in New York. At the Academy of Music on Fourteenth Street, which was then the city's most elegant thoroughfare, he was greatly relieved to find a normal-size orchestra of some seventy men, and in addition to some of his own works—*Artist's Life, The Blue Danube,* and the *Pizzicato Polka*—the program included such sturdy concert fare as the overtures to Rossini's *William Tell* and Wagner's *Rienzi.*

American journalism, at the time, was not yet paying much attention to the arts, and even *The New York Times* merely reported that the concerts took place without making any serious attempt to evaluate the performance. Besides, it was a Presidential election year and the paper devoted most of its scant space to the pithy utterances of Horace Greeley, who was fulminating against the incumbent Ulysses S. Grant. The tone of political discourse at that period can be gauged from the fact that so suave an orator as Greeley referred to his political opponents as "murderers, adulterers, drunkards, cowards, liars, and thieves." As the campaign fever engulfed New York, Strauss and his entourage boarded the steamer *Donau* in mid-July for their homeward voyage.

On arriving in Hamburg, Strauss received news that a more ominous kind of fever—cholera—had broken out in Vienna. His mortal fear was immediately aroused again. Instead of returning home, he and his staff headed for Baden-Baden, Germany's most fashionable resort, to recuperate from America and wait for the cholera to subside in Vienna.

At the request of Emperor Wilhelm I, who was spending the summer at Baden-Baden, Strauss conducted several concerts of the local *Kurorchester.* The Emperor was particularly fond of *Tales from the Vienna Woods,* which Strauss had to repeat for him time and again. After one of the performances, the Adjutant General of the Prussian Court mounted the stage and presented the utterly surprised Strauss with the Order of the Red Eagle, one of Germany's highest decorations.

Another admirer in the audience at Baden-Baden was Hans von Bülow, the ranking symphonic conductor of his day. Like Strauss, Bülow was an ardent Wagnerite, as smitten with

Wagner's music as Wagner was with Bülow's wife Cosima. Even after losing Cosima to the composer's tempestuous courtship, Bülow remained Wagner's foremost champion. Describing the Strauss concerts at Baden-Baden, Bülow remarked in one of his letters: "Strauss is one of the few of my colleagues for whom I have unreserved admiration. One can really learn something from him. . . ." Through Bülow Strauss also made the acquaintance of Johannes Brahms, who was to remain a lifelong close friend.

Amid the ordered pleasantness of life at Baden-Baden, Strauss soon forgot his American travails. Summer and early fall passed in the leisurely routine of "taking the waters" and with long afternoon promenades in the *Kurpark*, usually in the company of Bülow and Brahms. Not until October did Strauss and Jetty return to Vienna.

The death of Jetty and the loss of Angelika in the latter part of the 1870s left Strauss's personal life in a rather precarious state.

The years with Jetty, though not always happy, had accustomed Strauss to the kind of domesticity attainable only in marriage. Angelika, of course, had failed him entirely in this as well as in other respects. And so, toward the end of the decade, Strauss once again faced the rather unsettling task of finding someone to marry.

It was quite convenient, therefore, that about the time of Angelika's departure a young acquaintance of Strauss's died, leaving an attractive twenty-one-year-old widow, who incidentally was also named Strauss. In many ways, Adele was the exact opposite of Angelika. Small, fine-featured, with raven hair, she had the appearance of a slender and rather wistful child, and in her dark eyes resided the kind of warmth that promised solace to the disappointed Strauss. She was a banker's daughter, and like many well-brought-up women of her class, she combined assured personal competence and efficiency with delicacy of manner and an air of self-effacement. Strauss was enchanted with this configuration of traits, for he valued basic management talent in a prospective wife as much as her more ethereal attributes.

At first his relation to Adele and her little daughter Alice was mainly a protective one, but their mutual affection soon reached a point where marriage seemed the most suitable arrangement for them.

Youth and femininity had always provided a profound psychic impetus for Strauss. His particular musical idiom was, in essence, a celebration of lovely women. The insinuations of his melodies reflected their grace of movement, their inflections of voice, their vivacity and tenderness. Adele, sprightly, gentle, and very pretty in a gossamer way, must have seemed to Strauss the embodiment of these qualities. She, in turn, feeling very much alone after her husband's death, gratefully accepted the love and solicitude of an older man.

Before a marriage could take place, some legal difficulties had to be resolved. Divorce was almost impossible to obtain in Catholic Austria, and divorced persons were not allowed to remarry. These restrictions stood in strange contrast to other prevailing sex attitudes. Premarital and extramarital liaisons, for example, were regarded quite tolerantly in Vienna as part of the local life-style. Such arrangements, however, had no legal status. Where official sanction was required, the church remained obdurate and kept its stranglehold on civil law.

Fortunately, Strauss had formed friendly connections with the Protestant aristocracy of Germany during his summer at Baden-Baden. He counted among his personal acquaintances Duke Ferdinand of Saxe-Coburg-Gotha, who brought Strauss's marital dilemma to the attention of his uncle, the reigning duke of that principality. If Strauss were to accept the Protestant faith and citizenship in the duke's domain, his difficulties might be resolved.

It was only with great reluctance that Strauss abandoned

his formal allegiance to Austria and to Catholicism. But for
Adele's sake, he converted to the Lutheran faith and became
a subject of the obliging Duke of Saxe-Coburg-Gotha. On
July 11, 1887, Duke Ernst II personally pronounced Johann's
divorce from Angelika, and on August 15 of that year, Johann and Adele were married in the royal chapel at Coburg.
They spent a brief honeymoon at the palace as the personal
guests of the Duke. Then they returned to Vienna, now
technically foreigners in their native city.

Strauss was fifty-eight at the time of this marriage, but his
love for Adele rejuvenated him. In her presence, his bearing
and his gait were that of a man half his age. Almost daily he
wrote her little love letters. Before going to the theater to
conduct a performance, for example, he would leave her this
note: "My dear Adele! I shall change the tempo from
maestoso to *allegro* so I can hurry back to you all the
sooner and kiss you a few minutes earlier. Your Jean." He
kept scribbling notes to her on no particular occasion, rang-
ing from little gallantries to exuberant declarations like: "You
are the queen of my happiness, of my life!" Writing to her
from Berlin, where he had gone to see Fritz Simrock, his
publisher, the normally inarticulate Strauss was moved to
rococo flights of imagination: "I need my publisher to be
able to adorn you. The publisher has an important part to
play. There are arrows to be shot. Arrows of love—and they
cost money. I am able to buy them through [my music
which is] a love-token I send to the publisher Simrock at
Berlin, Friedrichstrasse 171. It is the only address I can remember. And why? *Cherchez la femme.* Sleep well, you
black-eyed Adele, the only woman on earth. . . ."

For Adele's sake he wanted to be young. He dyed his
graying hair and his moustache, and he kept himself trim by
riding the fine horses he collected at his newly acquired
country estate at Schönau, in the Danube region of Lower
Austria. His love of the graceful, the lively, extended even to
horses. A spirited horse touched his imagination. If on occa-

sion, he still fell into those dark moods that beset him during his final years with Jetty, just watching his horses canter about would dispel his gloom. At that stage of his life, he rarely accepted invitations for concert tours. But when a Russian impresario promised him two rare blooded stallions if Strauss would conduct a concert in Moscow, he could not resist. He was so delighted with the horses his Russian host presented to him that he immediately gave them a workout. Later he wrote home: "My nerves are just as run down as those of my horses. Both the horses and I exerted ourselves too much. . . . The horses were too young for the work, and I was too old." It was the only time that Strauss, always conscious of age and mortality ever mentioned his advancing years.

Despite his domestic happiness, Strauss remained rather withdrawn. He seldom gave large parties at his spacious town house in the Iglgasse, and only a few friends visited him regularly. Among those were Alexander Girardi, the famous comic who played leading roles in many Strauss operettas, the composer Carl Goldmark, the piano manufacturer Bösendorfer, and Johannes Brahms. The visitors usually came after lunch for a game of billiards or to play Strauss's favorite card game, Taroc. There was one main social rule: serious talk had to be avoided. Strauss could not bear to hear anything of an intellectual or problematic nature discussed in his presence. It would upset him for days, making him unable to compose.

Among these acquaintances, Strauss's closest personal bond was with Brahms—an attachment difficult to fathom. Musically, the two men stood far apart: Brahms probing music for ultimate depth; Strauss, as a public entertainer, always conscious of surface effect. In music, Brahms was a philosopher, Strauss a magician. Temperamentally, too, they were at opposite poles: Strauss always suave and socially adroit while Brahms affected a gruff, bearish manner to hide the profound tenderness so evident in his music. Yet there grew a silent affinity between the two that allowed them to sit together in the garden for long afternoons, rarely speaking a word, each happy in the company of the other.

At times, Brahms would go to the piano to play his own version of Strauss waltzes, enriching them with elaborate improvisations. Goldmark recalls in his diary a performance of *The Blue Danube* by Brahms that was a marvel of spontaneous evolution of the musical material. One can only regret that no attempt at notation was ever made.

It was Adele, no less than Johann, who drew Brahms to the Strauss mansion. The old bachelor was an inveterate admirer of other men's wives, a pattern dating back to his youth, when he fell so lastingly in love with Clara Schumann. Brahms always respected the marital loyalties of his friends, never attempting any intrusions. To the arch-romantic Brahms, being in love was a creative necessity. Perhaps his devotion to categorically unattainable women was his assurance of *staying* in love. The ostensibly chaste homage provided a workable area for emotionally productive encounters. But it is sad to reflect that the profound lyricism of his music—particularly the ardor and tenderness of his love songs—was inspired by women he had known only from a distance.

Brahms once quipped that he and Strauss were both "in service at the Court of Adele—Brahms for fugues, Strauss for waltzes." Another time he inscribed Adele's fan with the opening bars of *The Blue Danube*, signing it "unfortunately not by J. Brahms." He was rarely given to such self-effacement. In contact with others, he invariably assumed a defensive pose of bitter and biting sarcasm that eventually alienated most of his acquaintances. Johann and Adele Strauss were the only exceptions, and he treated them with an affectionate courtesy and a warmth shown to no one else. The quality of this relationship must have been a great comfort to Brahms in the darkening mood of his last years, which found such penetrating expression in his *Four Serious Songs*, the Clarinet Quintet, and the last *Intermezzi*.

For Strauss it was a time of contentment and respite. In the circle of his friends, nourished by Adele's devotion, Strauss lived quietly into the acceptance of being old. Adele had succeeded in arresting the tide of melancholy that had swept over him in the years just before he met her. Though he never recovered his former élan, it was through her that he attained a certain tranquillity. She gave him the emotional shelter he so needed. She was his anchor in the sea of time and held him to the end of his life.

12

Twilight

Softly the rain fell. Now and then a gust of wind drove the water against the window pane in the gray afternoon.

This was Strauss's favorite weather. Even in summer, at his villa in Ischl near Salzburg, he always hoped for rain. He liked to stand near the window, especially at dusk, his eyes tracing the drops running down the pane while the fir trees in the garden slowly swayed their branches like the thick arms of dark-green ghosts.

"I love this miserable weather," he wrote to Girardi. "If only it keeps that way. Composing is so easy in the rain. . . ."

Occasionally he interrupted his work to play the newly written melodies for Adele on the piano, or he went into the kitchen to putter. "To clear my head from too much concentration," he told Girardi, "I like to pick peas from their pods or cut the ends of string beans, or pull the stems from gooseberries. Such activity at least promises a certain pleasure. . . ."—adding that the pleasure to be derived from his compositions was by no means as certain.

His invasions of the kitchen often embroiled him in arguments with his cook which he vastly enjoyed. The cook was a firm believer in the traditional Austrian five-course meal, with soup being followed by fish before the roast was served. Strauss was all in favor of the fish. He loved fresh brook trout as an appetizer. But he firmly held that soup—especially the Austrian kind of *Lungenstrudelsuppe* or *Leberknödelsuppe* with chunks of lung hash or liver dumplings swimming in it —merely swamped the stomach and spoiled the meal. He preferred to skip soup at table, a heresy for which the cook never ceased to upbraid him.

When it wasn't raining, he would play in the garden with his little stepdaughter, who was fond of laying out seashells in decorative patterns among the flower beds. The shells were her special treasure—she had gathered them at the beach in Ostend during a vacation trip. Often Strauss, in his white flannel trousers, would crawl around on his hands and knees to help the little girl with her shell game.

But his only true repose was work. Late into the night he would scribble on his score sheets at his stand-up desk near the window, stopping at times to write a short letter to Adele, who was sleeping in the next room. In the morning she would find messages like this piled on her night table:

"Dearest Adele! I wish you a very good night, and a good sleep, and a good mood when you wake up! Let us be merry as we go through life. *On ne vit qu'une fois.* Especially women should always smile. . . . It looks so pretty on them and prevents wrinkles. . . ."

He had no hobbies now, no recreation. Ceaselessly he composed. The music sprang up within him and had to be let out. Measure after measure tumbled onto the score paper. But the wealth of his invention was wasted on the inanities supplied by his librettists. Indeed, few art forms are as predictable and simple-minded as Viennese operetta, except perhaps American cowboy movies. Yet furbished with Strauss's music, even this literary sop captured the audience. Works such as *Blind Cow*, or *Waldmeister*—long forgotten except for their sparkling overtures—ran hundreds of performances on all the stages of Europe. To contemporary audiences and critics alike, the sheer charm of the music hid the basic failure of the total work.

Few of these scores maintain a consistent level of inspiration. Like all popular music, they contained platitudes. That, after all, is what makes music accessible to the musically naïve. A broad public can accept only what falls within a common denominator of its comprehension. Or, putting it another way, popular music must be at least partly commonplace. But in Strauss scores, these platitudes are neither obtrusive nor predominant. They are always redeemed by freshness of melodic invention.

With impresarios clamoring for new operettas, Strauss now rarely found time to write orchestral waltzes. Yet in 1888 he made a notable exception. Forty years had passed since the revolution of 1848, and Franz Josef was celebrating the fortieth anniversary of his reign. Strauss, the former revolutionary, was now the Emperor's official Director of Court Ball Music. As such, he wanted to pay special tribute to his sovereign, who had become a unique figure in political history, regarded by many as a saint rather than a ruler.

In his great and genuine modesty, Franz Josef would have never encouraged such sentiments; yet something in his character invited veneration. He never was a heroic monarch, never a triumphal figure. His was a different grandeur: a gentleness combined with unbending decency. Responsibility and a sense of duty were the motive forces that kept him working at his desk each day as if he were just another government official. Even the humblest of his subjects with a deserving cause could personally petition him in audience. He was unfailingly courteous, and those in personal contact with him were touched by his sense of compassion. He embodied gentlemanly correctness, justice, and probity—qualities he believed necessary to give moral sanction to the wielding of power. No biographer or historian has ever captured the essence of this rare and humble man, whose frail, stooped figure belied all vulgar notions of dominance. He had the dignity of a true monarch, an aura of natural majesty that stemmed as much from his humaneness as from his rank.

It was this charisma of the Emperor, more than anything else, that kept Austria from crumbling. The divisive forces within the empire had become nearly overwhelming. The various nationalities under the Austrian crown were agitating ever more virulently for secession. Nationalism, that cancer in the soul of humanity, had spread to every ethnic faction, setting each group against all others in unreasoned hate. Poles, Czechs, Hungarians, Serbs, Slovenes, and Slovaks had little love for each other, but they were united in their enmity for Austria. They hated the empire not because it was exploitive; for Austria had never been imperialistic in the economic sense. They despised Austria because it had the idea of a supranational community as its basic tenet.

Austria stood for the concept of human community integrated by the spiritual force of the crown—an idea linked to the Catholic notion of a universal church and the ethos of the Holy Roman Empire. This kind of mystic centralism ran counter to the new vogue of ethnic nationalism, and it enraged the nationalists. Perhaps the idea of such spiritual centrality—the ideological basis of absolutism—had really been untenable ever since Copernicus suggested that the earth was not the center of the universe. But Europe had yet to learn—and still has to learn—that the ideals so fervently sought in the name of nationalism were attainable only by seeking the deeper meaning within the Copernican world view in a new social synthesis based on a more generous vision of shared humanity.

On a more mundane level, one might argue that Austria's deepening troubles were at least partly the by-product of the telegraph. As long as it took provincial authorities several days to contact the government in Vienna by courier, they were free to make decisions on the spot, based on their insight into the local situation. As a result, public administration rested on tolerant rapport between local population and local governance. Authority was muted by *Schlamperei*—an emollient blend of bumbling inefficiency and conciliatory temper.

If Vienna sometimes displayed an attitude of colonial condescension toward the ethnic groups in the provinces, little of it showed at the local level. Provincial administrators would make sure that rich local merchants were invited to festivities at the military casino and that their wives and daughters would be asked to dance by the handsomest Austrian officers on hand. The guiding principle was *Fortwursteln* —a precept only roughly rendered into English as "muddling along." Austria's secret strength lay in this calculated ineptitude, resulting in unofficial local autonomy.

Regrettably, this amiable mode of government fell victim to electricity. By 1870 or thereabouts, telegraph lines stretched from Vienna to even the remotest parts of Montenegro or the Bukovina. Local officials now had orders tapped out directly from Vienna, where the central bureaucracy had little understanding and less consideration for local sentiment. Indulging the usual bureaucratic fantasy of power at the expense of political realism, they called for blunt repression of reasonable provincial dissent, shattering the workable accommodation of the past and sharpening the growing crisis of nationalist demands.

Thus the Austrian idea of the supranational state foundered on human mediocrity and bureaucratic incomprehension. These qualities, of course, had always been plentiful. But now they were potentiated by instant communications. The telegraph had turned banality into evil.

Ethnic fractionation was not the only rift in the failing empire hymned by Strauss in the *Emperor Waltz*. The rapid growth of industry, combined with total absence of adequate social legislation to protect factory workers from exploitation and the vicissitudes of a free market, had created an urban proletariat in the larger cities. Vienna, grown in Strauss's lifetime from 300,000 to more than a million, now included endless rows of slums that stood in shameful contrast to the splendors of the Ringstrasse. With an increasing portion of the population working twelve hours a day for a pittance— if they were lucky enough to find work—the egalitarian *Gemütlichkeit* that had so amiably bridged social differences in the past was fast giving way to the open animosity of class struggle.

A surprising number of the solidly bourgeois Viennese intelligentsia, stirred by the wretched conditions of the poor, became receptive to the thinking promulgated through the International Workers' Association, founded by Karl Marx in London in 1864. For the first time in absolutist Austria, where parliament was a mere charade, there was an open call for "the emancipation of the working class from capital" and the "social question" became an uncomfortable topic of conversation. As one Viennese editorialist observed, "A lot of people may not know what it is, this social question, but everybody feels it."

At the time, nobody in Austria had the historical perspective to formulate the question clearly, but the more perceptive Viennese intellectuals realized that the issue went far beyond the need for adequate social legislation. Basically, the unthinkable question was whether an absolutist monarchy, evolved as a social order suited to an agrarian economy, could survive in an industrial age. Like a specter, the unspoken question lingered in the background. It never was allowed to interfere with the sybaritic pleasures of the more visible Viennese, who lived in comfort, if not opulence, and produced during the last decades of the empire some of the most dazzling intellectual and artistic achievements. But softly and persistently, a discordant undertone now sounded in the city of music.

In the waning century, Austria lay in the heart of Europe as a lovely baroque anachronism. Premonitions of its end made it seem even lovelier. "The atmosphere of Vienna," recalls the historian Cohen-Portheim, "was like that of Paris before the Great Revolution; there was that same incomparable refinement and elegance mixed with foreboding of disaster."

Amid the whirlpools forming in the stream of time as it approaches a sharp bend, one figure seemed firm, unchanging, timeless: the Emperor. Even those who dreamed of the downfall of the monarchy, both nationalists and socialists, held Franz Josef in deep personal affection. That is why Austria's survival hinged on his personal survival. "As long as he lives . . ." people used to say in Vienna. They never finished the sentence. What they meant was, "As long as he lives, the catastrophe can be postponed." This was too grim a thought to be uttered in the balmy evening of Austria. So it was the incomplete allusion that became the whispered password by which the Viennese reassured each other: "As long as he lives . . ." This was the monarch whom Johann Strauss immortalized in the *Emperor Waltz*.

In its musical structure, the *Emperor Waltz* transcends any of Strauss's concert waltzes. The long introduction is not a waltz at all, but a soft, hesitant march suggesting courtly pomp and splendor in haunting understatement. After the shift to three-quarter time, the first waltz theme emerges— not sensuous as so many other Strauss melodies, but lyrically chaste: the declaration of affection of one man for another. In this respect, the *Emperor Waltz* differs from all the other Strauss waltzes, which were conceived as seductive tributes to women, and in its final theme the music attains a jubilant festiveness that is the essence of exalted celebration.

Among all the waltzes of Strauss, the *Emperor Waltz* is the most symphonic, more tone poem than dance. The critic William Ritter describes it as "the most beautiful flower the fantastic tree of Strauss's music has borne." A certain characteristic of Austrian music, particularly evident in Schubert and Bruckner, enters into Strauss here more strongly than elsewhere. It defies precise description, being as it were a mystery of the senses, an almost hypnotic immersion in the tonal color of a certain chord, the surprise of modulation, the tension of melodic architecture in the line of a phrase.

In some passages of this waltz, it seems as if Strauss, at this point in his life, had suddenly found a connection to the deepest substrate of Austrian musicality—a line of feeling that runs discernibly from Mozart to Mahler. It is a sensory intoxication that goes beyond music as sound and beyond music as structure. The Viennese poet and dramatist Franz Grillparzer, who ranks with Goethe and Mann among the supreme masters of the German language, described something of this quality in his novella *Der arme Spielmann*. He tells of a musician improvising in solitude on his violin, savoring "the never-failing bounty and grace of a single note, the musical essence itself . . . miraculous in its satisfaction to the thirsting, languishing ear."

Elsewhere in the literature of German romanticism we find reflections of this particular mode of perceiving music. E. T. A. Hoffmann, whose fevered, demon-ridden stories survive in Offenbach's *Tales of Hoffmann*, was obsessed with what he felt as the power of music over mind and soul. Heine asserts that "music begins where words end." Correspondingly one senses in the work of Schubert, Bruckner, and Mahler that they saw music not as a manipulable craft but as revelation speaking through them. To them, music was communion, otherwise ineffable, related in kind to the communion symbolized by the holy sacrament.

Perhaps this deeper musicality flourished in Austria precisely because Catholic mysticism dramatized and made credible by the overwhelming backdrop of Alpine landscape, had been at work for generations to create a mental climate in which such metaphysical perceptions could burrow so deeply into the imagination that even the dance bore their mark. In its more expansive moments, the *Emperor Waltz* contains the vistas of a Bruckner symphony.

As Court Ball Music Director, Strauss had been repeatedly in the Emperor's presence, both at the summer palace in Schönbrunn and at the Hofburg in the Inner City. But in the last decade of his life, he apparently also had occasion to meet the emperor in privacy at the villa of the actress Katherina Schratt. The relation of the Emperor to this young woman has caused a good deal of speculation both among scandalmongers and serious biographers. It seems fairly well established that it was Empress Elisabeth herself who, in 1883, arranged a meeting between Franz Josef and the twenty-nine-year-old Kathi Schratt. The erratic Empress, always restless, always traveling, had grown emotionally distant from her rather prosaic strictly duty-minded husband. Franz Josef, on his part, did not in the least share her artistic interests and could not stand the company of her literary friends, and only on rare occasions did the imperial couple spend any time together.

Elisabeth had the insight and generosity of spirit to perceive that the aging Emperor needed the companionship of a woman—preferably a young one—to retain his élan and to ward off the loneliness that is the cost of eminence. Noticing during a visit to the Burgtheater that the Emperor seemed taken with more than Frl. Schratt's performance onstage, she saw to it that—by discreetly contrived happenstance—he would have opportunity to meet the actress. In the years that followed, Kathi Schratt's leading role as the Emperor's *Freundin* became an accepted feature in the social repertoire of the court. To forestall any doubt in the matter, Elisabeth frequently allowed herself to be seen both at court and in public together with the Emperor and Kathi, so that Kathi's position appeared fully sanctioned. Kathi, on her part, developed a profound admiration and liking for Elisabeth, who managed this curious *ménage à trois* with cool elegance and aplomb.

To keep Kathi within convenient reach, the Emperor furnished her with a charming villa in the Gloriettegasse, a quiet, tree-shaded street just outside the garden walls of Schönbrunn palace. His solitary morning walks through the great park of Schönbrunn usually took the Emperor in the direction of Kathi's villa, and during the warm season of the year it was his custom to have breakfast there. One morning, arriving a little earlier than usual, he found Kathi's garden gate still locked. Perplexed, he simply stood in the street and waited. Never before had a door been closed to him. The Emperor did not know that one could ring a bell.

Strauss also was a frequent visitor at Kathi's house. His mansion in Hietzing was just around the corner, and Kathi often invited him for his favorite snack—crayfish and gooseliver pâté, served with very dry champagne. On such occasions, according to Viennese hearsay, Strauss and Franz Josef would meet informally—the King of the Waltz and the Emperor of the Realm enjoying each other's company in a summer garden.

Yet only one conversation between Strauss and Franz Josef has been historically authenticated. It took place in 1894 when Strauss was celebrating the fiftieth anniversary of that now legendary night at Dommayer's, when he had defied his father by giving the first concert of his own. In a week of nearly continuous festivities, Vienna entered into the spirit of the occasion as if it were a national holiday. One event was a gala performance of *The Gypsy Baron* at the opera. Just before curtain time, all eyes turned in delightful surprise to the great, two-story-high royal box. The Emperor himself had come to pay homage to the composer. Franz Josef had no ear for music and his rare attendance at the opera was for him a ceremonial duty rather than a personal pleasure. Usually he left before the end of the second act. The stage manager, Frau Aleandrine von Schönerer, therefore went to the royal box during the first intermission and, after a long and low curtsy, asked if the Emperor wished to receive Strauss at once. Unexpectedly, the Emperor replied that he intended to stay to the end of the performance and would talk to Strauss afterward.

"This time I didn't want to leave," Franz Josef told Strauss after the last curtain and the thunderous ovation that followed. "I enjoyed myself immensely. It is strange, but your music ages as little as you do. You haven't changed at all in the long years I have known you. I congratulate you on your opera. . . ."

Strauss was beside himself with happiness. "Opera! The Emperor said opera!" he later exclaimed to his friends. He thought the Emperor was passing musical judgment by referring to his operetta as opera. In his joyful agitation he did not even consider that the musically illiterate Franz Josef was obviously incapable of making such a distinction. It may have been nothing but royal malapropism, a mere slip of the imperial tongue, but for Strauss it was ecstasy.

Later that week the Vienna Philharmonic gave a banquet in honor of Strauss after which the composer delivered the only public speech of his life. It was hesitant and short:

"Gentlemen, I am not a talker. The honors you bestow on me today I owe to my predecessors—to my father and to Josef Lanner. They have indicated to me the way in which some growth may be attained: it is possible only through the expansion of form. That was my contribution—my small contribution. That is all I have done. I feel that I am too much honored, one ascribes too much merit to me."

For a moment, Strauss stood silent seemingly struggling with himself. It was as if he realized that, perhaps unwittingly, he had touched on a profound topic of musical aesthetics. Such explication, he may have felt, was not his métier. He broke off abruptly: "I have talked too much . . . Nothing more . . . nothing more . . . It is already over."

An ovation drowned his embarrassment.

Later in the evening, a gift from a group of American admirers was unveiled: a garland of fifty laurel leaves of solid gold—one for each year of his musical life.

His final years Strauss spent in the quietly ordered domesticity of his four residences: the town house in the Iglgasse, the house in Hietzing at the outskirts of Vienna, the country estate at Schönau, and the summer villa in Ischl, the picturesque little city in the Salzburg lake district where half a century earlier the young Emperor Franz Josef first saw the radiant Bavarian princess who was to become his tragic Empress. He still composed every day, methodically assembling his ill-fated operettas. He still enjoyed a physical vigor uncommon for his age. But the sheer weight of time past—the accretion of memory that Mehring calls *l'édifice immense de souvenir*—seemed to burden him. Despite his never-dimmed affection for Adele, his moods of melancholy withdrawal became more frequent, and again he went for days on end without speaking.

It was not that Strauss was unhappy. He would still on occasion enjoy the company of friends, though the death of Brahms in 1896 had taken from him his most cherished companion. Toward Adele, he showed an invariant tenderness compounded of love, gratitude, and delight. But time itself, the somber mutability that changes all things, foreshadowed the border between living and no-longer-living and engulfed this silent man with its own muffled music.

May 22, 1899, was the Feast of the Assumption, Austria's traditional springtime holiday. A special performance of *Die Fledermaus* was scheduled for this cheerful occasion. As a special treat for the holiday audience, Strauss himself was to conduct the overture. He threw himself into the score with the vitality of a youngster, and in the course of his vigorous conducting he sweated freely. To relax from the happy exertion and to enjoy the cool air of the spring evening, Strauss decided to walk home from the Opera instead of taking his carriage. It was the time of year when the fragrance of lilac and acacia sweeps through Vienna and the white-blossoming horse-chestnut trees along the streets are in full flower. Under their baldachin and with his music still ringing in his ears Johann Strauss took his last walk.

The fever came in the morning and would not pass. This did not keep him from composing. For a few days, he would still work at his desk, wrapped in heavy robes but shivering, setting note after note on the score of *Cinderella*. This was to be his first ballet music. Strauss was so enthusiastic about the project that he was determined to go on with it despite the rising fever and the racking cough. Some days later, he abandoned the desk and took to bed. But as long as he could hold up his head, he kept writing.

Because of the fever's obstinacy and the apparent involvement of bronchi and lungs, Dr. Lederer, Strauss's physician, called into consultation the famous Professor Nothnagel of the University of Vienna, which then boasted the world's foremost medical faculty.

"Please cough," said the Professor, laying his stethoscope against Strauss's back.

Strauss did as he was told, then added with a wan smile: "Is that all I can do for medical science?"

There certainly was not much that medical science, at that time, could do for Strauss. Professor Nothnagel told Strauss that he had a severe cold. He told Adele that he had double pneumonia.

By June 1, Strauss was in delirium. Adele tells the rest: "Suddenly he sat up in bed, and under his tortured breathing, softly, there was a song! An old song, which even my little daughter knew, but I had never heard him sing it. Now it came softly from his pale lips. Solemnly, almost ghostlike, the song floated into the room:

> *Brüderlein fein, Brüderlein fein*
> *Einmal muss geschieden sein. . . .*
> *Scheint die Sonne noch so schön,*
> *Einmal muss sie untergehn. . . .*

[My little friend, My little friend,
Now we must part. . . .
No matter how beautifully the sun shines,
Sometime it must set. . . .]

"In the morning of June 3, he took my hand and kissed it twice without words. It was his last caress. In the afternoon at a quarter past four he died in my arms."

At the Volksgarten, the long rows of roses were in bloom. The great park, extending in front of the Hofburg toward the Ringstrasse and the filigree towers of the Rathaus, was the site of many outdoor concerts. That afternoon, between two selections, someone stepped up to the podium of conductor Eduard Kremser to whisper something in his ear.

Kremser stood quite still for a moment. Then he spoke briefly to the first violinist. From him the message passed in whispers through the ranks of the orchestra. The men changed the sheet music on their stands. All the string players put mutes on their instruments.

The audience, murmuring, expected an announcement of a program change. But the conductor said nothing. He raised his right arm for a downbeat, his left arm stretched out with the palm down to indicate pianissimo.

In a whisper, the orchestra began the luminous opening of *The Blue Danube*—much slower than usual. The orchestral volume never rose above a sigh. The audience understood and quietly dispersed. It was so that Vienna learned of the death of Johann Strauss.

13

Coda

There is a certain fitness in the fact that Strauss, dying in
1899, did not see the dawn of the twentieth century. He
would not have been at home in it at all. The spirit of his
music arises from the optimism, the sentiment, and the aura
of conciliation by which the nineteenth century patched together the compromises that smothered and postponed imminent conflicts until, in our own time, they tore the world
apart.

Strauss wrote waltzes for people who could still accommodate their hearts within the general scheme of things—not
for a generation so alienated from its world that such concepts as melody and harmony themselves are no longer rele-
vant in the art of music.

Among the inclusive changes in the entire mode of human
existence since the death of Strauss was the collapse of the
old order of Europe in the wars of 1914 and 1939, a change
nowhere more drastic than in Austria. According to a Viennese joke, "Franz Josef ruled until the death of Johann
Strauss." The joke contains historic truth: with the passing
of the Waltz King, the real authority and cohesion of the
Austrian empire had gone. After all, Austria had never been

an empire in the usual political sense but, as historian Crane Brinton puts it, "a congeries of peoples, administrative areas, legal systems, quite lacking in any common patriotism." What held Austria together was the force of myth—perhaps the most profound influence on the political imagination. Johann Strauss, without anyone knowing it in his lifetime, had become a keystone in the structure of that myth. With him gone, not even Franz Josef could make the center hold. Without magic, the fairyland crumbled. The Austria of a thousand years was at its end.

Of course, to ascribe the downfall of a civilization to the absence of its most characteristic musician is sheer hyperbole, though Orpheus probably plays a much larger role in the totality of human affairs than "practical" people accord him. The forces that were to shatter the world of the waltz were already gathering strength at the time of Strauss's death, and the men who embodied these forces were already at work in Vienna, though obscured in the general pleasantness of Austria's *fin de siècle*. One would find them sipping *Mocca* at the coffeehouses along the Ringstrasse, enjoying the way of life they were about to destroy.

Arnold Schoenberg was already shaping assumptions that would negate the premises of music. "A simple chord," he would expound to his coffeehouse cohorts, "is a very special effect that should be employed sparingly and then only after careful preparation."

At another table, one might find the young neurologist, Dr. Freud, whose notions about sexual repression and sublimation made the romantic yearnings expressed in the waltz seem either clinical or ridiculous. Dr. Freud, though, never made it clear just what he proposed in lieu of romance in civilized society.

In the political arena, Vienna's coffeehouses at that time harbored the makings of more ominous changes. Leon Trotsky, who liked the Café Central in the Herrengasse, already dreamed of a state far different from that of Emperor Franz Josef, and so did Adolf Hitler, who was painting the apartments of Vienna's largely Jewish bourgeoisie.

Indeed, it was Hitler who, among his other grotesque accomplishments, would write by far the oddest footnote to the chronicle of the Waltz King.

For more than a hundred years, Johann's grandfather Franz, the tavern keeper who had drowned in the Danube, had lain forgotten. Then, in 1938, a document turned up among the matrimonial records at St. Stephen's cathedral proving that Franz Strauss's parents had been Jews who were later baptized.

This discovery came at an awkward moment. Hitler had just invaded Austria. The standard policy of his regime in regard to "racially putrid" (*rassisch verseucht*) composers was to destroy them. Even for those long dead, there would be ceremonial denunciations followed by burning of scores, melting of printing plates, tearing up of library index cards, and smashing of records to eradicate every trace of their creative existence.

In the case of Strauss, this raised problems. The Ministry of Culture might pronounce Mendelssohn and Mahler as unfit for the Germanic soul; but to assert that *The Blue Danube* or *Wine, Women, and Song* were malignant concoctions of the international-Jewish conspiracy to pollute the Aryan mind—not even Goebbels could bring that off.

Dr. Goebbels, however, was rarely intimidated by facts. He ordered the *Reichssippenamt*, the government agency entrusted with the investigation of blood lines, to purify Strauss. They did this by confiscating the cathedral's matrimonial fascicle and preparing an expert forgery deleting all evidence of the Jewish roots of the Strauss family tree. The fraud was officially published, on vellum, dated February 20, 1941, bearing the swastika seal of the Third Reich and a statement of certification by the powers of Berlin, who believed that they were reshaping the world for a new millennium. As far as the government was concerned, the music was now fit for Aryan ears.

Of course, there were still those luckless scholars who had discovered the embarrassing facts in the first place. They were summoned to Vienna's splendidly gothic Rathaus, where an armed officer in the black uniform of the SS—his dagger embossed with the motto *Blut und Ehre* (Blood and Honor) —suggested to them some scholarly revisions. He pointed out that their findings constituted an ideological error that could possibly be atoned by blood and dishonor but might also be eradicated by their silence. The scholars took this instruction very seriously.

This brainwashing of history may well have succeeded but for the act of a single person. In the spring of 1945, during the weeks of senseless fury and destruction that marked the final spasm of Nazism, a man stumbled through the burning wreckage of Vienna, carrying back to St. Stephen's the original document the Germans had confiscated. No one ever ascertained who he was, how he had obtained the abducted document, or what were his reasons for returning it. Perhaps in the chaos of the gutted city, amid disorder, plunder, rape, and mass death a solitary musicologist remembered his primary loyalty to scholarship and felt impelled to rectify a fraud he had abetted. One likes to think that this kind of a moral act could still take place under such circumstances.

In the deep vault beneath the church, the parchment page survived even after, a few days later, the great cathedral itself fell victim to the malice of the Germans, who deliberately shelled St. Stephen's as their farewell to Vienna.

When the flames died down after the Battle of Vienna in April, 1945, Strauss's house in the Iglgasse lay in ruins, along with a major portion of the Inner City. Most of his personal belongings, kept in Austrian archives and museums, disappeared when the Red Army pillaged Vienna as part of the liberation. Even Strauss's violin was gone.

For Europe, now poised between new centers of power in East and West, the interregnum following the collapse of the old order still continues. But Vienna is still a lovely city. The rubble of war has been swept under the patterned rug of memory; much of the Ringstrasse has been restored; and elsewhere, neat new buildings with neon signs rise from former bomb craters.

With its many surviving mementos of the Habsburg era, the city stands today like a stage set for a play that has folded. It still has charm, and it still has manners. The older inhabitants, as Edmund Wilson observes, "act like attendants of the palace awaiting the return of the long-gone owners."

The persistence of memory never seems out of place in Vienna. More than elsewhere, one still senses that continuity with the past for which we hunger in our disjointed era. Not the least among the things creating this sense of unity within time is the music of Johann Strauss. It still pervades the Stadtpark on balmy afternoons when small orchestras play his waltzes in rococo pavilions.

The music, more durable than empires, remains. Because it was so much of its time, it is for all time. For, as T. S. Eliot observes:

> Time present and time past
> Are both perhaps present in time future,
> And time future contained in time past.
> . . . . . .
> What might have been and what has been
> Point to one end which is always present.

Through his music we still see the world of Strauss. For in his art he has held and vitalized that oneness of time of which the poet speaks.

Sources

The biographer or historian often finds himself in difficulties similar to those of a man genuinely devoted to two women of very different temperaments. One is his humane interest in his subject, which leads him to be expansive; the other is his commitment to scholarship, which demands that he be rigorous. He knows that neither can satisfy him without the other and that he must, in his own particular way, reconcile their divergent claims.

Despite my striving for historical accuracy, I conceived this book less as a scholarly account than as a synoptic glimpse of a moment in time, of a world mirrored in the transient sparkle of the Viennese waltz as the reflection of the sun is caught in a raindrop.

On such a premise one may dispense with at least the outer trappings of academic stringency. Accordingly, I shall not burden this bibliography with the tedious listing of primary sources, which are scattered in countless contemporary publications, concert programs and reviews, personal correspondence and reminiscences, and those airy effluences of European journalism known as *feuilletons*.

As a congenital bookworm, I enjoyed the dusty job of digging for such materials in the excellent collections of the National-bibliothek in Vienna and the Wiener Stadtbibliothek. It added to my pleasure that both these libraries are housed in splendid

buildings that figure prominently in the narrative—the National-
bibliothek is located in the Hofburg, where Strauss conducted
his orchestra at the Habsburg court balls, while the Stadtbibliothek occupies part of Vienna's flamboyantly gothic City Hall,
one of the landmarks along the Ringstrasse. I also found contemporary materials concerning the French setting for Chapter
9 in the Bibliothèque Nationale in Paris, practically across the
street from the Palais Royal where the elder Strauss played for
the king of France.

Since I did not regard my task as that of historical sleuthing, I
admit without regret that I uncovered no unpublished primary
sources; but many biographic and historical details presented
here had not been previously available in the English language.
This book is also the first Strauss biography in any language
to take account of the German wartime attempt to expunge evidence of the Strauss family's Jewish antecedents—an incident
ominously typifying the "control of truth," even in the historic
dimension, by the modern corporate state.

I was fortunate in being able to obtain many important and
some rare secondary sources through the help of several anti-
quarian booksellers in Vienna, who went to considerable trouble
to track down what I needed. For the rest, I relied mostly on
the ample and excellent facilities of the New York Public Library, both at the Central Branch and the Music Division. The
Austrian Institute in New York also helped by providing me
with introductions to the Viennese libraries and by allowing me
to consult its own collection of books on Austrian history and
art.

The following references will be useful to those wanting a
more particularized account of matters covered in this book. The
relative abundance of sources in German allowed me to be se-
lective in their listing, but I included most of the applicable
books available in English.

BOOKS ABOUT STRAUSS

Brodszky, Franz, *Wenn Johann Strauss ein Tagebuch geführt
hätte.* (Budapest, 1967)

Decsey, Ernst, *Johann Strauss—Ein Wiener Buch.* (Vienna, 1948)

———, *"So voll Fröhlichkeit,"* Oesterreichische Musikzeitschrift, Vienna, May 1949.

Ewen, David, *Tales from the Vienna Woods—The Story of Johann Strauss.* (New York, 1944)

———, *Wine, Women and Waltz: A Romantic Biography of J. Strauss, Son and Father.* (New York, 1933)

Grasberger, Franz, *Die Wiener Philharmoniker bei Johann Strauss.* (Vienna, 1963)

Jacob, Heinrich Eduard, *Johann Strauss und das neunzehnte Jahrhundert: die Geschichte einer musikalischen Weltherrschaft.* (Amsterdam, 1937) Also available in an English translation by Marguerite Wolf under the title *Johann Strauss—Father and Son: a Century of Light Music.* (New York, 1939)

Jäger-Sunstenau, Hans, *Johann Strauss—de Walzerkönig und seine Dynastie.* (Vienna, 1965) A collection of documentary material pertaining to the Strauss family.

Jaspert, Werner, *Johann Strauss: sein Leben, sein Werk, seine Zeit.* (Lindau, 140)

Knosp, Gaston, *Johann Strauss—La vie une valse.* (Brussels, 1951)

Kronberg, Max, *Johann Strauss—La grande valse.* (Paris, 1939)

Lange, F. *Josef Lanner und Johann Strauss, Vater: Ihre Zeit, ihr Leben und ihre Werke.* (Leipzig, 1919)

Loewy, Siegfried, *Johann Strauss, der Spielmann von der blauen Donau.* (Leipzig, 1924)

Neuwald-Grasse, Anny, "Die Beziehungen von Johann Strauss, Vater, und seinen Söhnen zu Russland," *Der Merker*, Vienna, 1917.

Pastene, Jerome, *Three-Quarter Time: The Life and Music of the Strauss Family of Vienna.* (New York, 1951)

Procháska, R., Freiherr von, *Johann Strauss.* (Berlin, 1900)

Reich, Willi (editor), *Johann Straus—aus Briefen und Erinnerungen.* (Zurich, 1950)

Ritter, William, "Les dernières oeuvres de Johann Strauss," *Magasin littéraire et scientifique*, Paris, 1892.

Schönherr, Max, "An der schönen blauen Donau: Marginalien zur 100. Wiederkeh des Tages der Uraufführung," *Oesterr. Musikzeitschrift*, Vienna, January 1967.

———, *Johann Strauss Vater—Ein Werkeverzeichnis*. (Vienna, 1954)

Schnitzer, Ignaz, *Meister Johann: bunte Geschichten aus der Johann-Strauss-Zeit*. (Vienna, 1920)

Teetgen, Ada, B., *The Waltz Kings of Old Vienna*. (New York, 1940)

Weigel, Hans, *Die Flucht vor der Grösse: Beiträge zur Selbsterkenntnis Österreichs*. (Vienna, 1960) Contains a psychologically illuminating essay on Strauss.

———, *Das kleine Walzerbuch*. (Salzburg, 1965)

OF TIME, PLACE, AND SPIRIT

d'Artiste, Paul, *La vie et le monde du Boulevard (1830–1870)*. (Paris, 1930)

Barea, Ilsa, *Vienna*. (New York, 1966)

Bauernfeld, Eduard von, *Aus Alt- und Neu-Wien*, vol. 12 of Gesammelte Schriften. (Vienna, 1872)

Brion, Marcel, *Daily Life in the Vienna of Mozart and Schubert*, tr. Jean Stewart. (New York, 1962)

du Camp, Maxine, *Paris—ses organes, ses fonctions et sa vie dans la seconde moitié du 19e siècle*. (Paris, 1879)

Carner, Mosco, *The Waltz*. (London, 1949)

Conte-Corti, Egon Caesar, *Elisabeth*. (Salzburg, 1934)

———, *Franz Josef I*. (Graz, 1960)

Crankshaw, Edward, *The Fall of the House Habsburg*. (New York, 1963)

l'Exposition universelle à Paris; guide pour les visiteurs. (Paris, 1867)

Friedell, Egon, *A Cultural History of Modern Times*, vol. III. (New York, 1955)

Galloway, Tod, *The Music of the Waltz and its Creators*. (London, 1930)

Grun, Bernard, *Kulturgeschichte der Operette*. (Munich, 1961)

Hanslick, Eduard, *Musikalisches Skizzenbuch: Kritiken und Schilderungen.* (Berlin, 1896)

Hennings, Fred, *Ringstrassensymphonie*, 3 vols. (Vienna, 1964)

———, *Solange er lebt.* (Vienna, 1968)

Herrmann, Willy, *Der Walzer*, vol. 8 of Musikalische Formen in historischen Reihen. (Berlin, 1931)

Journal des arts, des sciences et des lettres et de l'exposition universelle. (Paris, 1867)

Kann, Robert A., *The Multinational Empire.* (New York, 1950)

———, *A Study in Austrian Intellectual History.* (New York, 1960)

Kelen, Betty, *The Mistresses.* (New York, 1966)

Kracauer, Siegfried, *Pariser Leben—Jacques Offenbach und seine Zeit—eine Gesellschaftsbiographie.* (Munich, 1962)

Kralik, Richard, *Wien—Geschichte der Kaiserstadt und ihrer Kultur.* (Vienna, 1912)

Laube, Heinrich, *Reise durch das Biedermeier*, new edition. (Vienna, 1946)

Mackinley, Malcolm Sterling, *Origin and Development of Light Opera.* (London, 1927)

Maurois, André, *Miss Howard and the Emperor.* (New York, 1957)

May, Arthur J., *The Hapsburg Monarchy, 1867–1914.* (Cambridge, 1951)

Mendelssohn, Ignaz, *Zur Entwicklung des Walzers* in Studien zur Musikwissenschaft, vol. 13. (Vienna, 1926)

Niecks, Frederick, "Historical and Aesthetical Sketch of the Waltz," *Monthly Musical Record.* (London 1917)

Nicolson, Harold, *The Congress of Vienna.* (New York, 1946)

Rath, R. John, *The Viennese Revolution of 1848.* (Austin, 1957)

Redlich, Joseph, *Emperor Francis Joseph of Austria.* (New York, 1929)

Schroeder, Paul W., *Metternich's Diplomacy at Its Zenith.* (Austin, 1962)

Sigmond, Charles, *La vie parisienne au 19ᵉ siècle.* (Paris, 1901)

Tamir, M., *Les expositions internationales à travers les âges.* (Thèse pour le doctorat de l'Université de Paris, presentée en 1939.)

Trollope, Frances, *Vienna and the Austrians.* (London, 1838)

Weigl, Bruno, *Die Geschichte des Walzers nebst einem Anhang über die moderne Operette*. (Langensalza, 1910)

Werfel, Franz, "An Essay upon the Meaning of Imperial Austria," in *Twilight of a World*; tr. H. T. Lowe-Porter. (New York, 1937)

Witeschnik, Alexander, *Musik aus Wien*. (Vienna-Munich-Basel, 1955)

Compositions

Listed by Opus Numbers

JOHANN STRAUSS I

36 Ungarische—Galopp
37 Wiener Tags Belustigung—
   Potpourri
38 Souvenir de Baden—Walzer
39 Wiener Tivoli-Rutsch—
   Walzer
40 Wiener Damen—Walzer
41 Fra Diavolo—Cotillion
42 Sperl—Galopp
43 Der Raub der Sabinerinnen
   —Walzer
44 Contre-Tänze
45 Tivoli-Freudenfest—Walzer
46 Musikalisches Ragoût—
   Potpourri
47 Vive la Danse!—Walzer
48 Heiter auch in ernster Zeit!
   —Walzer
49 Das Leben ein Tanz, der
   Tanz ein Leben—Walzer
50 Cotillion on *Die Unbekannte*
51 Hofball-Tänze
52 Bajaderen—Galopp
53 Bajaderen—Walzer
54 Contre-Tänze
55 Ein Strauss von Strauss—
   Potpourri
56 Alexandra—Walzer
57 Zampa—Walzer
58 Mein schönster Tag in
   Baden—Walzer
59 Die vier Temperamente—
   Walzer
60 Karnevals-Spende—Walzer
61 Tausendsapperment—Walzer
62 Zampa-und Montecchi—
   Galopp
63 Frohsinn mein Ziel—Walzer
64 Robert Tänze (from *Robert
   le Diable)*
65 Mittel gegen den Schlaf—
   Walzer

66 Erinnerung an Pest—Walzer
67 Erste Walzer-Guirlande
68 Gabriellen—Walzer
69 Fortuna—Galopp
70 Pfennig—Walzer
71 Elisabethen—Walzer
72 Cotillion on *Der Zweikampf*
73 Original—Parademarsch
74 Venetianer Galopp
75 Iris—Walzer
76 Rosa—Walzer
77 Zweite Walzer-Guirlande
78 Erinnerung an Berlin—
   Walzer
79 Gedankenstriche—Walzer
80 Huldigungs—Walzer
81 Grazien—Tänze
82 Philomelen—Walzer
83 Merkurs-Flügel—Walzer
84 Heimatklänge—Walzer
85 Reise—Galopp
86 Ballnacht—Galopp
87 Erinnerung an Deutschland
   —Walzer
88 Die Nachtwandler—Walzer
89 Eisenbahn-Lust—Walzer
90 Jugenfeuer—Galopp
91 Krönungs—Walzer
92 Cotillions on *Les Huguenots*
93 Galopp on *Les Huguenots*
94 Künstlerball—Tänze
95 Brüssler Spitzen—Walzer
96 Ball-Raketen—Walzer
97 Cachucha—Galopp
98 Pilger am Rhein—Walzer
99 Bankett—Tänze
100 Der Karneval in Paris—
   Walzer
101 Paris—Walzer
102 Original—Parademarsch
103 Huldigung der Königin
   Viktoria—Walzer

104 Boulogner—Galopp
105 Freudengrüsse—Walzer
106 Musikalischer Telegraf—
    Potpourri
107 Versailles—Galopp
108 Gitana—Galopp
109 Exotische Pflanzen—Walzer
110 Taglioni—Walzer
111 Indianer—Galopp
112 Londoner Saison—Walzer
113 Die Bergmeister—Walzer
114 Furioso—Galopp
115 Rosenblätter—Walzer
116 Wiener Gemüts—Walzer
117 Ghibellinen—Walzer
118 Myrthen—Walzer
119 Tanz-Rezepte—Walzer
120 Cäcilien—Walzer
121 Dritte Walzer-Guirlande
122 Palmzweige—Walzer
123 Amors-Pfeile—Walzer
124 Wiener Karnevals—
    Quadrille
125 Elektrische Funken—Walzer
126 Erinnerung an Ernst, oder
    Der Karneval von Venedig
127 Deutsche Lust, oder Donau-
    lieder ohne Texte—Walzer
128 Apollo—Walzer
129 Adelaiden—Walzer
130 Jubel-Quadrille—Walzer
131 Die Wettrennen—Walzer
132 Die Debutanten—Walzer
133 Sperl—Polka
134 Egerien-Tänze—Walzer
135 Die Tanzmeister—Walzer
136 Stadt-und Landleben—
    Walzer
137 Annen—Polka
138 Mode—Quadrille
139 Die Fantasten—Walzer
140 Musikverein-Tänze—
    Walzer

141 Die Minnesänger—Walzer
142 Haute-Volée—Quadrille
143 Latonen—Walzer
144 Parademarsch
145 Minos-Klänge—Walzer
146 Die Lustwandler—Walzer
147 Walhalla-Toaste—Walzer
148 Saison—Quadrille
149 Die Dämonen—Walzer
150 Künstlerball-Tänze—Walzer
151 Quadrille zur Namensfeier
    Kaiser Ferdinands
152 Tanz-Caprizen—Walzer
153 Quadrille zur Namensfeier
    der Kaiserin Maria Anna
154 Lorelei-Rhein-Klänge—
    Walzer
155 Bruder Lustig—Walzer
156 Asträa—Tänze
157 Volksgarten—Quadrille
158 Redoute—Quadrille
159 Nur Leben!—Walzer
160 Waldfräulein Hochzeits—
    Tänze
161 Salon—Polka
162 Orpheus—Quadrille
163 Frohsinns-Salven—Walzer
164 Aurora-Fest-Klänge—
    Walzer
165 Fest—Quadrille
166 Rosen ohne Dornen—
    Walzer
167 Wiener Früchteln—Walzer
168 Willkommen-Rufe—Walzer
169 Haimonskinder—Quadrille
170 Masken-Lieder—Walzer
171 Eunomien-Tänze—Walzer
172 Odeon-Tänze—Walzer
173 Marianka—Polka
174 Musen Quadrille
175 Faschings-Possen—Walzer
176 Geheimnisse aus der Wiener
    Tanzwelt—Walzer

JOHANN STRAUSS II

136 Vermählungs-Toaste—
    Walzer
137 Neuhauser—Polka
138 Pepita—Polka
139 Kron Marsch
140 Knallkügeln—Walzer
141 Wellen und Wogen—
    Walzer
142 Wiedersehen—Polka
143 Schneeglöckchen—Walzer
144 La Viennoise—Polka-
    Mazurka
145 Bürgerball—Polka
146 Novellen—Walzer
147 Musen—Polka
148 Schallwellen—Walzer
149 Erzherzog Wilhelm-Gene-
    sungsmarsch
150 Ballg'schichten—Walzer
151 Elisen—Polka
152 Karnevals-Spektakel—
    Quadrille
153 Nordstern—Quadrille
154 Myrthen-Kränze—Walzer
155 Haute-Volée—Polka
156 Napoleon Marsch
157 Nachtfalter Walzer
158 Alliance Marsch
159 Schnellpost—Polka
160 Ella—Polka
161 Panacea-Klänge—Walzer
162 Souvenir—Polka
163 Glossen—Walzer
164 Sirenen—Walzer
165 Aurora—Polka
166 Handels-Elite—Quadrille
167 Man Lebt Nur Einmal—
    Walzer
168 Leopoldstädter Polka
169 Bijouterie—Quadrille
170 Nachtveilchen—Polka-
    Mazurka

171 Freuden-Salven—Walzer
172 Gedanken auf den Alpen—
    Walzer
173 Marie Taglioni—Polka
174 Le Papillon—Polka-Mazurka
175 Erhöhte Pulse—Walzer
176 Armenball—Polka
177 Juristenball—Tänze
178 Sans-Souci—Polka
179 Abschiedsrufe—Walzer
180 Libellen—Walzer
181 Grossfürstin Alexandra—
    Walzer
182 L'Inconnue—Polka-Mazurka
183 Krönungsmarsch
184 Krönungslieder—Walzer
185 Strellna-Terrassen—
    Quadrille
186 Demi Fortune—Polka-
    Française
187 Une Bagatelle—Polka-Fran-
    çaise
188 Herzel—Polka
189 Paroxysmens Walzer
190 Etwas Kleines—Polka-Fran-
    çaise
191 Controversen—Walzer
192 Wien, mein Sinn—Walzer
193 Phänomene—Walzer
194 La Berceuse—Quadrille
195 Telegrafische Depeschen—
    Walzer
196 Olga—Polka-Française
197 Spleen—Polka-Mazurka
198 Alexandrinen—Polka-
    Française
199 Le Beau Monde—Quadrille
200 Souvenir de Nice—Walzer
201 Künstler Quadrille
202 L'Enfantillâge—Polka-
    Française
203 Helenen—Polka

333 Wein, Weib und Gesang
—Walzer
334 Königslieder—Walzer
335 Egyptischer Marsch
336 Im Krapfenwald—Polka-
Française
337 Von der Börse—Polka-
Française
338 Slovakiana—Polka on
Russian melodies
339 Louischen—Polka-Française
340 Freut euch des Lebens!—
Walzer
341 Festival—Quadrille on
English motifs
342 Neu-Wien—Walzer
343 Shawl—Polka-Française
(*Indigo*)
344 Indigo—Quadrille (*Indigo*)
345 Auf freiem Fusse—Mazurka
(*Indigo*)
346 Tausend und Eine Nacht—
Walzer (*Indigo*)
347 Aus der Heimat—Polka-
Mazurka
348 Im Sturmschritt—
Schnellpolka
349 Indigo Marsch (*Indigo*)
350 Lustiger Rath—Polka-
Française
351 Die Bajadere—Schnellpolka
352 Russische Marsch-Fantasie
353 Russische Marsch-Fantasie
354 Wienerblut—Walzer
355 Im Russischen Dorfe—
Fantasie
356 Vom Donaustrande—
Schnellpolka
357 Karnevalsbilder—Walzer
358 Nimm sie hin—Polka-
Française
359 Grüsse aus Osterreich—
Polka-Française

360 Rotunde—Quadrille
361 Bei uns z'Haus—Walzer
362 Die Fledermaus—Overture
(*Fledermaus*)
363 Fledermaus—Quadrille
(*Fledermaus*)
364 Wo die Zitronen blüh'n
—Walzer
365 Tik-Tak—Schnellpolka
(*Fledermaus*)
366 An der Moldau—Polka-
Française (*Fledermaus*)
367 Du und Du—Walzer
(*Fledermaus*)
368 Glücklich ist, wer vergisst
—Polka-Française
(*Fledermaus*)
369 Cagliostro Quadrille
(*Cagliostro in Wien*)
370 Cagliostro—Walzer
(*Cagliostro in Wien*)
371 Hoch Osterreich!—Marsch
(*Cagliostro in Wien*)
372 Bitte schön—Polka-Française
(*Cagliostro in Wien*)
373 Auf der Jagd—Schnellpolka
(*Cagliostro in Wien*)
374 Licht und Schatten—
Polka-Mazurka (*Cagliostro
in Wien*)
375 O schöner Mai—Walzer
(*Prinz Methusalem*)
376 Methusalem Quadrille
(*Prinz Methusalem*)
377 I-Tipferl—Polka-Française
(*Prinz Methusalem*)
378 Bareditter Galopp
379 Kriegers Liebchen—
Polka-Mazurka (*Prinz
Methusalem*)
380 Ballsträusschen—Schnellpolka (*Prinz Methusalem*)

420 Die Wahrsagerin—Polka Mazurka (*Der Zigeunerbaron*)
421 Husaren—Polka (*Der Zigeunerbaron*)
422 Zigeunerbaron—Quadrille (*Der Zigeunerbaron*)
423 Wiener Frauen—Walzer
424 Adelen—Walzer
425 An der Wolga—Polka-Mazurka
426 Russischer Marsch
427 Donauweibchen—Walzer (*Simplizius*)
428 Reitermarsch
429 Quadrille (*Simplizius*)
430 Soldatenspiel—Polka-Française (*Simplizius*)
431 Lagerlust—Polka-Française (*Simplizius*)
432 Mutig voran!—Schnellpolka (*Simplizius*)
433 Spanischer Marsch
434 Kaiser-Jubiläum—Jubel-Walzer
435 Sinnen und Minnen—Walzer
436 Auf zum Tanze—Schnellpolka
437 Kaiserwalzer
438 Rathausball-Tänze—Walzer
439 Durchs Telephon—Polka
440 Gross-Wien—Walzer
441 Ritter Pasman—Piano Arrangement
442 Unparteiische Kritiken—Polka-Mazurka
443 Seid Umschlungen, Millionen!—Walzer
444 Märchen aus dem Orient—Walzer

445 Ninetta—Walzer and Herzenkönigin—Polka-Française (*Fürstin Ninetta*)
446 Ninetta—Quadrille (*Fürstin Ninetta*)
447 Ninetta—Marsch (*Fürstin Ninetta*)
448 Diplomaten—Polka
449 Neue Pizzicato Polka
450 Ninetta—Galopp (*Fürstin Ninetta*)
451 Übersprungen
452 Festmarsch
453 Hochzeitsreigen—Walzer
454 Auf dem Tanzboden
455 Ich bin dir gut—Walzer (*Jabuka*)
456 Zivio!—Marsch (*Jabuka*)
457 Höh'!—Schnellpolka (*Jabuka*)
458 Tänze mit dem Besenstiel—Polka-Française (*Jabuka*)
459 Sonnenblume—Polka-Mazurka (*Jabuka*)
460 Jabuka Quadrille (*Jabuka*)
461 Gartenlaube—Walzer
462 Klug Gretelein—Walzer
463 Trau, schau, wem!—Walzer
464 Herjemineh—Polka-Française (*Waldmeister*)
465 Liebe und Ehe—Polka-Mazurka (*Waldmeister*)
466 Klipp-Klapp—Galopp (*Waldmeister*)
467 Es war so wunderbar—Marsch (*Waldmeister*)
468 Waldmeister—Quadrille (*Waldmeister*)
469 Hochzeits—Praeludium

470 Deutschmeisterjubiläums-
marsch
471 Heut' ist Heut'—Walzer
(*Die Göttin der Vernunft*)
472 Nur nicht mucken—Polka-
Française (*Die Göttin der
Vernunft*)
473 Wo unsere Fahne weht—
Marsch (*Die Göttin der
Vernunft*)

474 Husarenlied (*Die Göttin
der Vernunft*)
475 Solowalzer (*Die Göttin
der Vernunft*)
476 Potpourri on motifs from
Die Göttin der Vernunft
477 An der Elbe—Walzer
478 Aufs Korn!—Bundesschüt-
zenmarsch
479 Klänge aus der Raimundszeit

Unpublished Works (Incomplete)

Aschenbrödel—Ballet
Traumbilder—Orchestral
Fantasia
Overture Comique

Josefinen-Tänze (Piano 4-hands)
Graduale
Romulus, Operetta
(Act 1 complete)

Operas and Operettas

Die Lustigen Weiber von Wien, never produced
Indigo, February 10, 1871, Theater-an-der-Wien
Karneval in Rom, March 1, 1873, Theater-an-der-Wien
Die Fledermaus, April 5, 1874, Theater-an-der-Wien
Cagliostro in Wien, February 27, 1875, Theater-an-der-Wien
Prinz Methusalem, January 3, 1877, Carl Theater
Blindekuh, December 18, 1877, Theater-an-der-Wien
Das Spitzentuch der Königin, October 1, 1880, Theater-an-der-Wien
Der Lustige Krieg, November 25, 1881, Theater-an-der-Wien
Eine Nacht in Venedig, October 3, 1883, Friedrich-Wilhelmstrasse
Theater, Berlin
Der Zigeunerbaron, October 24, 1885, Theater-an-der-Wien
Simplizius, December 17, 1887, Theater-an-der-Wien
Ritter Pasman, January 1, 1892, Hofoperntheater, Wien
Fürstin Ninetta, January 10, 1893, Theater-an-der-Wien
Jabuka, October 12, 1894, Theater-an-der-Wien
Waldmeister, December 4, 1895, Theater-an-der-Wien
Die Göttin der Vernunft, March 13, 1897, Theater-an-der-Wien
Wiener Blut, October 25, 1899, Carl Theater

Posthumous Revisions of Unsuccessful Operettas

Gräfin Pepi (combination: Simplizius, Blindekuh), July 5, 1902,
Vienna
1001 Nacht (Indigo), June, 1906, Vienna

INDEX